no. 35

the irish
review

editors

•

MICHAEL CRONIN
COLIN GRAHAM
CLARE O'HALLORAN

CORK **c** UNIVERSITY
u
p PRESS

The Irish Review is a refereed journal. Since it first appeared in 1986 it has established itself as a journal of record. It provides a forum for critical and creative writing in English and Irish. Its editorial policy is pluralist and interdisciplinary; pluralist in its commitment to involving writers from all parts and traditions of the island and from other countries; interdisciplinary in its desire to publish articles on the arts, society, philosophy, history, politics, the environment and science. Our aim is to serve a general rather than a specialist readership.

Published by Cork University Press, 2007

Copyright © The Irish Review and Contributors
ISSN 0790-7850
ISBN 978-1-85918-391-5

Typeset by Tower Books, Ballincollig, Co. Cork
Printed by ColourBooks Ltd, Baldoyle, Co. Dublin

Order Information

Institutional rate, two issues €110.00/£75/$140

Individual rate, two issues €32 /£22/$42

Single copies €16/£11/$21
Subscriptions with payment to:
Cork University Press, Youngline Industrial Estate, Pouladuff Rd, Togher, Cork, Ireland.
Payment can be made by cheque, postal order, Access, Visa or Mastercard.
Trade orders are distributed by Gill & Macmillan Distribution Ltd, Hume Avenue, Park West, Dublin 12, Ireland.

The Arts Council
An Chomhairle Ealaíon

The Irish Review receives financial assistance from The Arts Council / An Chomhairle Ealaíon

Contributions are invited from Ireland and abroad – to be sent to
The Editors, *The Irish Review*, Cork University Press, Youngline Industrial Estate, Pouladuff Road, Togher, Cork, Republic of Ireland
Telephone +353 21 4902980; Fax +353 21 4315329;
E-mail corkuniversitypress@ucc.ie
Contributors should, in the first instance, provide an electronic submission saved using Word or rich text format (.txt or .rtf), and PC compatible. Send submissions by e-mail to corkuniversitypress@ucc.ie or by post to the address given above. If the article is accepted a typescript will be required along with a disc. Please follow the style of the journal and include a short biographical note.

www.corkuniversitypress.com

Contents

Reviews

Editorial:
The Contemporary Ballroom of Romance

WANDA BALZANO and MOYNAGH SULLIVAN

With terms like 'post-feminism' used liberally in the media, and young women and men under the vague impression that we all live in an equal world – because, in the world of consumer choice, all seem to have equal opportunities to spend it in order to be 'worth it' – it becomes even more of the essence to keep the discourses of gender and feminism alive and open. Until the old issues have been resolved and the movement towards social justice has ceased to be relevant, this question remains one of the central grounds of contention in modern society. If the use of the term 'post-feminist' reveals in its 'consumers' a desire to be at all costs modern, and post-modern, in other words progressive and trendy (shedding the old clothes is seemingly the fastest way to abandon things of the past and urgently embrace a carefree, fashionable attitude), then this dangerously mirrors the more alarming aspects of a winning Celtic-Tiger mentality. One cannot but remain unconvinced of this kind of entrepreneurial, self-congratulatory, *à la mode* feminism that follows the capitalistic model closely and is an indulgent form of bourgeois individualism, encoding a contradiction in terms that pits the group (women) against the self (woman).

It is the responsibility of educational analysts to revitalize the defining terms of the feminist question and to regenerate a critical discourse that is at risk of being hijacked by conservative political forces. Resistance to conformism through grassroots organization and social activism needs to be complemented by other, more widespread, gestures coming from academia, so that there will not be an ideological division, but a more concerted effort among various types of study and activism. In third-level education this also means that the field of Irish Studies within and outside the island invariably has to include the discursive construction of gendered identities as well as, for instance, that of minority groups and the disabled, in the past, present and future, so that literary studies, cultural studies and gender studies can be considered to be a relevant part of a cross-categorical and genealogical grammar of the representation of Ireland. Often, however, the field is not recognized as standing on its own and, because of the multi-disciplinary and interdisciplinary approach of feminism, it is consequently (dis)regarded as broad and not deep. That is why in universities and colleges Women's (and Gender) Studies have found it difficult to be included in the curriculum; apparently, that is also why they are relegated to a marginal position within the institutions, dwelling in centres and programmes more regularly than in departments. Similar reasons for the exclusion of Women's Studies are given by its detractors within Irish Studies. Such diffidence is also reflected in the compilation of some recent compendia and encyclopaedia of Irish culture, where, regardless of the growing attention to its subject matter, feminism is not included as an entry. Yet, in spite of these unconstructive responses, it is increasingly difficult to ignore the vitality of the contemporary feminist debate in intellectual circles, as it has been there for a long while, being laid bare amidst the controversies surrounding the publication of the first three volumes of *The Field Day Anthology* and then sharpened with the publication of volumes IV and V, devoted to Irish women's writing.

In July 2005, during the Irish Seminar of the Keough Centre of the University of Notre Dame, which took place in Dublin, the exchanges that followed Siobhán Kilfeather's Madden-Rooney Public Lecture on 'Genealogies of Irish Feminisms' illuminated one of the fundamental problems faced today by feminist scholarship in Irish Studies: was the male standard, or canon, a compromisingly influential point of reference for Irish feminism? In the course of that informal debate, Joe Cleary suggested that many Irish feminists treated the initial publication of the first three volumes of *The Field Day Anthology* as pivotal, or even as a starting-point, to its own detriment. While he was voicing some people's view of the project, the question could be addressed more productively from a different angle: must feminist scholarship give up the territorial claims of public visibility and leave the canonical status to patriarchal texts altogether, while trying to claim a different space? Would that not be seen as a self-marginalization? Why should there be a separate space? Since the first three volumes of the anthology were promoted in America as 'the most comprehensive exhibition of the wealth and diversity of Irish literature ever published',[1] with the claim of being inclusive and diverse, why should feminist scholars and intellectuals be made to relinquish public ground and therefore seek a separate territory of their own? It is of course the case that the ostensibly shared agendas of the two sets of *The Field Day Anthology* are in fact structurally underwritten by very different visions and subject identities. While the three-volume anthology is a good example of Irish writing (mainly by men) in historical contexts, the two new volumes appropriately reflect the main strength of modern feminist thought: its multi- and interdisciplinarity, and its resistance to easy categorization.

Another question, however, surfaces here, and it has to do with the risk of transforming *The Field Day Anthology* case as a defining *cause célèbre* or as a Trojan horse (as a destructive scheme that masquerades as a benign project) for Irish feminism, as if 2002 was its *ANNUS MIRABILIS* – or, rather, the *ANNUS DOMINAE*, before the Canon (b.C.) and after the Canon (a.C.) – thus deflecting attention from the very values contained within its covers, and from the whole import of the women's movement, both within Irish Studies and Irish society, in theory and in practice. Present-day feminism was not born in 2006 and also, as Hilda Tweedy puts it so well, 'the women's movement was [not] born on some mystical date in 1970, like Aphrodite rising from the waves. It has been a long continuous battle in which many women have struggled to gain equality, each generation adding something to the achievements of the past.'[2] The issue of public space (in academia, in the media, and in different shaped and sized halls of power) will continue to be a prominent feminist concern until full equality is achieved. The idea of 'sharing', in equal terms, is top priority in any agenda which sees itself as democratic. The fact that women and men are inherently of equal worth is the fundamental belief underlying many definitions of feminism – in Ireland and everywhere else – but what are the issues that continue to impede the realization of this belief?

Patronage is a central problem for feminists. It is a fact that women in the artistic and academic world have emerged in large numbers in the last decade, but they continue to have very limited success when it comes to large-project funding, institutional power and public visibility, resulting in almost secret 'genealogical' lineages in academic circles, where the assumption is that women will look after women, so that the so-called mainstream arena tends to be more sympathetic to young men. Over the years such an attitude has contributed to further polarization of men and women in Irish society and in Irish Studies, with feminists treated with the same sort of distrust accorded to the 'bould wimmen' of Ireland, with all their sexual lures, from the 1920s to the late 1970s. The fear of sexual contamination, to say the least, appears replicated in much of what passes for Irish Studies practice, so that it begins to resemble the same sex segregation of Irish education and social practices of the early Free State. Given that much of the necessary scholarly work on women has been carried out by women, this sort of distrust of women by men is ever more accentuated. The enriching possibilities of feminist scholarship are minimized, to everyone's detriment: in this ballroom of critical romance, we all, like the character from William Trevor's tale, become Bridies of a sort, men and women both.

Irish education is still segregated in many ways, at least in the way many disciplines are taught, at all levels. For feminism to move on considerably and make an impact on the future generation, education needs to be targeted. No matter how insightful its politics, feminism feels deeply threatening to many people, both women and men. By providing a powerful critique of the idea of a timeless social hierarchy, in which God or nature preordained women's dependence on men, feminist scholarship exposes the historical construction and potential deconstruction, of categories such as gender, race, class and sexuality. Fears that feminism will unleash changes in familiar class, family, sexual and racial relationships can produce antifeminist politics among those who wish to conserve older forms of social hierarchy. In a former colony such as Ireland, suspicion, if not fear, of feminism may result from its association with Western (British) colonialism, or with 'outside' or foreign forces. For some, feminism connotes a form of rampant individualism associated with the worst features of contemporary Western, particularly American, society. Feminism forces all women and men to think about social inequalities and about their own relationship to systems of power. For some, it conjures up the fear of losing taken-for-granted privileges; for others, it brings up the pain of acknowledging lack of privilege. Neither is a very pleasant prospect, especially if feminist-led scholarship is presented in the oversimplified language of male oppression and female victimization. By necessity, the vocabulary will have to change and adapt to new perceptions. Portraying a movement as blaming one group and denying the resilience of another will keep it unpopular, even though feminism at its best offers much more complex interpretations of the dynamics of gender, race/ethnicity, and power. The 'F' word can only be demystified through a proper management of educational strategies.

Struggles over definitions are important. Since 1937 the definition of 'family' and 'woman' has been the source of much contention. The location of women in the domestic setting and in the role of mothers urgently needs revision. Also, the privileged position of the married family in the Irish Constitution should be ended to prevent discrimination against unmarried couples and children. Unmarried couples, same-sex couples, lone parents and children – whose rights are not explicitly recognized in the Constitution of the Republic – experience serious inequalities and suffer discrimination in areas such as taxation, housing, inheritance and welfare because of the State's failure to recognize their relationships and families. The family based on marriage should no longer be privileged, in order to protect children's rights in particular, while there should be an express right for all persons to marry in accordance with the law and found a family, regardless of their gender identity or sexual orientation. A gender-neutral provision recognizing the work of carers in the home should replace the current outmoded reference to women's domestic 'duties'. As a case in point, it would be an instructive lesson to study the case of South Africa, which in 1996 became the first country to explicitly include protection from discrimination on the grounds of sexual orientation in its Constitution. Families should be valued for what they do rather than how they are labelled. Quite simply, the children's best interests are served by recognizing and protecting their relationship with their primary carers irrespective of biology, gender or sexual orientation. One can only hope that Ireland will learn from the experience and progress of other countries which have set a leading example in these cases and, again, the intelligentsia must help move things forward.

Has Irish feminism, at this point, passed the historical test of time? Has it been able to redefine itself in response to local and global politics? How is it responding under the pressure of the new influx of immigrants, where non-Western women, from Muslim countries and with different beliefs, for example, are eager to join the national debate as equals? It is of course useful to remember that the fractured tradition of Ireland has always offered the challenge of difficult borders, such as that between North and South, Nationalist and Unionist, revisionist and postcolonial, Irish and English, or academia and community, rural and urban. Yet, the topics of ethnicity and racism offer a new and urgent challenge that should be treated with caution, resisting both the temptation of forced assimilation (rather than accommodation) and discrimination.

Feminism moves forward precisely through dissension about its identity and in different forms, languages and cultural locations. The international exchange of experiences with new generations of women will increasingly pose the question in terms of the relationship between women's subjectivities and the new forms of social and linguistic reproduction in the age of the cyborg. As the relation between 'centre' and 'margin', with a hierarchical division between 'first' and 'third' world, is overturned, our critical thinking will require us to reflect and to act within troubling spaces, establishing unusual connections, living among changing categories that will allow us to make close what is far, and to jump between the borders. The histories, images, the places that women traverse and of which they are agents do not allow essentialist views or simple dichotomies. We are going to enter the space and time of transnational feminisms.

In order to understand the (multicultural) future of women (and of Women's Studies) in Ireland, however, we must appreciate the history of feminism that has brought us to the present moment. The emergence of research projects (importantly) funded by the government of Ireland such as 'The Irish Women's Movement Project' constitutes the measure of a considerable achievement, since this is the first time that any Irish government has funded a university-led study and analysis of the legacy of feminism and the women's movement in recent Irish history. A variety of other projects, such as the 'Women's History Project', the 'Munster Women Writers Project' and the increasing publication of volumes of feminist research – to mention only a few: Linda Connolly, *The Irish Women's Movement: From Revolution to Devolution* (2002); Linda Connolly and Tina O'Toole, *Documenting Irish Feminisms: The Second Wave* (2005); Rebecca Pelan, *Two Irelands: Literary Feminisms North and South* (2005) – confirm that Ireland has reached a critical stage in the important task of recovery work and appreciation. The fact that many of these projects have established a basis for linking national and international research, websites and archives in the comparative study of the women's social movement has opened up the Irish frontiers to a transcultural and transnational dimension.

The records of the Irish women's movement are valuable not only to political activists and scholars interested in understanding social change in Ireland; they are also relevant to the debates among the media, community workers, educationalists and writers regarding feminism and Irish identity. In this issue of *The Irish Review* Ailbhe Smyth, Pat Coughlan, Gerardine Meaney, Maria Luddy, Pat O'Connor, Susan McKay and Ivana Bacik either revisit essays of their own which had significant critical influence within their disciplines, or revisit points in Irish legal, constitutional or social history to illuminate present-day practices and beliefs. The wide-ranging essays assembled here should prove a valuable part of that ever-evolving discussion, reflecting, as they do, upon history, literature, sociology and politics.

Notes and References

1 Patricia Ferreira, in 'Claiming and Transforming an "Entirely Gentlemanly Artifact": Ireland's Attic Press', *Canadian Journal of Irish Studies*, 19:1 (1993), 97.
2 Hilda Tweedy, *A Link in the Chain: The Story of the Irish Housewives Association, 1942–1992* (Dublin: Attic, 1992), p. 111.

Momentary Views:
A Personal History

AILBHE SMYTH

Part One: 'Iron Inklings'

> There are outsiders always. These stars –
> these iron inklings of an Irish January,
> whose light happened
>
> thousands of years before
> our pain did: they are, they have always been
> outside history.
> (Eavan Boland, from 'Outside History')

Decades, years, an entire century, millennia before and after them.

How to make sense of it all, without fixing the centre, tidying the edges, distorting the relation of one to the other?

How to encompass those volatile rhythms, subtle cadences, cycles without apparent pattern? How to embrace the 'lies, secrets and silences' as much as the achievements and celebrations?

How to account for it all, without denying the continuity of becoming which is reality itself, mine and that of women everywhere, differently, unequally, arrogantly, rebelliously, dangerously, tentatively, hopefully, joyously (even)?

How to step 'outside history' – that space I have fought so hard to inhabit – so as to see it whole and entire, yet always in transit to the future perfect?

This is a view from the moment, site-specific, limited in each of its always particular angles of vision, subject to the gravity of time, altering even as I speak, extracted by stealth and sleight of mind from the flowing mass of partial views and halting voices.

Le Siècle est mort! Vive le Siècle!

Battle cry and *cri de coeur.*

I have no time for the death of centuries or the birth of millennia. Deflectors and attention-seekers in the flux, they may or may not enable us to think more clearly, imagine more vividly, act more strategically, love more compassionately: all moments are transitional, carrying what we have gained, lost, never had, from then and now to a future never perfect.

Perfectly poised, I have lived my way through a millennial cusp, one foot rooted in the second half of the last century, the other intending to leave its trace in the first half of this one, at least. I can't afford the breaks – and they never come all that easy, do they? We construct them arduously – like children making jigsaw puzzles of marvels they have never seen – earnestly attaching retroactive meanings to a succession of moments in the questionable light of our own still-incomplete histories and (self-) interests.

I grow increasingly wary of historical totalization as I become more aware of whose moments are historicized and whose are not.

What of all those I do not know, cannot see?

Feminism is Dead! Long Live Feminism!

Battle cry and *cri de coeur.*

I pay no heed to triumphalist or fatalist pronouncements on the death of feminism.[1] I continue to believe in the motivating potential of a future perfect as a political and personal imperative. I am a pragmatic idealist, when it comes down to the bottom line, as far away as it's possible to get from *angst* and abstraction. You cannot not be, as a feminist. However it plays and gets represented in local and global arenas, feminism is a radically progressive philosophy, politics and practice. Its most basic premise is rooted in optimism: nothing is immutable, including the internal dynamics of feminism itself. There is so much that must change for so many; so much we must make for the future.

Making for the Future

Feminism has uprooted and overturned so much that seemed certain in our lives – the most intimate aspects of our sexual and personal relations as much as wider social and political structures and values. The once-tightly patrolled borders between genders, and between individual, family, community, state and nation, are shifting with great speed, becoming daily more fluid. They bring more openness and the possibility of greater freedoms, of course, but also the converse: the loss of familiarity and security, engendering anxiety, tension and an often acute sense of disorientation.[2] The sexual and emotional economies shift even more seismically than the social, affecting us at levels of our selves that can be extraordinarily difficult to understand and articulate in the everyday, and almost impossible to map in concrete and objective ways.

Feminism has been a major transformational force in modern Ireland for the past three decades, but the changes it has generated and expedited are volatile, incomplete and unevenly beneficial. Gender transformations impact on people differently, *and above all unequally*, and always intersect with other experiences, locations and regimes of social control, including class, ethnicity, sexuality, age and (dis)ability, among others. To consider feminism is therefore a complex business, requiring attentive, knowing, empathetic and imaginative scrutiny of the ways in which specifically located women can and do live their lives.

Still, assessing the extent and nature of change at the present moment, in all its (perfectly) normal partiality and multiplicity, is a vital project, not for the survival of feminism (logically and entirely expendable in the future perfect) but for the realization of a world – the world – where freedom and equality have meaning and can be realized by everyone. Women breaking rank with our bodies, our hearts and our minds have profoundly and acutely unsettled the social order. It is important for us to know in all kinds of different ways what that dis-ordering signifies, how it is experienced in its dailiness and, above all, where it may lead.

Facts, statistics, flow-charts are important in mapping the trends and processes of social change, but they are not enough.[3] Changes in perception and feeling, in the economy of affect, are not so readily amenable to measurement. We need other kinds of knowledge to understand and tell the multiple dis/re-locations of the present and their erratic connections with the past. We need stories, poems and dreams, I am sure, in making for the future:

> Because what matters to us most
> can seldom be told in words
> the heart's moods are better charted
> in its own language –
> (Moya Cannon, from 'Between the Jigs and the Reels')

Part Two: Momentary Views

Over the past few years, much like so many others I have known since the 1970s, I have been serially and sometimes simultaneously exhilarated, frustrated, amused, weary, inspired, sceptical, bored (occasionally), provoked and energized by activism occurring in the myriad spaces a political – specifically feminist and lesbian – activist activates: in meetings, streets, bars, media, conferences, classrooms, courtrooms, boardrooms, bedrooms, living rooms, non-living rooms and everywhere else you try to live your life (and change the world).

What follows is an intricacy of stories, flashes from a 'life'. Not the whole life, for some things remain outside this kind of discourse, still. They are momentary and entirely partial views, 'iron inklings'.

Apples and Oranges

An invitation arrives to present myself at 11a.m. sharp at the Gaiety Theatre for a 'historic photograph' of one hundred women of influence.

Not power, or authority – just influence.

Not one or ten thousand or one or two million – just the Chosen Few, happy or not.

Just as much as the system can stand, for the moment, as it re-enacts and reproduces that very moment we stand in.

A chilly autumn morning. I dress carefully, doubtfully, in my very best leathers: statement, defiance, or trivial pursuit?

> I am as different as apples and oranges.
> I will not be boxed.
> I have come (after all) for the photograph.

Along with the other ninety-nine women who have changed the face of Ireland, they said. What do they mean? What does it mean to participate? What will it keep in place, this representation of change? What do I represent? Will it matter?

Why am I here? As an academic? But there are others. As a feminist radical activist? There are one or two others. As an explicitly 'out' lesbian? Maybe. There are no others. Nobody tells me why I am a woman of influence – and would I believe them even if they did?

I feel nervous, flattered, slightly ashamed. Arriving too early, I loiter without intent in Habitat – global goes local, like everywhere else in the rich world – meet a friend, as bemused as myself, I think. We smile ruefully, catch up on news, pat our hair, and one another, comfortingly.

Good morning ladies! No bridling at 'ladies', although 'girls' stirs up a breeze of altogether girlish giggling protest, we're so polite, too polite, not politic. But we are not girls. We are 'established' women, getting on, and surely beyond giggling. Sit here, there, move over that way, smile again please, yeah, keep it going there, head up the one on the left half-way down, mobile phones ring discretely, ladies speculate about why this one or that is not here, and – *sotto voce* – why the other one is. We know one another, by name, by sight, the chosen few.

Where are you, who are you, why are you if you're not here?

And when they arrived at the gates of heaven, still flustered after the long jour-ney, St Peter, the head gatekeeper as ever was, asked them sternly: Were you a woman of influence? Were you polite not politic? Did you pat your hair, put your best foot forward, learn to row but never rock the boat? Did you change the face of Ireland, avoiding its limbs and vital organs at all costs? Can you pay the heavenly price? Have you a photograph to prove it?

But surely it's those *not* in the picture who pay the price, always?

I am angry with myself. Have I learned nothing, I who have taught for so long, about the seductive deceits of the Janus faces of power? That selling your politics for a picture destroys your soul, however much you dress it up or down?

What have we changed for the better, all one hundred of us, by whose reckoning, for whom, for how long? And are they the better for it? Who are we? Who are they? By what right have we few been chosen in the place of so many? Has all our influence really shifted the structures of power more than an inch in our favour?

I know the answers, most of all when I'm sliding over them.

Coats and Bags of All Kinds

The very same afternoon, still doubtful in leather, I carry on down Grafton Street to a conference in Trinity where I am to speak, where I will need to bare my politics and my soul.

WOMEN AND SOCIAL EXCLUSION
RECLAIMING and TRANSFORMING
THE WOMEN'S MOVEMENT

Up bleak concrete stairways to a large, untidy room. Coats and bags of all kinds, yellow programmes, paper cups, I fall over a small child, inhale the combined smells of onion sandwiches and cigarettes. I like this disarray on hallowed university ground – proof of disorderly conduct, signs of condi-tional inclusion maybe, at least for two days.

> We, a group of women community activists for equality and inclusion and against racism, we – disabled women, women of colour, Muslim women, Jewish women, lesbians and others, who feel excluded from women's movement events, are organising an inclusive conference. This event is unique in that it is you who will be setting the agenda.[4]

We're setting it in papers and discussions, in speak-outs, dialogues, mime, drama, dancing, singing and however else women feel moved to express themselves, the like of which is never heard in this stern, sterile environment. Bright reflections of the refusal to desiccate.

There are about seventy of us and again I meet many women I know. None was included in this morning's photograph. The contrast is a sharp pain in my belly. These worlds are utterly different. The women in this room know that there is nothing simple about gender, that socio-economic 'difference' is about unequal relations of power and that political analyses and agendas disconnected from the realities of experience and which do not explicitly challenge the *status quo* are not worth a button.[5] They say so movingly, wittily, intelligently, angrily, powerfully. There is respect here. No one giggles. 'Ladies' need not participate.

I hear someone talk about how she has always felt excluded by the Women's Movement. I am ashamed because there is much truth in this and no amount of personal breast-beating can erase the ignorance or (worse) indifference of many years. The failure to think about the inequalities between women, the unwillingness to make space and the inability to take on issues of literally vital importance to women in marginalized positions are facts. That many women feel the women's movement is not about or for them is neither very new, nor particular to Ireland and certainly there are reasons which at least partly account for it. That doesn't make it any the less real and painful. It most definitely does not lessen the urgent need for revolutionary change within feminism in this place, now.

And that is exactly what is happening in this large, untidy room. This *is* the Women's Movement in action, collectively reflecting, analyzing, arguing, exchanging experiences, information and ideas, defining agendas, strategizing, networking, dealing with the present, making for the future.

But are the women in this room 'women of influence'?

The women in the picture are rarely the Women's Movement (however we define it), and even those few who are, are never all of it. Women's organizations (including Women's Studies centres) are not the Women's Movement either, although their investment is great and they may stake claims to *de facto* ownership. But no one owns a social movement: it is not a commodity or a piece of property: it is ideals and ideas, politics and projects, it is a process constantly in the (re)making.

It is difficult for those (myself included) who have been feminist activists for a long time to acknowledge the failures and silences of a movement which has fought so hard to lay the foundations of women's autonomy and freedom in Ireland, and around the world.[6] It is difficult because there have been costs to pay and we have so often been vilified, ostracized and demonized. Defensiveness becomes a second skin, necessary for the protection of sensitive scars. But it cannot be allowed to prevent us embracing some of the consequences of the very changes so many have struggled to bring about: women everywhere, with coats and bags of all kinds, willing, able and determined to take matters into their own hands.

And indeed there has been great change, some of it even measurable and concrete – contraception, anti-violence legislation, divorce, homosexuality decriminalized, equality legislation, improved educational and employment opportunities, more comprehensive healthcare – although still no childcare. But this must not mean that we take positive change for granted, or assume that it floats all the boats to the same degree. Equality is being 'main-streamed' – or so they tell us – but what is left out of the picture, who is not in the picture, is almost everything we've been talking about here in this room today.

My Body is a Battleground

Remember the Barbara Kruger billboard?

YOUR BODY IS A BATTLEGROUND[7]

Sometimes, and maybe it's (only) the effect of age, I feel it in the brittle-ness of my bones, the slackness of my flesh. All those marks and scars, not necessarily all my own.

The process of modernization is underscored by tensions, confusions and contradictions, with ownership and control of women's sexuality and reproduction as the arena where the struggle between tradition and mod-ernism is fought out most bitterly. This has been the experience of women in Ireland for over a quarter of a century. Men's violence, divorce, reproduc-tive rights, abortion the most hotly and divisively contested of all. The absorption of the entire country in the abortion controversies since the early 1980s signals how abortion is identified as the defining 'boundary' between the old and new versions of Ireland.

In all of this, what about women, what about our bodies, what about independence? Batted around from court to court and referendum to refer-endum, 'the women themselves, they just don't come into it'.[8]

But we do, we do, and we won't go away.

A quarter of a century ago now, a young Irish woman I know well became pregnant without intending to. She had been using contraception, but, for some reason or another, it failed. There is nothing unusual about this – it happens to women of childbearing age all the time, all over the world.

This young woman went ahead with her pregnancy, because (I believe) she didn't see herself as having any option – she had to go ahead, whether she wanted to or not, and indeed she did not. She was just eighteen, and in no position financially or socially to raise a child – and certainly in no state of mind or maturity to take on the responsibility of raising a child on her own, the man having disappeared like snow off a ditch. She had to go ahead because the legal, social and cultural prohibitions against abortion were so total and powerful that even the very notion of 'choice' was unthinkable and unspeakable for her. Her baby was adopted. This was not a 'decision' she made in any real sense of that word, implying some ability to choose freely between one option and another. Her baby was adopted, because there was nothing else she could do. And she was devastated. I don't really know how she dealt with that, and she had to deal with it almost entirely on her own. I don't really know how she thinks and feels about it now, and I suspect she doesn't talk about it. I do know I will never forget the pain on her face, the pain that held every bone and muscle in her body tight and rigid, when I saw her a short while after the adoption. I will never forget it because it was terrible and cruel, and because no woman, anywhere, should ever have to go through that.

Seeing that young woman's experience made me incandescent with anger. I am still angry about how we continue in Ireland to deny women the freedom to make our own reproductive decisions, because of the absence of adequate sex education (or any at all), and because there is still not easily accessible, safe and free contraception for all women everywhere throughout the country.[9] I am deeply angry at how we turn our backs on women's needs by pretending that information and the 'right to travel' are somehow enough for a woman who decides rationally and in the fullness of her own conscience – that she needs an abortion. A leaflet and a ticket to England are not an abortion. And they most certainly do not ensure the well-being, liberty and dignity which women are entitled to, as self-determining human beings. The reality is that at least 5,000 women in Ireland need an abortion badly enough, every year, to make a demeaning and often desperately lonely journey to England to get one.

How many more don't go because they have no money, no information, no support – no sense of a choice? I don't know.

So this evening I am going to a meeting of the Abortion Reform Campaign. We are girding yet again for the fight, already shaping up for the year to come. How many abortion campaign meetings have I been to over the past fifteen, seventeen, eighteen years? I've lost count, and sometimes, it's true, my energy flags. But I'm campaigning again because it matters.

Reproductive freedom has been a central issue for feminism and the Women's Movement since the nineteenth century because reproduction has been – is – a central part of women's lives and the arena in which male control has been consistently exercised. In the White West, the struggle has focused on contraception, abortion, and more recently on the development of reproductive technologies. For many women with disabilities, for Black and many ethnic minority women in the West, as for millions of women elsewhere in the world, the struggle has often centred around other reproductive issues – notably around population control strategies such as enforced sterilization and limitation of family size.

Depending on class, race, ethnic origin, global location, it can seem as if women are demanding diametrically opposed 'freedoms' and 'rights'. But this is not so: what women consistently seek is the freedom to live our bodies as part of our 'selves', the freedom to make sexual and reproductive decisions appropriate to our social, economic, physical and psychological needs. And whether that entails having more or fewer or no children, it is always about women's capacity and right to exercise choice.

The issue of abortion and its bitterly divisive politicization over the past thirty years is just the most recent chapter in the long history of women's fight for freedom. In the second half of the twentieth century, abortion became one of the primary arenas for the playing out of the struggle for patriarchal control – a struggle which has always been waged on women's bodies, whether through reproductive control, violence and violation or through other forms of bodily appropriation.[10]

The reality of abortion, and women's need for it, will not go away because we try to pretend it doesn't exist. Abortion is not a question to which there is a 'right' or 'wrong' answer.[11] It is a need and a reality which must be clearly named and recognized and placed in the context of women's slow and often painful struggle to achieve liberation.

'I Don't Think They Can Hear Me'

> I don't think they can hear me, she went on, as she put her head closer down, and I'm nearly sure they can't see me. I feel somehow as if I was getting invisible.
>
> (Lewis Carroll, from *Through the Looking-Glass*)

So the first question is, was Alice a dyke?

A grey, wet Sunday afternoon in Dublin, yet the room is crammed for the first-ever all-time great All-Ireland Coming Out Day celebration, complete with radio advertising (Mozart on the backing track, oh how Euro we've become), speeches and media hype.

Maybe my mother will see a photograph?

I think about the lightning changes in this small, no longer so Catholic country. I wouldn't have spoken at an event like this ten years ago, so much would have been on the line. But then, there wasn't an event like this a decade ago. The Robinson era, sherry in the Áras,[12] years of campaigning leading to the decriminalization of homosexuality (male – lesbians were always unthinkable) have exposed the mechanisms of sexual control.[13]

Now, although still with some residual trepidation – old prohibitions die hard and long – I can say what I think and who I am, with no omissions. So I do.

When I came out as lesbian nearly fifteen years ago, I really didn't come out at all, except, I suppose – and then quite prudently – to other lesbians and gay men. Except for my daughter, I didn't come out to my family, to most of my heterosexual friends, or at work, because I didn't feel free to say I was lesbian, knew it would have negative consequences, knew it would be too hard for me to say it. It did indeed have an impact on my personal life, which I still cannot talk about in public, because it is still too painful. It has affected my professional and political life too, although I have learned to live with that more easily, and to see it, in some ways, as even strategically useful. To be marked is, at the very least, to be visible, a sign of difference, a tiger of another stripe.

The fact is, I still don't find it easy to stand up in public and say 'I am lesbian', even though I am a middle-class, white, settled woman with a well-paid, high-status job. These powerful privileges give me advantages and protections in all other parts of my life – but not here. I can be, and sometimes am, ignored, marginalized or discriminated against because I am lesbian. Yet my lesbian sexuality is an important part of my identity and the Irish woman I am, and I want that to be acknowledged and valued in the same way as all the other connected parts of me.

Over the past twenty or thirty years, we have been experiencing a long transition from repression and closure, to openness and greater ease of sexual identity and expression. In many respects, we have in Ireland been re-inventing or re-generating ourselves as a society through a profound and often volatile interrogation of sexuality, initiated by feminists and supported and diversified by lesbians and gay men since the early 1980s.

Now, in the 2000s, Irish laws, policy and attitudes reflect a society which is less fearful, repressive and punitive. But the transition is slow and frequently painful, with responsibility for the contesting of the dominance of heterosexuality still borne massively by lesbians and gay men: campaigning, lobbying, researching, teaching, publishing, creating social, political and cultural space(s), and providing services. Marginalization, discrimination, exploitation, shame, silence and invisibility continue to be realities lived daily by countless lesbians and gay men in this country. Acceptance, ease, visibility are unpredictable and piecemeal (now you see us, now you don't), and conditional upon the terms set by ruling groups: don't draw attention to your lesbian/gay sexuality, except the terms set by the hetero-patriarchal world; don't disrupt its norms and values; don't disturb its homely beliefs and comforts.

Because of persistent and brave feminist, lesbian and gay activism over many years, we are certainly making progress in this country.[14] But we all know that laws are not enough in themselves to radically change the deep-rooted myths and stereotypes, the attitudes and behaviours which maintain homophobia and discrimination.

Which is why today is important.

The Ecology of Bogland

Then there was the time in 1992 when I was in Boston with about fifty other Irish women at a conference organized (and financed) by American women. We were a disparate lot, with little connection between the Northern and Southern women. The Southern group were mainly 'public' and professional women from middle-class, Dublin backgrounds – the 'liberal agenda' incarnate. The Northern women were mostly community activists and working class, from both Protestant and Catholic communities, with a quarter of a century of war behind them, whatever lies ahead.

Entitled 'Reaching Common Ground', the conference aimed to bring together women from the two parts of Ireland to talk about our differences and how we might overcome them. In the event, we did and we didn't. We talked across the dividing lines of class and religion, and even tried, *sotto voce*, to talk about why they keep us apart. What we didn't do was reach the promised land of 'common ground'. We glimpsed it from time to time in moments of discovery, exchange and pleasure, in workshops, midnight bars and Cambridge cafés. But did any of us (Irish women) really think we would do more? Common ground, after all, where it has been cut from under you by the ruthlessness of colonial history, cannot grow again overnight, or even in a week.

> The ecology, conservation and exploitation of bogland is complex . . .
> Boglands can be dangerous; it is unwise to visit them alone or to walk on
> a bog, as some of the pools are very deep.

It was a difficult week, full of the wariness and tensions stemming from our complex differences, not least our different experiences of war and peace. Where some (mainly American and Southern Irish) insisted on enthusiasm, even euphoria, others (mostly Northern Irish) were more cautious: 'Everybody in Northern Ireland is holding their breath', as one of the Northern women put it. 'Peace is not normal', another young woman said. And it is disturbingly unfamiliar. After twenty-five years of war, a whole generation of young people in Northern Ireland have never lived in a state of peace. But no women in Southern Ireland have lived in a state at war. Peace and war cannot mean the same things to those who have known only the one, but not (yet) the other. Northern women told us so many times, and in so many ways, that it is a fragile thing, this peace. Unlike war, which is tough, durable, unyielding.

But when we listened, what did we make of what we heard?

So who are you to tell us what our peace should mean? What it should live like? How it should feel? Who are you to tell us that it will cost so much, and not more, that the $$$ and £££ must be spent on these things rather than those? How do you know anything about the cost of war and the price of peace? 'This is a peace very bitter to the taste', a Unionist woman said.

Northern women spoke of their anxieties about the 'peace process' and its provenance: 'We have peace by courtesy of the paramilitaries.' And where, they asked, is the process anyway if the brokers behave as if peace were a commodity to be capitalized on the world market? They were angry at women's exclusion from the 'peace talks'. What is democratic and open about a process that shuts women out?

In Boston, we made much small talk, but discovered at least (if we didn't know before) that talking about war and the wounds it leaves is both necessary and difficult:

> Two decades later, I listen
> look mostly in vain
> for signs
> that the wounds of the dead
> heal
> that children are not born
> with stigmata
> of those old bullet wounds.
>
> (Marie Smyth, from 'Bloody Sunday Revisited')

In Northern Ireland, the two communities (Protestant and Catholic) rarely talk to one another; Northeners and Southerners don't know how to talk to one another; North or South, the middle class doesn't bother to talk with the working class. In such untalkative circumstances, perhaps we didn't do so badly, after all, in at least trying to find the words to ferry us across the deep divides that have kept us in our separate states of mind and place. The habits of different histories and experiences are not easily put aside, even in a sunny Boston week.

> Many would not talk
> for fear
> of bursting the scars
> or fear of weeping

or that I
would put them on tv
or twist their words
to prove something.

(Marie Smyth, from 'Bloody Sunday Revisited')

I am uncertain about what we achieved in a week in Boston. But we did talk, and we didn't (on the whole) twist each other's words. I don't think we proved anything, except that our confusions and uncertainties about ourselves and each other, about the past, the present and the future, will take a lot of talking to sort out.

Bogland, they say, takes a long time to regenerate.

Unfamiliar Families

I've been asked to give a public lecture in a very public library on 'Changing Families'. Very few people show up, and the organizers clearly don't know what to do with me. I'm embarrassed. All those ads. My nose is out of joint. I spent ages thinking, reading, worrying about it, writing it, but you have to not take it personally. You have to tell yourself that in this part of the city they might be just a mite wary (with entirely good reason rooted in experience) of what a middle-aged, middle-class, white academic and (to boot) a 'self-professed' feminist, lesbian, queer radical, if that is not entirely oxymoronic, might have to say, or not, about 'the family'. And anyway, they're probably mostly so busy trying to live in one, love in one, survive in one, support one, escape from one, that they don't have time, much, for thinking about it all. Thinking is a terrific luxury and a huge privilege – I try to remember to remind myself every day, and not to give up on it – even if it doesn't mean you know how to do it any better than the next person. Or the one over there.

Everywhere I look around me, I see unfamiliar families. I mean, families not at all like the one I grew up in and around. Including my own. I am part of a family that is, in terms of my experience, unfamiliar to me. I think we're inventing it as we go along. As queer as can be.

I am the eldest of a family of six children, all of us still living, which already tells you a great deal about my background – middle-class, white, sedentary, Western European – the resources we had access to, and my parents' aspirations for us. My mother was one of eleven, but I have just one child, Lydia, who is twenty-six. I grew up in a conventional patriarchal, nuclear family: father (out at work all day), mother (in at work all day and often much of the night – who tends to the crying babies?), and with a vast extended family (I have very approximately seventy-three first cousins, almost all of us living within shouting distance of one another. Lydia's father and I weren't married to each other – I was still technically married to someone else

because divorce was not permitted and I never wanted to marry ever again anyway –
and we lived in different cities, although we raised our daughter together. She lived
with me first, then went to live with her father when she was eleven, coinciding (or
not) with my coming out as lesbian.

One Christmas, when she was little, my mother asked Lydia and myself if we
would like to spend it 'with the family', to which my daughter instructively replied:
'But Granny, we are a family'. Last Christmas, Lydia, her dad, my then girlfriend,
and another friend spent the day together in my house in Dublin. Lydia got mar-
ried, most romantically, on a Californian beach not long ago. I live on my own, and
my mother has lived on her own too, ever since my father died over twenty years ago.

Who is a family now?

My Mother, My Daughter and I

On Sundays, I go to see my mother. We make extraordinary efforts to meet
somewhere in the middle between all that divides us. Each week we confront but almost never talk about the differences between us. Differences of
disposition and temperament to be sure, fewer maybe than we want or
imagine, and clear as the day except for their entirely unsimple, inexorable
inflection by the massive upheavals spanning the decades of our lives, hers
and mine. Lives overlapping and intertwining for so many years, yet without continuity at their extremities. Born just after the first (Western) world
war and Irish independence, she raised me to the very best of her means
and abilities for a life like hers, as her mother had raised her. But that was
not how it turned out. Born after the second (Western) world war, child of
the decades of (Irish) economic expansion, I grew up into a far bigger
world, full of possibilities my mother couldn't even dream of.

My mother was born in Belfast, but grew up and still lives in Dublin. She
left school after the Inter Cert and did clerical work until she married. She
had six children, and worked full-time at rearing us, as hard as anyone I've
ever known, for no pay and no independent social status. She looked after
our father, made our clothes and hot dinners, grew vegetables, bottled fruit
and managed to make ends meet. She taught us to say the rosary, mind our
manners, do our homework and turn the lights out, more or less in that
order of priority. When we grew up (not all of us altogether as expected),
she went on caring for her children and then her grandchildren in all kinds
of ways. Although she has always had numerous friends, her family and
home are the centre of her life, or so it seems to me.

This tells you nothing about who my mother is, what she is like – her
intelligence, humour and energy, or her rarely indulged penchant for
extravagance. It tells you nothing of how she too must have struggled and
changed over the years. The decisions, choices, dilemmas, pain, pleasure,

hopes and disillusionments that have marked her life are not here. It would not be for me to tell you or anyone these very private things, even if I could. But indeed I cannot, for so much remained hidden, buried, silent in the lives of women of my mother's generation and upbringing. I don't know clearly what being a woman has meant to her, how she experienced her sexuality, what she might have done differently if she had had half a chance.

I went to university, and have been in paid work since my early twenties. I married briefly, chose to have one child – by another man – and discovered my lesbian sexuality when I was in my mid-thirties. My life has been so much more public than my mother's – teaching, writing, broadcasting, always politically involved – and I have been able to make many more decisions about how I live. I no longer believe in most of what I was taught when I was a child. I don't fear god or the neighbours, or believe in the unquestioned rightness of the State and the Constitution. I am appalled by the desperation of poverty and of war, by the terrible inhumanity of some towards the majority. Although I bow to no man, often I am afraid. I am afraid of loneliness, lies, cruelty, my own above all. I am afraid of fear itself. I believe in my right to take nothing for granted and to leave no stone unturned.

Last Sunday, my mother and I talked about my daughter, her granddaughter: loving, admiring, acknowledging her difference and her distance from us both. The privileges I inherited have been passed on to her with interest accruing, for my generation of urban middle-class women in Ireland has gained a great deal. There is an irony in finding myself worrying about Lydia's future the way my mother (still) worries about me. I've always wished she wouldn't, of course, and know Lydia feels just the same. I hope, as I believe my mother did, that I have raised her to be able to confront the challenges of her generation and to act creatively, fearlessly and generously in the world. But I think this is not enough – and I'm not sure I can even dream far enough ahead to say precisely why. I have raised a daughter for a future I cannot even imagine. So I do worry, because I am sometimes fearful about this future that is being made so fast and carelessly, without the participation of so many.

Sometimes one or other of us, my mother or I, can make the huge imaginative leap that enables us to understand the truths and realities of the other's experience, but it is not easy. Generational cross-talk almost never is.

I am aware of how I drown out my mother's halting voice with my fluent assertions, and of the vulnerability of my own voice in the passage of time and the growing up of daughters. Generations are such provisional things, like centuries.

Part Three: Coming to Terms

> We have reached a point of historic crisis. If humanity is to have a recognisable future, it cannot be by prolonging the past or present. If we try to build the third millennium on that basis, we shall fail. And the price of failure, that is to say, the alternative to a changed society, is darkness.
>
> (Eric Hobsbawm)[15]

Yes, I am often ashamed in the present and fearful for the future, but I don't fear the apocalypse, because I believe in human agency. I believe that the alternatives which will provide us with foundations for the future are right here and right now. Everywhere, throughout the world, and whether men take heed or not, women have been refusing to prolong the past or to make do with the half-truths, the partial realities, the sleights of law and policy, the volatile inadequacies of the present. And much has shifted, whether we can measure it 'accurately' or not, as a consequence.

I still believe in the necessity of revolution, in justice, equality and freedom. I no longer believe these are simple matters. There is so much (still) to learn, to construct, to invent, to imagine.

LEXICON

I am not so good
At letting go, moving on
Leaving my bags at the door
Or out on the tarmac.
What I have, I hold
(Mantra from an old lexicon)

'You're in a funk'
She used to say, always cool, whenever she came back
From another sortie
Over to the deep blue yonder
Clutching on, for all she was worth,
To here and to there, all in one breath

Enough to drive you over the edge
To the other side.

I'd laugh of course, nonchalant as ever was,
Splaying my fingers to stop the shake
(Made me feel so old, way over the hill)

It was all about sides, when I think about it,
Lexicons that couldn't make the crossing

I think it's time now
To come to terms
Learn new words for other worlds

No more trips
Just the big jump, once and for all
Yet again
Into God knows where.

Notes and References

1 I pay even less heed to the alleged non-existence of 'women'. Feminists do indeed have to discover ways of resisting amnesia and oblivion, as much as the tyranny of (always incomplete) memory.

2 For an interesting discussion of processes of social change and the 'colliding discourses' they generate, see Kieran Keohane and Carmen Kuhling, *Collision Culture: Transformations in Everyday Life in Ireland* (Dublin: Liffey, 2004). See also Colin Coulter and Steve Coleman (eds), *The End of Irish History? Critical Reflections on the Celtic Tiger* (Manchester: Manchester University Press, 2003).

3 I set out, originally, to write a 'real' paper about changing gender relations in contemporary Ireland, complete with facts and statistics, neatly arranged in highs and lows, replete with requisite references. I abandoned it because it said so little about the remarkable, complicated and contradictory trajectories of women's lives, and therefore of the lives of men and of children, of everyone in the place I live in. The weft and woof of change continued to float somewhere above and beyond my careful deployment of information and the kinds of explanations I was capable of advancing. For an excellent history and analysis of contemporary feminism in Ireland, see Linda Connolly, *The Irish Women's Movement: From Revolution to Devolution* (Dublin: Lilliput, 2003). Also, see Linda Connolly and Tina O'Toole, *Documenting Irish Feminisms* (Dublin: Woodfield, 2005).

4 'Women and Social Exclusion', Trinity College Dublin, September 1998.

5 'Social Inclusion', to be achieved largely via the extension of 'Social Partnership', is now a key mantra within Irish policy-making élites and much of the 'third sector'. I have my reservations. Inclusion has an oddly hollow sound when defined by the included. I know, because I am an 'included' in terms of my social class, ethnicity, current ablebodiedness, and all the cumulative privileges they give me: a house, education, job, security, confidence, access to women and men of influence. What concerns me acutely about 'inclusion' is its political weakness, conceptually and practically: 'inclusion' effectively disallows the fundamental critiques of the existing order that are crucial to transformative action, and leave binary systems (of 'insiders' and 'outsiders') intact.

6 See Cathleen O'Neill, 'Reclaiming and Transforming the (Irish) Women's Movement', *f/m (feminist magazine)*, Special issue on 'Movement', 3 (1999), 41–3.

7 Barbara Kruger, *Love for Sale*, text by Kate Linker (New York: Harry N. Abrams, 1996).

8 This is a quote from Ruth Fletcher's study of five Irish women who went to the UK for

an abortion. Ruth Fletcher, 'Silences: Irish Women and Abortion', *Feminist Review*, 50 (1995), 44–60.

9 Countless women in rural areas in particular have told me how difficult it is still for them to openly seek to purchase contraceptives or to request a prescription for the pill from their local doctor.

10 See Ailbhe Smyth (ed.), *The Abortion Papers: Ireland* (Dublin: Attic, 1992).

11 And beyond the factual realm, there are remarkably few questions permitting of direct answers.

12 President Mary Robinson invited members of the lesbian and gay community to visit her at her official residence, Áras an Uachtaráin, in 1992. This was the first time such an honour had been extended to lesbians and gay men in Ireland and signalled President Robinson's commitment to creating a more open and egalitarian society.

13 Male homosexuality was decriminalized in 1993 without acrimonious public debate. For an account of the campaign to achieve decriminalization and gay liberation more broadly, see Kieran Rose, *Diverse Communities: The Evolution of Gay and Lesbian Politics in Ireland* (Cork: Cork University Press, 1994).

14 See Eoin Collins and Ide O'Carroll (eds), *Lesbian and Gay Visions of Ireland: Towards the Twenty-First Century* (London: Cassell, 1995).

15 Eric Hobsbawm, *The Age of Extremes: A History of the World, 1914–1991* (New York: Vintage, 1994).

'The Whole Strange Growth':
Heaney, Orpheus and women

PATRICIA COUGHLAN

And if you set it within the context of this kind of criticism, and relate it to the resurgence of women and the vehemence of the Women's Movement in Ireland, then you have dialogue, you have answer back, and you have provocation. Why not? It is a dialogue.

(Seamus Heaney, Interview, 2002)[1]

. . . Her fate to be a consequence of passion,
His love songs practised, but unpleasant to her ear.

(Vona Groarke, from 'Grace Notes', 1994)[2]

In 1990 I became interested in how two leading Irish poets, John Montague and Seamus Heaney, wrote about women, gender and sex. This started out as quite a tentative enquiry, but took on the character of a critique as I gathered evidence about the representations of women and femininity in this influential and distinguished body of poetry, and about both poets' appropriation and redeployment of female figures and ideas about gender from earlier Irish traditions. After its publication in 1991 as '"Bog Queens": The Representation of Women and Femininity in the Poetry of Heaney and Montague', the essay began, rather to my surprise, to be received as polemical and combative, and has now been widely cited and reprinted three times.[3]

Soon after having had the present essay commissioned, my attention was drawn to interesting comments by Heaney himself in 2002 on my essay, in the extensive, US-published interview quoted above. The interview was conducted by a group of college students and has a relatively loose weave and a meditative tone. With apparent casualness, the discussion ranges over a constellation of topics, among which questions of gender appear prominently. While the discussion focuses successively on an alleged femininity as characteristic of Irish Catholicism, on gendered metaphors for poetic inspiration, on the current culture of political correctness internationally, or on feminism and Irish poetry, the interview affords a clear and unified impression of his recent thinking on gender as a whole, particularly in its relation to the writing of Irish history and identity.

A questioner refers to Heaney's remark (in the 1980 Haffenden interview) that 'you saw Irish Catholicism as having a definite feminine presence', and asks how 'that sense of the feminine presence' has affected his poetry.[4] Evidently choosing not to focus on the religio-cultural aspect of the question, he responds as follows:

> I used to think that my poems came out of something passive, brooding, womb-like. But the longer I live I realize that's not the whole truth. I must admit it was a kind of myth, that there was a kind of wilfulness in it. These terms, of course, 'feminine presence' and 'masculine drive' and so on, are now regarded as sexist and suspect and agin' the law somehow. I was basing my distinctions on the biological facts of siring and mothering, you know? One is a forced entry, as it were, and the other is a suffered consequence. So you can think of poems as a consequence of something, as a matter of waiting, or you can think of them as wilful entering.[5]

This response, full of counter-currents, first evokes a self-presentation by the poet as not only feminine but, when writing, in the process of female gestation: 'passive, brooding, womb-like'. At first he disavows this as a conscious construction ('a kind of myth'), with 'a kind of wilfulness in it'. Then he refers to the alleged policing nowadays of the use of stereotyped gender terms ('"feminine presence" and "masculine drive" and so on'). A mild defensiveness is first shown in the shift of register to the deliberately informal phrase 'agin' the law somehow'; this develops into a rejection of the idea he has himself just advanced, of myth as a construction and of representations as willed and cultural, in a stubborn 'I was basing my distinctions on the biological facts of siring and mothering, you know?' The 'you know?', more than just phatic in seeming to petition his hearers' assent, is followed up by an even more sharply antithetical characterization of gendered roles and application of them to notions of poetry-making: 'One is a forced entry, as it were, and the other a suffered consequence.' Poems, then, he says, can be understood either as 'a matter of waiting' or as 'wilful entering'.

I have quoted the whole passage to show the fascinating to-ing and fro-ing of Heaney's thinking, which moves between two quite disparate positions before settling emphatically upon one of them. Several interlinked instances of unspoken slippage, or perhaps of cavalier extrapolation, occur here. The fallback on 'the biological facts' shows how the whole train of thought ignores distinctions between male and masculine, female and feminine, and thus implicitly rejects any kind of belief that gender is constructed in society, rather than in nature. There is also a move from *gender* adjectives ('masculine', 'feminine'), themselves already remarkably fixed and polarized by the nouns 'drive' and 'presence', to a description of genital *sexual* intercourse, or rather of rape (unless there is some other way of understanding 'forced entry' and 'suffered consequence'). 'Siring', 'forced', and 'wilful' line up against 'mothering', 'suffered' and 'consequence'. The glaring lack of congruity between 'siring' and 'mothering', which re-effects that collapse of 'woman' into 'mother' familiar in Irish Catholic ideology as well as in Freud and many other patriarchal writings, deserves a discussion in itself.

There is another extrapolation from the processes of human sexual interaction and reproduction to those of poetic composition: it's not just that women's role in real life is presented as 'a matter of waiting' and men's in 'wilful entering': poems too – those highly skilled, prestige cultural artefacts – can be divided into two sexed categories. The strangeness of this idea has been muted by its recurrence in literary history and criticism. Such uses of the sexual metaphor for artistic creation have a long history in the discussion of writing – certainly that of men – and are important in the tradition of Romanticism, as Gilbert and Gubar showed in their classic anatomy of the process in *The Madwoman in the Attic*.[6] Furthermore, the strong, indeed inextricable, association of lyric poetry in particular with masculine subjectivity – 'the great male writing "I"' – has long been noted by critics, by poets themselves and, since the 1970s, by feminists.[7] In Irish cultural rhetoric it is, of course, closely interwoven with the powerful figure of the nation as feminine figure, which appears later in Heaney's interview. Poets engaged in the assertion of nationhood are especially liable to strike virile poses, as Whitman does in 'A Woman Waits for Me':

It is I, you women – I make my way,
I am stern, acrid, large, undissuadable – but I love you,
I do not hurt you any more than is necessary for you,
I pour the stuff to start sons and daughters fit for These States – I
    press with slow rude muscle,
I brace myself effectually – I listen to no entreaties,
I dare not withdraw till I deposit what has so long accumulated
    within me.

Through you I drain the pent-up rivers of myself,
In you I wrap a thousand onward years,

On you I graft the grafts of the best-beloved of me and America . . .[8]

Whitman's adoption of the vatic, national-bardic role seems to demand the degree of *machismo* – so evidently performative – which his speaker expresses here. However, his characterization, in surrounding stanzas, of the American women who will be recipients of this seminal surge is startlingly at odds with Heaney's passive figure uneasily abstracted in the phrase 'a suffered consequence':

They are not one jot less than I am,
They are tann'd in the face by shining suns and blowing winds,
Their flesh has the old divine suppleness and strength,
They know how to swim, row, ride, wrestle, shoot, run, strike, retreat,
    advance, resist, defend themselves,
They are ultimate in their own right – they are calm, clear, well-possess'd of
    themselves.[9]

As Heaney's readers know, gendered metaphors of creativity have also been especially significant to this particular poet and are closely interwoven with his sense of both Irish and masculine identity.[10] One of the curious aspects of this metaphorical projection of reproductive upon artistic acts is the tendency of male writers to gather in the roles of both sexes. Metaphors of involuntary conception, long gestation and painful bringing forth are all common instances of this appropriation by male authors of female physical experiences and reproductive capacities, which become added to male ones, sometimes in the exaggeratedly *macho* forms we have just seen.[11]

In the interview, Heaney next circles back to his own sense of 'waiting': 'I used to think that I wasn't "a wilful writer", that wilfulness was somehow agin' the laws of imagination which I took from Wordsworth and Keats and the Romantics.'[12] It is interesting that he repeats the phrase, 'somehow agin' the laws', which he has earlier used about the imperatives of political correctness in the context of gender: an echo which, in such a conscious craftsman of words, is more likely to be parodic and playful than symptomatic. He then elaborates the idea of a quasi-feminized passivity as important in his writing, illustrating it by quoting from the *Prelude* about Wordsworth's sense of being nurtured, even mothered, into his poet's capacities by the river Derwent. The passage figures the poet as an infant being harmoniously nurtured by figures of both genders: his nurse and Nature, feminine, and the river, masculine, who 'blend[s] his murmurs with my nurse's song' (*Prelude*, I.269–275). Heaney continues:

> Without thinking of it at the time, I was totally sympathetic to that idea
> of poetry as something that came naturally, a process out of a condition
> . . . I took the fire in the flint, the Yeatsian, dominant, metrical, affirma-
> tive, commanding strength as being opposite to this kind of passive

waiting. I thought of my own poems as growths, multiplying, spawn-like.

And yet, that's too simple, because all artistic work is to a greater or less extent a doing: it's an entry into an action.[13]

Here, the idea of a 'process out of a condition', influenced by Wordsworth's gentle, unforced scene, seems at first to develop towards a merging of gender differences. Then, however, comes the now-familiar oscillation back towards a position of masculine active vigour: Heaney sets this 'passive waiting', and the impression of his work growing almost involuntarily, as 'multiplying, spawn-like', against the 'dominant . . . affirmative, commanding strength' associated with Yeats.[14] He then reinforces this conception of the poet's position as having to be one of 'dominant . . . strength' with the formulation of art as 'a doing' and 'an entry into an action'. Along with the recurrence of 'entry' here, it's hard to avoid hearing the ghostly accompaniment of its adjectives 'forced' and 'wilful', from the earlier specifically sexualized account.

In the process of these oral reflections, we see Heaney in debate with himself, not just about the overt topic – the contemporary viability of the sexual metaphor in envisioning poetic acts and states of mind – but about gender itself and how it may be spoken of. Showing a recurring impulse towards self-identification with a decisive masculinity, he goes on to adopt Philip Sidney's word 'forcibleness', Greek *energeia*, appealing to an imagined community ('we') by calling it 'the thing we admire in poets and poetry'.[15] Ultimately, however, he returns to a proposed synthesis of these active–passive antinomies, at least so far as the production of poetry is concerned, when he observes how in Hopkins' fierce, tortured work a 'very masculine . . . deliberate, forcing way with words' co-exists with a 'helpless . . . suffering [of] his own linguistic processes' and of the 'English language . . . hatching in him'.[16] This imagined coupling provides an excellent instance of the reproductive appropriation I have mentioned: finally 'there was a kind of birth-giving process there'. With characteristic – and characteristically disarming – self-awareness, he concludes this phase of his discussion by wryly acknowledging that 'one of the difficulties of doing criticism by metaphor is that you get into, I get into, questions like this which I have to answer by more metaphors'.[17]

Later, Heaney is more explicitly drawn to discuss feminism and feminist criticism, and the responses are complex and intriguing. Asked about 'the idea of women as nature and men as culture' in 'Digging' (an interpretation his interlocutor reports having encountered during a year spent at University College Cork), he refers specifically to my essay as 'a polemical article'. He grants that feminist criticism is 'a critical language, it has a new approach', that 'it's necessary that those inherited tropes be interrogated', and 'I think it's a fair comment, within its own terms'.[18] Nevertheless, he attributes to feminist readings a failure to recognize the role of form in poetry and therefore an intrinsic partiality and unreliability:

> Nevertheless, poetry isn't just its thematic content. Poetry is in the musi-cal intonation. What is missing in a lot of that criticism is any sense of the modulation, the intonation, the way the spirit moves in a cadence. It deliberately eschews the poetryness of poetry in order to get at its the-matic and its submerged political implication. That's perfectly in order as a form of intellectual exercise and political protest, but it is not what the thing in itself is.[19]

Here, in order to resist feminist critiques of the political ideas in his own work he seems to fall back on and entrench the formalist position that ide-ology drives out aesthetics, and therefore to disavow the thematic content of poetry. Yet to enquire into the meanings of poems is not necessarily to strip them of their characteristic formal qualities.[20] It is perfectly possible, and is the ideal of all responsible criticism, feminist or not, to arrive at an interpretation which takes account both of form and of meaning, in their inextricable interweaving. Indeed at an early point of this interview Heaney himself has acknowledged that, while poems have 'no ethical duty to stand between the goalposts of history', they have 'to know at least that there is a game going on'.[21]

In practice, of course, Heaney always has combined mythic-imaginative work that conveys large-scale statements about the world, historical and ideological, with his formal imperatives: hence his major public role as bard and vatic seer of the North of Ireland, at least from *North* onwards. The recourse to religious language in the above passage – 'the way the spirit moves in a cadence' – is a protective mystification (invoking the Orphic mysteries), which is also revealing.[22] In his ensuing meditation on the possi-ble contemporary relation between women and poets, he sets up a further imaginative structure, in which he embeds the feminists-*versus*-poet con-tention in a larger mythic-literary pattern, combining the Orpheus legend in Ovid's version with Brian Merriman's eighteenth-century poem *Cúirt an Mheán-Oíche* (*The Midnight Court*). Both these canonical works pit women against male poets, in the Orpheus story with fatal results. In 1993 Heaney had reworked parts of both Ovid's and Merriman's texts and published them together. Subsequently, in his 1995 lecture 'Orpheus in Ireland' col-lected in *The Redress of Poetry*, he developed a reading of *The Midnight Court* which further explained this connection between Orpheus and Merriman's poet-speaker, narrowly saved at the end of the poem – by waking up – from a brutal fate at the hands of the band of incensed women.

There has been lively discussion and contestation since 1980 about the meaning and uses of Merriman's poem, which involves complex questions. *Cúirt* is vigorously bawdy, anti-romantic and anti-clerical, and, ever since Frank O'Connor made a forceful English version in the 1940s, it served as a rallying point for libertarians against the forces of censorship and hyper-Catholic prudery in Ireland. It is true that it constructs eloquent and forceful female speakers and, within its fiction, enacts an empowerment of women, even to the level of ruling over a court of law and giving judgement. Despite being written in the 1780s, it also strikes notes opposing sexual abstinence and emotional barrenness and withholding which have had a deep resonance in the nineteenth- and earlier twentieth-century Irish contexts of late marriage age, uniquely high female emigration, rural depopulation, and social stagnation.[23] Aesthetically, *Cúirt* is sure-footed, linguistically rich and deeply engaging, and it occupies a justifiably high place in the canon of Irish literature. However, the heartfelt endorsement of its gender representations by vocal culture-critics has begun, over the last twenty-five years, to arouse dissent.[24] When sovereignty and sexuality are envisioned together, the result is generally not liberating to women, and in this case the imagined empowerment of female figures seems inextricably embroiled with sexual arousal, via the sado-masochistic effects invoked at the end of the poem, where the poet is sentenced to whipping by the women (in his dream(s), as we might say). My purpose here is to explore Heaney's thinking about gender and sexuality, not to attempt a definitive judgement of *Cúirt*. Merriman's conscious and pervasive ironies, and the unreliability of all the poem's speakers, render it suggestively indeterminate, and it is a task for scholars of the language, genre and period.[25]

Heaney's essay on the poem, originally one of his Oxford Poetry Lectures, has the character of a debate, deftly conducted: it oscillates between views of gender and sex which are in underlying tension with each other. He argues that Merriman should be seen as proto-feminist because he 'gave [women] bodies and brains' and 'let them speak as if they lived by them'.[26] He half-playfully calls the poem's sovereignty-figure, justice Aoibheall, 'a kind of aisling promise of Mary Robinson', and even proposes that *Cúirt*

> has become a paradigm of the war initiated by the movement for women's empowerment, their restoration to the centre of language and consciousness, and thereby also to the centre of all the institutions and functionings of society.[27]

He does acknowledge the 'unease' a contemporary 'sensitised reader' may feel about the 'normative status' which the poem grants to marriage, and notes that Merriman's representation overwhelmingly stresses the female reproductive role and 'mostly ignores [woman's] potential as a being independent of her sexual attributes and her reproductive apparatus'.[28] This markedly positive and enlightened attitude to the feminist project, enthusiastically celebrating the prospect of more agency for women and aptly naming a central cause of their protest, is hard, however, to reconcile with other passages in the essay. He rebukes the republican and feminist radical Máirín de Burca for allegedly labelling the *Cúirt* 'sexist rubbish' in a robust 1980 critique both of the poem and of its reputation as a text of sexual liberation. De Burca was articulating a widely held view in her scepticism of 'the curiously male notion that Liberation [sic] for women coincides exactly with the principle of free love'.[29] By contrast, Heaney argues ('slyly', in one critic's word) that Merriman 'was surely something of a progressive when it came to the representation of women', and should be spared 'the common feminist castigation of Irish men poets for representing women (and Ireland) in the passive, submissive roles of maiden and mother'.[30] He thus insists on the interpretation of *Cúirt* as fundamentally libertarian and anti-repressive, and finds it a precursor to sexually frank poems by Nuala Ní Dhomhnaill, which he appreciatively cites (as evidence for the easing of 'literary and moral constraints' in 1980s and '90s Ireland). One might question his apparent assimilation of the generically mocking, satirical tone of Merriman's rhetorically mediated female personae to Ní Dhomhnaill's rather different lyric speakers.[31]

It is intriguing, however, that he does implicitly grant some justification for de Burca's judgement about the crudeness and tendency towards voyeurism of the poem's account of sexuality.[32] Frank O'Connor, whose English version is where most non-Irish-speaking readers encounter Merriman, observed that it seems impossible to render in English the frank humour and sense of bodily delight and play which characterizes sexual discourse in Irish. He admitted to a coarsening, in his version, of the poem's explicit sex-talk, partly for this reason and partly from a deliberate motive to shock the prudish, especially in the form of the Irish censors. Heaney says that this emphasizes 'those aspects . . . most likely to offend a contemporary feminist'.[33]

Finally, despite his previous approval of women as speakers and social agents, Heaney's 1995 interpretation of the *Cúirt*'s famously abrupt ending would seem definitively to disavow the process of female empowerment and to contradict his own earlier approval of women's right to equal subjecthood. He draws on ideas of Seán Ó Tuama's to develop an interpretation of the poem as re-enacting an allegedly vital and recurrent task of psychosexual containment, a process in which order must be periodically re-established after a provisional and circumscribed outburst of feminine power and antagonism to men and therefore to a whole social order implicitly gendered masculine.[34] Despite endorsing Ó Tuama's observation that the complaint of the wronged young woman given voice in *Cúirt* is in a direct line of descent from the medieval *chanson de la malmariée*, the wronged victim of enforced and unhappy marriage, Heaney goes on to propose a vision of culture as predicated on and largely consisting in the containment of the feminine, and as driven by an alleged immemorial fear of women on the part of men:

> [A]n archaic beast has indeed stirred under the poem's surface and the reader experiences a vague need to see it unleashed into action . . . the Merriman poem has a mythic potency which its comic mode unleashes and defuses.[35]

It would seem, then, that women may be permitted to attain empowerment only in dreams, whether their own, cast as utopias, or, as here, those of men, humorous, bawdy and satirical nightmares. Like the one-day toppling of customs and norms in medieval feasts of fools, the exercise surely serves to reinforce, at the finish, the status quo, after the temporary titillations of a strictly provisional reversal of gender-power arrangements. As Máirín Ní Dhonnchadha points out, 'at the end of the poem female "liberation" is associated with anarchy and poses a threat to the narrator and, by extension, to the male sex'.[36]

A further point follows this, concerning the denouement. Quoting from his own vividly energetic versions, Heaney compares the startlingly violent language of the sentence pronounced upon the sleeping poet-narrator with Ovid's description of the killing of Orpheus. Both dwell graphically on the overpowering of a man by a group of enraged women and their violent infliction on him of extreme physical pain (in Orpheus's case, unto death; in Merriman's, prospectively). In his Merriman version the clear affect is of masochistic sexual excitement ('[t]est all your whips against his manhood').[37] The Ovid text, by contrast, aims for and achieves bloody horror.[38] By the end of the essay, then, moments of Apollonian rationality, which discern the genders' equal share in being, seem to have been supplanted by others where male–female relations are a dog-eat-dog contestation, Dionysian in their intensity, where the risk of women's gaining the upper hand is half-pleasurably, half-fearfully entertained and attended by a moment of quasi-masochistic arousal before being recognized as a threat to civilization. In Merriman's version, ultimately comic, the danger is safely – safely, that is, for the male poet – averted by the waking-from-the-nightmare device. In Ovid's, Orpheus's enchanting song and his eternal romance with Eurydice are recalled and renewed in a narrative of transcendence to immortality. Orpheus's fate asserts the masculine prerogative of creating symbolic artefacts which instate and further cultural creation by rising above the merely natural state of the destroying women: their fate is to be forcibly rooted and muted, as oak trees in the containing earth.

Seven years later, in the 2002 interview, however, there is a significant development in Heaney's use of the Ovid–Merriman material. This further step involves his own explicit self-identification with the Orpheus–Merriman figure as beleaguered culture-carrier, and the corresponding assignment to his feminist critics of the rage and frustration of both Bacchantes and fictional Clarewomen. The repudiation of de Burca's radical position is now extended to feminist criticism generally, which is represented, with a significant hardening and simplification of Heaney's attitudes, as monolithic in character and, as we have seen, as blind to the aesthetic qualities of poetry. In 2002 Heaney focuses first on Ovid, and on the generally less familiar episode in the Orpheus legend: how, well after his loss of Eurydice in the underworld, the great poet is torn to pieces by a band of women called Maenads (meaning 'mad women'), who are ritually intoxicated as part of the cult of the wine-god Dionysus. The dead Orpheus's head is thrown into the river Hebrus and floats down it to the sea, in some versions still chanting poetry.[39] With humorous relish, Heaney explains how he devised the phrase 'Orpheus, the misogynist' for his version of Ovid, and describes Merriman's poem as 'about frustrated sexual appetite', with 'all of these old, traditional motifs' and as 'full of vigo[u]r and interest'.[40] He follows Ovid's version of the murder of Orpheus as occasioned by the archetypal poet's turning 'away from the love of women', after his loss of Eurydice, and towards that of a young boy.[41]

The poet in Merriman, subjected in his mock-*aisling* to a primarily verbal mauling, is much more explicitly presented as a version of Orpheus, the archetypal poet torn apart by the archetypal unreason and excess attributed to women. And Heaney now additionally describes his own interest in the Orpheus theme specifically as 'a response to that development' (i.e. feminism) and relates it directly to 'the critical wars and the polemical wars between feminist critics and male poets: Dead-White-European-Male versus the rest, so to speak'.[42] Thus we are invited to place him, too, in the succession from Orpheus to Merriman via Ovid and Rilke, all under attack by maddened Maenads and feminists. He wryly positions himself in this homosocial sequence of beleaguered poets by adding: 'And poor Orpheus is super-dead, super-white, super-European.'[43] So Orpheus, the Apollonian and semi-divine singer, lines up with Merriman's persona and Heaney the allegedly reviled poet, and all are represented as glorious individual martyr-victims of destructive, irrational Dionysian women from Thrace, East Clare and modern feminism respectively.

This mythopoeic move involves a remarkably tendentious and reductive representation of feminism, namely as a displaced expression of sexual frustration. As we have seen, Heaney merges the alleged sexual chagrin of the Dionysian women as cause of the death of Orpheus, and the political protest of the modern women's movement, with the complaints of Merriman's female figures:

> And if you set it [Merriman's poem] within the context of this kind of criticism, and relate it to the resurgence of women and the vehemence of the Women's Movement in Ireland, then you have dialogue, you have answer back, and you have provocation. Why not? It is a dialogue.[44]

No doubt all of this is partly mischievous and humorous in tone. But he characterizes feminism as a censorious, joyless position: 'that criticism is very Puritan: extirpate the mistaken'. In 1995 he had referred to the 'moralistic criticism' of 'a new feminist consensus'.[45] Here some strain is evident in the argument: there is a rather odd shift from the idea of women as Dionysian and overwrought by emotion to that of a 'political point being made'.[46]

However threatening the observations of feminist critics may be to the patriarchal *status quo*, it is hard to see the attempt to account for feminist thinking as a displacement of sexual frustration and a disguised claim for sexual attention as other than a defensive response, with a basis in irrational, perhaps unconscious, anxiety about a shift in power relations, in this age of an alleged crisis of masculinity. Such responses were not uncommon during the 1970s, the years of the decisive emergence of the Irish Women's Movement and its open self-alignment with the international second-wave struggle for women's rights, as those who recall those years will be aware.[47] In the early 2000s it should no longer be necessary to explain that feminism was and is about the seeking by and for women of rights, equality and full civil subjecthood, but the 2002 Heaney seems to withhold or to have lost the understanding which he evinced in 1995 of that central vision of empowerment and agency which has motivated feminism from the first wave to the present. The perennial quest by individual persons of all genders for sexual happiness is perfectly distinguishable from the collective one for due rights and an equal voice, which all feminisms share.

Along these lines, *Cúirt an Mheán-Oíche* itself may partly express real social protest. Merriman's ribald social satire no doubt catches some elements of women's indignation against their material disempowerment as well as their emotional and sexual neglect, within the poem's more general critique of aspects of the social order of North Munster in the late eighteenth century. This is so despite the fact that, as in Aristophanes' *Lysistrata* in late fifth-century Athens, women in Merriman's text are more spoken for and ventriloquized – providing an occasion of ribaldry – than positively envisaged as the primary or true originators of this critique, and that there is a voyeuristic aspect to the whole thing.[48]

Heaney's mini-myth also has a clear further implication. This is that the female speakers' complaints in Merriman, primarily sexual, are more authentic than the protest of women in our own era (as exemplified by my essay, taken as an example of feminism). *Cúirt* has historical priority and impeccable native and Gaelic credentials, unlike the alleged 'vehemence of the Women's Movement in Ireland', which is thereby displaced into a superficial position, with more than a hint of the forced and shrewish. This move seeks to go behind and beneath the arguments of contemporary feminism (including critiques of the masculinism of Irish men's poetry), and as it were to trump these arguments and the position from which they are made. This is done not only by insisting that what (in men's minds) women *really* want is sexual happiness; that insistence is also secured by grounding it in an *echt*, canonical Irish text which long pre-dates the Women's Movement. The latter is thus presented as a phenomenon merely of modernity or post-modernity. Furthermore, either Irish feminists are deviating from true native traditions and should go back to berating poets and priests for withholding their sexual attentions and neglecting women's real needs, here redefined as primarily sexual, or else their voices are part of an alleged 'dialogue', a set of ongoing exchanges whose mode of discourse is contention, flyting, or 'provocation'. This model, of the genders trading quasi-humorous and often bawdy accusations, deliberately disclaims post-Enlightenment ideas of rational debate in the public sphere. It reinstates the idea of a fundamental essentialized male–female binary which nothing can change, and which also underlies the earlier discussion of the gender of inspiration. True 'dialogue', on the other hand, is what takes place between equally empowered persons or groups; it is argument based on evidence which enables such dialogue. Instead, the Merriman-poet escapes by waking up out of that (dream-or nightmare?)-world in which women might get a real hearing and where a female authority-figure is empowered to bring about justice.

Once more Heaney here has recourse, via Merriman, to that very mythic realm which in 'Bog Queens' I had argued underlies his thinking about Ireland. It is significant that he uses the phrase 'the resurgence of women', which would suggest the existence of an earlier, originary state of affairs in which women were not subordinate (*re-* rather than *in-*surgence). It echoes the idea of women's '*restoration* [my emphasis] to the centre' in the passage of 'Orpheus in Ireland' quoted above. The belief in an *ur*-matriarchy in any society is, however, discredited among historians, and within feminism itself these days it thrives only at the New-Agey and Goddess-advocate end of things; during the 1970s, however, there were those within the Irish Women's Movement who drew inspiration and hope from versions of a Celtic past which had allegedly given women agency and power. I think its use here signals the subliminal presence of the quasi-psychological, quasi-mythic notion of the Great (omnipotent, phallic, pre-Oedipal) Mother.[49] Heaney in effect marshals, or perhaps falls back on, the mythic figure of the sovereignty goddess in another form, that of the queen Aoibheall, heroine of Merriman's poem in her role as judge of the women's complaints (Heaney calls her 'sort of a faerie guardian of Munster',[50] which may further link her to Spenser's Mutabilitie figure in *The Faerie Queene*, also a judge).[51] As I argued in 1991, the ostensible and *virtual* empowerment of such female figures is, in social reality, always capable of safe containment within the mythic realm. Here again, we have the fundamentally Oedipal structure of the prince (or poet) who can visit the woman who embodies power but does not wield it, and gain *his* power from the encounter (sometimes figured as sexual, sometimes not). Over this, in Merriman, is parodically laid the *aisling* narrative, which stages the otherworldly encounter as enabling the utterance of the poem, where earlier it granted possession of the land itself.[52]

As well as referring to the great tradition of Orpheus, Heaney's myth of poets-versus-women is another instance of that amalgamation of Romantic lyric subjectivity with the appeal to an originary Ireland as touchstone of authenticity − connected to irreducible, allegedly natural, facts, including gender categories, fixed in time − which has constituted his vision. On the question of Ireland, the interview has one further revealing moment. Immediately after his Merriman discussion, Heaney invokes the context of Irish history more generally:

> Patricia Coughlan did an article on the passive woman figure in the representation of Ireland. But, in fact, English armies did come in and do all that depredation and the Irish poets of the eighteenth century were remembering Elizabethan scorched earth and Cromwellian massacre and took that image of violation and rape pretty seriously because, I mean, these were not just literary tropes.[53]

This remark is both the most opaque and perhaps the most interesting of the interview. Heaney's argument seems to be that because Irishwomen had already been made victims *by history*, I should not have criticized him for deploying the 'passive woman figure' *in representation*. In structure, this recalls the apocryphal story of the German officer asking Picasso of the painting 'Guernica': 'Did you do that?' and Picasso's reply: 'No, *you* did'. The argument runs: real rape and violation did take place during 'Elizabethan scorched earth and Cromwellian massacre', therefore there can be no valid objection to their being represented in poems. Yet I have never argued either that violent acts did not happen in Irish history, or that they ought not to be represented in writing.[54] The point is not whether, but how they are represented. I was not alone among contemporary critics in finding a troubling ambiguity in the symbolic, poetic uses to which Irish poets at times put these terrible historical facts: I sought to draw attention to the uncertain boundary between the legitimate and the exploitative in all representations of violence and atrocity (a boundary memorably placed by Heaney himself in his best work, and specifically named in the 'artful voyeur' position identified in 'Punishment' and elsewhere in *North*).[55] I observed the especial permeability of this boundary where gender is concerned, because of the pervasive equation of active subjectivity with the male and passive with the female. In discussing Montague and Heaney, both ethnically Catholic and broadly nationalist, I also drew on international post-colonialist ideas about the need to adopt hyper-masculine stances felt by men among subjugated populations, rendered passive – 'feminized' – by defeat, expropriation and subordinate status.[56] Thus strong masculine impulses towards the exercise of power and control, blocked in the sphere of political and historical action, are displaced, and agent- or subject-men, turned into object-persons as women are expected to be, seek to re-attain the status of agent by intensified displays of domination over 'passive woman figure[s]'.

However, another important manoeuvre is taking place simultaneously in this condensed and elliptical paragraph of the interview. Heaney seems to argue that my critique is somehow less authentic than his representations, which he considers to have the status of originals, and he implicitly attributes an impulse of censorship to that critique. He clearly thinks of his own and other poets' *representations* of the 'passive woman figure' as somehow more legitimately connected to, or naturally continuous with, the *'fact'* [my emphasis] of 'all that depredation', and therefore not open to discussion. But he is here effecting a strange and double occlusion. First, both Heaney and his Irish eighteenth-century poetic avatars were themselves producing representations, intervening in social and cultural discourse. Why should they be considered nearer to 'fact' than a historian's or literary scholar's writing? Second, there is an intriguing shift between the land and women's bodies. Is raping women the same as scorching the earth? Is one real and the other metaphorical? Or is it that one (the rape of women) is somehow a symbol, or allegory, of the other (scorched earth and massacre)? In fact, accounts of real literal rape have not turned up often during the very extensive historical research and writing about the intensive phase of Elizabethan and Cromwellian settlement, to which Heaney here rightly refers as a key moment of trauma.[57] This glide from woman to land, which turns women as literal sufferers of rape into Woman as symbol of victimhood, resolves itself into a recapitulation of the Mother-Ireland, Cathleen Ni Houlihan, *aisling*-heroine motif. The motif is foundational in, and seemingly incapable of being severed from, nationalist discourse, Heaney's included, with all its deeply problematic appropriation (might one say colonization?) of the woman as iconic image of disempowerment. The passage also amounts, then, to the recurrence of a theme familiar in nationalist ideology, within which the call to acknowledge gender is received as the unwelcome and unacceptable challenging of a prior and overriding imperative to serve and sing the nation.

Heaney is not alone in the reiteration of this position. I quote from Terry Eagleton, writing in 1998 'to counteract . . . narrowness in contemporary Irish cultural studies', where

> [m]uch . . . is shaped nowadays by what one might loosely call a post-modern agenda, which brings into play some vital topics but tends to sideline others of equal importance. It is ironic that a discourse of marginality should have shoved so many other matters brusquely off stage. Religion and education, for example, are at least as weighty matters in Irish cultural history as gender or racial stereotyping, but they happen not to be such favoured items on the post-modern menu, or in North American academia.[58]

That is, the 'postmodern agenda' (clearly bad) shows a tendency, which he deplores, to drive out what he calls 'anti-colonialist' (clearly good) enquiry, and to sideline other questions of national importance. Eagleton goes on to engage in the tricky manoeuvre of telling the Irish what they should and should not be thinking about: 'One cannot coherently insist on the "otherness" of a culture like Ireland [*sic*] while attending almost exclusively to issues there, however vital they may be to the Irish themselves, which happen to be to the fore at the moment in one's own society.'[59] This seems to give the preservation of Irish 'otherness' a higher priority than the attainment of justice and civil equality, or indeed, for Eagleton at least, than the right of the Irish people, however heterogeneously constituted these days, to decide on their own priorities. This stated priority of The Nation shows a hierarchy of imperatives which unites Eagleton with Heaney, despite the differences of their general politics (Marxist and liberal human-ist respectively). This is the darker face of nationalism, which shadows and occludes its emancipatory potential, making it – for women, as for those of other ethnicities in postmodern Ireland – a narrative of control, contain-ment and subordination rather than one of liberation. Yet more than ninety years ago such prioritization of some rights over others was already being vigorously contested by female founding figures among nationalists. As Constance Markiewicz argued in 1909: 'No one should place sex before nationality or nationality before sex.'[60]

In this essay I have focused on highly influential, indeed canonical utter-ances by the English-speaking world's – and of course Ireland's – most famous living male poet. I turn for my conclusion to some women's words, so that we may remind ourselves that women in contemporary Ireland can and do other than perform 'a kind of passive waiting', or, in someone's fanta-sy, tear male poets apart. Let us reflect briefly on two practising and accomplished Irish poets, of a later generation than Heaney and of the other biological sex: Moya Cannon (born 1956) and Vona Groarke (born 1964). There are no queens, sovereignty goddesses, or hags, whether at wells, mills, or anywhere else, in Groarke or Cannon (and these personages are a more or less extinct species in contemporary Irishwomen's poetry in general). There are bogs in Cannon's poems (she is from North Donegal and lives in Gal-way), as well as mountains, stone walls and fields. Groarke (from near Athlone) realizes a flatter, more midland landscape with many lakes and rivers, but specializes in houses, even to the extent of naming her second collection *Other People's Houses*, and she often presents the kind of suburban milieu which might be said to sustain many Irish lives these days: des rezzes, all alike, in housing estates. Groarke is interested in uncanny effects, but not in mythology or in chthonic presences. Both poets rather pointedly avoid those mythic-metaphorical encounters with aspects of the Irish landscape which are a trademark of Heaney's poetic imagination and which, I have argued, are predicated on masculine and Oedipal self-positioning. Both Cannon and Groarke are intensely interested in history, but their framing and re-staging of that history is a much more materialist one, a pared-down topography which sets up encounters with the physical remnants and traces of Ireland's past: in Cannon the 'room-sized fields' of the West, which yield-ed bare subsistence lives, and its 'wild hills' and 'miles of acid land'.[61] Groarke's collections, meanwhile, juxtapose Big Houses, generally ruined, and strong farmhouses with workhouses, signs of oppression and destitution that we, the inheritors of the nineteenth century – and, since the mid-1990s, it seems, of the earth – have still not been able physically to convert or assimilate.[62] Neither poet sexualizes Irish landscapes, as both Heaney and Montague do; and different as Groarke and Cannon are in terms of form, style and setting, both conduct subtle explorations of human action and feeling which delicately and sometimes humorously enquire into conventionally gendered roles and do not assent to the fixing of these in immemorial positions. There are elements of explicit feminist protest against such fixing in Groarke's first collection *Shale* which play their role in the general thematic aims of her work; it resists, or silently eschews, those mythic structures which marginalize the feminine or represent it primarily in its relation to masculine hegemony, while drawing on the imaginative richness of more secular poetic traditions.[63]

Both these poets' work awaits, and will richly repay, full critical discussion as among contemporary *Irish* (not just *women's*) poetry at its best. Complex questions arise about the role of narratives and hypostases of the nation in this work, as in that of other gifted and promising contemporaries: for example, how can we imagine Ireland newly, reconceive the nation without that feminine personification, that 'whole strange growth' which catches women in its immobilizing toils?[64] For sceptics, as I am, of post-nationalist positions, can the old nation-narratives be recuperated?[65] In Irish postmodernity, it is not yet clear whether the baby (the sense of what, however loosely, unifies our various Irelands and makes the country its changing, developing self) must be thrown out with the bathwater of old-nationalist and patriarchal appropriation, subordination and containment of the feminine. But that is another day's work.

Notes and References

1 Seamus Heaney, 'Interview', *Talking with Poets*, ed. Harry Thomas (New York: Handsel, 2002), pp. 43–67.
2 Vona Groarke, *Shale* (Loughcrew: Gallery, 1994), pp. 38–9.
3 David Cairns and Toni O'Brien Johnson (eds), *Gender in Irish Writing* (Milton Keynes: Open University Press, 1991), pp. 87–111; Michael Allen (ed.), *Seamus Heaney*, New Casebooks series (London: Macmillan, 1997), pp. 185- 205; Elmer Andrews (ed.), *Seamus Heaney* (Cambridge: Icon, 2000), pp. 128–35; Claire Connolly (ed.), *Theorizing Ireland* (London: Palgrave Macmillan, 2002), pp. 67–91. I would wish to say that both Seamus Heaney and John Montague have always been personally pleasant and courteous to me about 'Bog Queens'.
4 Seamus Heaney, 'Interview', p. 52.
5 Ibid., p. 52.
6 Sandra Gilbert and Susan Gubar, 'The Queen's Looking Glass: Female Creativity, Male Images of Women, and the Metaphor of Literary Paternity', in *The Madwoman in the Attic: The Woman Writer and the Nineteenth-Century Literary Imagination* (New Haven: Yale University Press, 1980), pp. 3–44.

7 The phrase is Helen Kidd's, quoted in Sarah Maguire's helpful summary of this debate in 'Dilemmas and Developments: Eavan Boland Re-examined', *Feminist Review*, 62 (Summer 1999), 58–66. Maguire observes that the persona, or self, presented in lyric is the 'fiction of a desiring subject', while women 'are not traditionally able to take the place of desiring subjects in a patriarchal society; we are the desired objects' (p. 64). Timothy Morris observes, reviewing Cynthia Hogue's *Scheming Women: Poetry, Privilege, and the Politics of Subjectivity* (New York: State University of New York Press, 1995): 'From Ovid to Whitman to Yeats, the male voice has seized the center stage of lyric discourse and silenced or annulled women's voices . . . Recent feminist theorists like Kristeva and de Lauretis have not been able to theorize beyond the restrictions on poetic voice imposed by dominant binaries of gender', *Style*, 30:1 (Spring 1996), 178.

8 Walt Whitman, 'A Woman Waits for Me', from the 'Children of Adam' section, *Leaves of Grass* [1891–2], *Complete Poetry and Selected Prose* (New York: Library of America, 1982), pp. 258–60.

9 Ibid., p. 259.

10 Ian Gregson contrasts Heaney's conceptions of masculinity with Paul Muldoon's in 'Sons of Mother Ireland: Seamus Heaney and Paul Muldoon', in *The Male Image: Representations of Masculinity in Post-War Poetry* (London: Macmillan, 1999), pp. 120–39.

11 Catriona Clutterbuck considers more positively than I do what she sees as Heaney's tendencies to experiment with the adoption of 'feminine' positions: see 'Gender and Self-Representation in Irish Poetry: The Critical Debate', *Bullán*, 4:1 (1998), 43–59. This recalls Joyce's much more extensive engagement in such self-positioning (two familiar instances being the characterization of Molly Bloom and the dream-feminization of Leopold in the 'Nighttown' episode of *Ulysses*). In my view these are, to use Heaney's own word, 'wilful' and strictly temporary and playful moves, which do little or nothing to shift the normative status of masculine subjectivity, as the centre of power and importance, from which such moments away are exciting but strictly transient and, so to speak, touristic visits. In Joyce these also carry a masochistic sexual charge, which is itself an excellent indicator of where the real power lies.

12 Seamus Heaney, 'Interview', p. 52.

13 Ibid., p. 53.

14 Here Heaney cites his own discussion twenty-two years earlier in *Preoccupations* (1980), his ten-year collection of reflections on poetry.

15 Seamus Heaney, 'Interview', p. 53.

16 Ibid., p. 55.

17 Ibid., p. 55.

18 Ibid., p. 61.

19 Ibid., p. 60.

20 In the light of these comments (which Heaney is, with typical courtesy, careful to apply only vaguely to 'a lot of that criticism'), it is somewhat ironic that Michael Allen, editing his New Casebook on Heaney in 1997, finds my own essay 'inwardly responsive to the textures and rhythms of Heaney's verse': *Seamus Heaney* (Houndsmills: Macmillan, 1997), p. 13. Allen also compares it favourably in this respect to what he sees as David Lloyd's 'look[ing] outside the liberal consensus' in his 1993 'Pap for the Dispossessed' essay (also reprinted in Allen, pp. 155–84).

21 Seamus Heaney, 'Interview', pp. 46–7.

22 Heaney's priestly qualities have long been enthusiastically celebrated by critics and reviewers in secular Anglo-American milieus: Mick Imlah's review of *The Redress of Poetry* in *The Independent on Sunday* said 'the force of his book is as much spiritual as

critical; there is a priestly glow behind its intellectual sparkle'. Quoted on the back cover of the 1996 paperback edition.

23 There is a good summary of this topic, with ample further citations, in Tom Inglis, *Moral Monopoly: The Rise and Fall of the Catholic Church in Modern Ireland* (Dublin: UCD Press, 1998), pp. 165–9.

24 Noting that *Cúirt* is 'openly concerned with gender politics', Patrick Crotty observes that this has only been discussed since the advent of feminist criticism and that it 'can be construed alternatively as a recognition by a male poet of the validity of female desire or as an elaboration of male sexual fantasy' in Angela Bourke et al. (eds), *Field Day Anthology of Irish Writing: Irish Women's Writings and Traditions* (Cork: Cork University Press, 2002), headnote to Merriman excerpt, Vol. IV, p. 243.

25 See Liam P. Ó Murchú, *Merriman: I bhFábhar Béithe* (Baile Átha Cliath: An Clóchomhar, 2005).

26 Seamus Heaney, 'Orpheus in Ireland', p. 55.

27 Ibid., p. 53. This rather strangely suggests the existence of an earlier, originary state of affairs in which women were not subordinate: I discuss later the significance of Heaney's deployment of this notion of an originary matriarchy.

28 Ibid., p. 56.

29 For De Burca's text, see Angela Bourke et al. (eds), *Field Day Anthology of Irish Writing: Irish Women's Writings and Traditions* (Cork: Cork University Press, 2002); Clair Wills (ed.), 'Feminism, Culture and Critique in English'; Máirín de Burca, 'Analysis of *The Midnight Court*', Vol. V, pp. 1588–91; (the phrase I have quoted is on p. 1590). Heaney inaccurately says she describes the poem as 'sexist rubbish' ('Orpheus in Ireland', p. 54); it is worth revisiting what she actually says. Reading Merriman primarily (and therefore somewhat reductively) as a social document, her's is alone among discussions of Merriman I have read in expressing distaste at the poem's harsh mockery of physical ageing; citing historian Gearóid Ó Tuathaigh's remark that early-nineteenth-century Irishwomen were 'treated more like beasts of burden than rational beings', she remarks: 'That, I suspect, was nearer the reality for women than the sexist not to mention ageist nonsense of Merriman' (*Field Day*, V, p. 1590). I see the significance of de Burca's contribution more in its response to the contemporary masculinist uses of the poem than to the text itself.

30 Ibid., p. 55. Patrick Crotty finds Heaney '[m]ore slyly… recruit[ing] Merriman as a defence witness in the gender trials of contemporary poetry criticism', *Field Day*, V, p. 243.

31 Ibid., pp. 54–5. The poems he cites are 'Féar Suaithinseach' and 'Gan do Chuid Éadaigh'.

32 Or at least those of the English versions; both de Burca and Heaney acknowledge that they are responding not primarily to the original, but to translations: he uses Frank O'Connor's, she that by David Marcus.

33 O'Connor's 'intention was to taunt, to affront the prudes and goad the censorship board'. Ibid., p. 56.

34 Seán Ó Tuama, 'Brian Merriman and his *Court*', in *Repossessions: Selected Essays on the Irish Literary Heritage* (Cork: Cork University Press, 1995), pp. 63–77 (first published in 1981). Heaney also approvingly cites Gearóid Ó Crualaoich's 'The Vision of Liberation in *Cúirt an Mheán Oíche*' in Pádraig de Brún et al. (eds), *Folia Gadelica: Essays Presented to R. A. Breatnach* (Cork: Cork University Press, 1983), pp. 95–104.

35 Seamus Heaney, *Midnight Verdict*, p. 33.

36 See *Field Day Anthology: Irish Women's Writing and Traditions*, Vol. IV, p. 172.

37 A Freudian view might be that this, like other dominatrix scenarios, unconsciously invokes an *ur*-phase of infancy in which the infant, as yet polymorphously perverse, experiences its mother as all-powerful and as the source of all physical handling, from gratification to what Freud calls 'unpleasure'.

38 Seamus Heaney, 'Orpheus in Ireland', p. 60. *Midnight Verdict*, pp. 33, 39–40.

39 Seamus Heaney, *The Midnight Verdict* (Loughcrew: Gallery, 1993). Milton powerfully recounts the death of Orpheus in 'Lycidas' (pp. 58–63), making it part of that poem's homosocial sequence of poets laid low by mortality and nature, personified in the wantonly destructive Thracian women. For Milton, Orpheus was a pagan antetype of Christ. In *Orpheus Dis(re)membered: Milton and the Myth of the Poet-Hero* (Sheffield: Academic Press, 1996, p. 185, n. 46), Rachel Falconer gives a useful bibliographical overview of the whole Orpheus theme in European literature.

40 Seamus Heaney, 'Interview', pp. 61–2.

41 The classical tradition, however, itself offers varying versions of the women's motives for murdering Orpheus: some say it was because he adhered to the cult of Apollo, god of poetry, rather than that of Dionysus, others because he could not love any *other* woman after the lost Eurydice. Heaney's version stresses the women's emotions of fury at their rejection, but the *sparagmos*, the tearing apart of Orpheus, is markedly characteristic of Dionysian ritual. I thank Keith Sidwell for discussion of this point. See Paul Harvey, *Oxford Companion to Classical Literature* (Oxford: Clarendon Press, 1974), pp. 298–9.

42 Seamus Heaney, 'Interview', p. 59.

43 Ibid., p. 59.

44 Ibid., p. 62.

45 Seamus Heaney, 'Orpheus in Ireland', p. 54.

46 Ibid., p. 61.

47 First-wave feminism met similar reactions during the New Woman movement of the late nineteenth century.

48 Ó Murchú's research shows Merriman more clearly than before as part of a male coterie of competing poets, who copied sets of erotic verses into his manuscript, some by and some about priests and sex, many exemplifying and mocking sexual boasting by male speakers. He sees an open anti-masculinity and self-flagellation, accompanied by a consistent sympathy for women, in the poem ('nóta neamhchceilte frithfhireannach agus féinsciúrsach'), p. 80; he comments on an unhealthy, voyeuristic note evident in the elderly husband's speech (pp. 87–8), but also on the jealous fear the young woman expresses that she will be displaced by younger girls reaching sexual maturity ('tiocfaidh na cíocha'), p. 99.

49 Readers of Heaney's contemporary Thomas Kinsella will be aware of the interesting parallels between these moves by Heaney and the vital significance of witchy and threatening, but indispensable, grandmother-figures in the imaginative universe which Kinsella has elaborated from Jungian thought.

50 Seamus Heaney, 'Interview', p. 61.

51 See Edmund Spenser, *The Faerie Queene*, Book VII, 'Two Cantos of Mutabilitie', and my 'The Local Contexts of Mutabilitie's Plea', *Irish University Review*, Special Issue on 'Spenser in Ireland: *The Faerie Queene* 1596–1996', 26:2 (1997), 320–41.

52 C. L. Innes notes an 'intensification', after the collapse of bardic tradition, of the 'unreal and visionary imagining of Ireland' that had grown out of the much earlier sovereignty goddess figure, in *Woman and Nation in Irish Literature and Society* (Athens: University of Georgia Press, 1993), p. 26.

53 Seamus Heaney, 'Interview', p. 62.

54 Indeed, as it happens I have written several essays precisely on violent and traumatic Irish historical events and their associated discourses in the period from 1590 to 1660. See, for example, '"Cheap and Common Animals?" The English Anatomy of Ireland in the Seventeenth Century', in J. Sawday and T. Healy (eds), *Literature and the English Civil War* (Cambridge: Cambridge University Press, 1990), pp. 205–23,

which discusses the 1641 atrocity literature, among other things.

55 Such questions arise in many cases of the representation of violence in postmodernity. For instance, intense controversy has surrounded Ariel Dorfman's play *Death and the Maiden* (1991) about torture and retribution in and after Pinochet's Chile. Focusing on the body of a woman and her struggle for justice, it too is uneasily poised between voyeurism and emancipatory aims.

56 Ashis Nandy first analysed this effect in Hindu nationalist ideology and discourse in *The Intimate Enemy* (Oxford: Oxford University Press, 1983), but it is observable in much earlier Irish discourses too: see, for instance, William Drennan's 'Letters of an Irish Helot' in *Selected Writings*, ed. Brendan Clifford (Belfast: Athol, 1998), Vol. I, pp. 234–45. I thank Clíona Ó Gallchoir for the Drennan reference, and for helpful discussion of gender and nationalist discourse.

57 Without wanting to minimize the brutality of seventeenth-century wars, forcible settlements and dispossession of the various kinds of Irish by English armies and settlers, the nearest thing to reports of such specifically sexual violation that I have come across in the period are accounts of the stripping bare of settlers, male and female, and the ripping open of the bellies of pregnant women, a much-repeated motif in the atrocity literature of the 1641 Rebellion, which was gravest in the province of Ulster against Protestant English and Scots planters. These are attributions of terrible violence to the Catholic Ulster rebels, or, within the old binaries of Irish history, to the proto-nationalist side. I need hardly say that it has been nigh impossible for historians to ascertain the degree of veracity of the 1641 propaganda pamphlets, and fuller study of the primary sources, the 1641 Depositions themselves, remains to be done.

58 Terry Eagleton, 'Preface', *Crazy John and the Bishop* (Cork: Cork University Press, 1998), p. ix.

59 Ibid., p. ix. I thank Piaras Mac Éinrí for useful discussion of these points.

60 In 'Free Women in a Free Nation', *Bean na hÉireann*, 1:4 (February 1909), 9–10. Quoted in Innes (*Woman and Nation*, p. 138), who provides extensive other evidence of this contestation, as does Margaret Ward's edited collection of texts from the heroic period of nationalism in the first two decades of the twentieth century. See Margaret Ward (ed.), *In Their Own Voice: Women and Irish Nationalism* (Cork: Attic, 1995).

61 See Moya Cannon, 'West', 'Hills', 'The Foot of Muckish', in *Oar* (Galway: Salmon, 1990, reprinted Loughcrew: Gallery, 2000), pp. 19, 30, 32.

62 Vona Groarke, 'The Way It Goes', in *Flight* (Loughcrew: Gallery, 2002), p. 20; 'The History of My Father's House', in *Shale* (Loughcrew: Gallery, 1994), p. 26; and 'Workhouses', in *Other People's Houses* (Loughcrew: Gallery, 1999), p. 38.

63 'Grace Notes' and 'Daphne as a Modern Theme' (*Shale*, pp. 38, 40), both wry and satiric in tone, show Boland's influence, while the beautiful lyrics of 'The Idea of the Atlantic' (p. 20) and 'If There is a City' (p. 46) experiment with representations of mother and daughter personae as figures of sufficiency and reflexivity, both *en-soi* and *pour-soi*, not mere embodiments of roles ancillary to a dominant masculine.

64 The phrase is Heaney's, from the conclusion of 'The Death of Orpheus' (*The Midnight Verdict*, p. 42): 'So that you couldn't tell if the whole strange growth / Were a wood or women in distress or both'.

65 Though it is true that Groarke and the best of her poetic coevals, in Justin Quinn's phrase, do not further 'the myths of rural culture that animated Patrick Kavanagh's poetry', I disagree with Quinn's view that they 'are the first genuinely post-national generation', which I find a reductionist one (Justin Quinn, 'The Irish Efflorescence', in *Poetry Review*, 91:4 (Winter 2001/2), accessed 6 July 2005 at http://www.poetrysociety.org.uk/review/pr91-4/quinn.htm).

Race, Sex and Nation

GERARDINE MEANEY

'In post-colonial southern Ireland a particular construction of sexual and familial roles became the very structure of what it meant to be Irish.'[1] Working on this article sent me back to that sentence, which I wrote in 1989. Re-reading it, I feel there should be more of a rupture. Everything changed, didn't it? Ireland got rich, got sense, got free. It was terribly oppressive of course, very discriminatory, in the dark prehistoric mist which now envelops Ireland before 1997 or so. The very prevalence of images of how dreadful the Irish past was (such as *Angela's Ashes*, *Song for a Raggy Boy*, *The Magdalene Sisters*) makes it seem incredibly remote. The radical changes in attitudes to such basic and primal areas of experience as sexuality and children obscure their rapidity. And the rapidity of change obscures the depth of continuity. This is nowhere more apparent than in the way in which the drearily familiar concatenation of motherhood, nation, referendum and paranoia erupted in twenty-first-century Ireland. The narrative of rapid national progress is dependent on suppression of the evidence of the persistence of structures of conformity, domination and exclusion at the heart of Irish society and culture.

There is an extraordinary level of official denial of the existence of racism in Ireland, as Steve Garner has outlined previously in *The Irish Review*.[2] In that context, it is important to start from the acknowledgement that one observes it every day, in leafy suburbs far removed from the north inner city frontlines of racial conflict so easily analysed as an anomaly. One incident stands out from a general background of racist graffiti hastily removed from bus stops, mutterings in supermarket queues, half heard conversations about 'them'. A little girl, aged about eight or nine, is looking wistfully over a garden wall, watching a group of giggling older children arrive at a birthday party next door. There is a lot of commotion, the

Dublin summer rain has finally stopped and the bouncy castle is going up in the back garden, so the partygoers play around outside, handing over the presents, getting more and more excited. The little girl is joined by a few other children, all a little younger, obviously not invited. They whisper amongst themselves for a moment and then the first little girl hoists herself up on the wall and calls, 'Here you', to one of the boys going to the party. 'You,' her voice getting crosser, shrill, 'you black bastard. Go back were you came from.' She jumps back on her own side of the wall and runs laughing into the house.

The little boy stands with his present in his hand, the other children moving closer to him, the mother hosting the birthday party hurrying them all into the house and talking loudly about cake. It must be confusing, the proximity of welcome and rejection in a city that so fervently doesn't want to know its own racism. None of the adults present, myself included, knew what to say to him. We were all white and, though this kind of thing is part of the air we all breathe in with him in suburban Dublin, we are observers, not victims of racism.

Since this observance of racism is part of the fabric of my daily existence, it is important to breach the academic proprieties, to juxtapose experience and analysis. Feminist theory, after all, was born from just such juxtaposition. It is equally important to refuse the kind of authority – and innocence – which scholarly discourse offers a white academic talking about racism. Cultural criticism in Ireland has tended to analyze racism as if it were no more than the pique of the little girl excluded from the big party of national independence for so long that she vents her frustration on the first available scapegoat. This is to ignore the question of where she learned the language of racism and how to target her scapegoat. Racism in Ireland has antecedents and a history. National identities are structured by the binary of them and us, insiders and outsiders, natives and foreigners. Irish nationalism may have had within it the potential for all kinds of hybrid, liberationist, adulterated and inclusive versions of Irish identity. However, the dominant ideology of state and nation was for most of the twentieth century extraordinarily narrow and exclusive. Bryan Fanning has documented the 'othering' of Protestants, Jews and Travellers as part of the process of state nationalism in the Republic of Ireland.[3] The dominance of the postcolonial–revisionist debate in the formation of Irish Studies and the analyses it produced of Irish nationalism have not only long outlived their usefulness. Both sides of the debate have obscured the role of whiteness in the construction of Irish identity as well as the relationship between gender and race in that construction.

Postcolonial theory offered feminist critique in Ireland a vital way of understanding sexual conservatism, the relationship of the Catholic Church and the State and the gendering of national identity as elements that it shared with a wide variety of postcolonial cultures. Postcolonialism remains part of the context in which 'non-national women were made central to the racial configuration of twenty-first-century global Ireland, illustrating not only orchestrated moral panics about "floods of refugees", but also the positioning of sexually active women as a "danger to the state and 'the nation'".[4] However, as the sociologist and theorist of race, Ronit Lentin, points out:

> To date, theorizing Irishness as white privilege has been hampered by legacies of racialisation of Irishness as structured by anti-Irish racism in Ireland and abroad. However, Ireland's new position as topping the Globalisation Index, its status symbol as the locus of 'cool' culture, and its privileged position within an ever-expanding European Community calls for the understanding of Irishness as white supremacy. Whiteness works best when it remains a hidden part of the normative social order.[5]

The emerging field of 'whiteness' studies offers a necessary development which illuminates the extent to which race performed a key function in the construction and policing of Irish identity throughout the twentieth century and of the origins of contemporary social and institutional racism in Ireland. It is vital to deconstruct the binary of colonizer and colonized, agency and victimization, pure and hybrid, and acknowledge the extent to which complex processes of accommodation, resistance and opportunism have shaped the concept of 'Irishness'.

Feminism and Nationalisms

If 'all nationalisms are gendered',[6] the Mother Ireland trope merely indicates the operation of a fundamental structuring principle recognizable in both official and insurgent nationalisms. It is one instance of the structural interdependence of gender and national identities. 'The hegemonic process of constructing a nationalist ideology depends upon distinguishing between self and other, us and them, in the creation of a common (shared) identity; women as symbol, men as agents of the nation, colonized space as feminine, colonial power as masculine.'[7] Miroslav Hroch argued in the 1990s with regard to both the then resurgent European nationalisms and to nineteenth-century nationalisms that:

> Identification with the national group . . . includes . . . the construction of a personalized image of the nation. The glorious past of this personality comes to be lived as part of the individual memory of each citizen, its defeats resented as failures that still touch them. One result of such

personalization is that people will regard their nation – that is, themselves – as a single body in a more than metaphorical sense. If any distress
befalls a small part of the nation, it can be felt throughout it, and if any
branch of the ethnic group – even one living far from the 'mother-
nation' – is threatened with assimilation, the members of the
personalized nation may treat it as an amputation of the national body.[8]

If the nation is experienced as 'a body', then the body in Western culture is
primarily figured as and through the female body. The systematic violation
of individual women's bodies in a way which understands itself as destroying both an organic community and an abstract nation was a horrific
validation of Hroch's analysis of the new nationalisms in this respect.
According to Anne McClintock:

> All too often in male nationalisms, *gender difference* between women and
> men serves to symbolically define the limits of national difference and
> power between *men*. Excluded from direct action as national citizens,
> women are subsumed symbolically into the national body politic as its
> boundary and metaphoric limit.[9]

Women are obviously crucial to national expansion and consolidation in
their role as biological reproducers of the members of national collectivities,
but something more complex than the desire to see the nation's population
expand is at stake. Peggy Watson offers an explanation that would indicate
why certain nationalisms seem more and some less prone to obsession with
control of women through and as mediums of reproduction. Watson offers
an example with striking parallels to Ireland. She recounts a response from
an unnamed member of the post-Communist Polish senate that:

> The reason for concentrating on the abortion issue at the expense of
> other pressing problems was simply because it was regarded as something
> which *could* be done . . . the regulation of women was seen as an area
> which required action, but also one where power could readily be exer-
> cised, whereas the economy engendered feelings of powerlessness . . .
> Attempting to legislate against the right to abortion in effect serves both
> to institutionalize the power of men, and to legitimate this power by
> providing a platform for new, more radical and 'modernized' definitions
> of women as *exclusively* grounded in domesticity.[10]

A range of legislative measures to promote just such ends occurred in
newly independent southern Ireland after 1922, culminating in the delin-
eation of women's social function within the home in Article 41.2 of the
1937 Constitution. The elision of women's role as activists into idealized
passivity and symbolic status is again characteristic of the transition from

national movement to state authority internationally. (The analogy with Poland is another reminder that the conjunction of white faces and histories of colonization and migration is not nearly as unusual as Irish cultural theory has sometimes made it seem.) Gender resurfaced as an area where reassurance could be sought against political violence, mass unemployment and rapid social change in the 1980s, a decade characterized in the Republic of Ireland by bitter constitutional campaigns to control the domain of reproduction and the family and ferocious divisions over sexual, familial and religious values. [11]

It might be assumed that the emergence of a prosperous post-Celtic Tiger Ireland would have eliminated the need for this kind of policing of the internal border constituted by women's bodies. In some regards that has been the case. In most important respects, however, the work of national scape-goat has simply been outsourced, as so much other domestic labour, onto immigrant women. The ease with which popular hysteria about pregnant migrants 'flooding' Irish maternity hospitals with their non-national babies could be translated into 80 per cent electoral support for a constitutional amendment limiting Irish citizenship on the basis of ethnicity and affiliations of kinship and blood indicates that racism was never a marginal factor in Irish political life nor a specific historical response to the numbers of actual migrants arriving in Ireland in the late 1990s. It was and is now constitutionally enshrined as a structural principle in national identity. Liberal appeals for Irish sympathy with immigrants on the basis that previous generations of Irish emigrants shared their experience ignore the extent to which the Irish cultivated, traded in and still exploit the valuable commodity of their white identity both abroad and at home. Kingsley's cry of horror that Irish white chimpanzees were so much worse than black African ones is perhaps too much quoted for a reason. It obscures the extent to which subsequent generations of Irish have been able to trade on their difference from the Africans with whom Kingsley's racist perceptions were more comfortable. The Victorian parlour game that Luke Gibbons so influentially described halted, like Kingsley, at the one point in the map of the British Empire where the natives were white.[12] As I have argued elsewhere, however,[13] far from subverting racial hierarchies the existence of liminally white groups has always been a functioning part of the racist system. Colonized or ethnically distinct whites such as the Irish and Scottish provided the British Empire with a highly expendable soldiery and an army of civil servants to deploy around the empire in the nineteenth century. As the Irish emigrated to the US, they progressively 'became white'[14] without at all disconcerting racist structures. (The way in which certain kinds of white ethnicities such as Irish and Polish function in the construction and control of working-class identity in the US is an increasing area of study.)[15] Long overdue, as studies of Irish emigration develop, is a thorough analysis of the way in which the experience of Irish emigrants abroad had an impact on how the Irish who remained at home viewed themselves, particularly in relation to race. It is certainly the case that a highly racialized and rigidly gendered identity was promulgated by both Church and State in Ireland as true Irishness.

Virgin Mother Ireland

Without rehearsing in detail well-known arguments, it may be useful to summarize. The psychodynamic of colonial and postcolonial identity often produces in the formerly colonized a desire to assert a rigid and confined masculine identity, against the colonizers stereotype of their subjects as feminine, wild, ungovernable. This masculine identity then emerges at state level as a regulation of 'our' women, an imposition of a very definite feminine identity as guarantor to the precarious masculinity of the new state. The specific role of the Irish Catholic Church in this maelstrom of economic, political, social and psychological forces is rather more than one among a number of regulatory institutions. It is after all sometimes very difficult to ascertain where Church began and State ended in regard to the institutionalization of individuals, public health and education. The fissure between whiteness and the colonial (not typically white) historical experience of Ireland was traditionally concealed by radiant images of Ireland itself in terms of what Richard Dyer calls 'the supreme exemplar of . . . feminine whiteness', the Virgin Mary.[16]

Dyer's work on whiteness is very suggestive in the Irish context, though his own analysis is primarily of whiteness in imperial and post-imperial cultures, and his research on the function of white women in colonial culture and of liminally white groups and the porous boundaries of white identity are particularly relevant. I want to put forward an argument here that the centrality of Mariology in Irish Catholicism and the extent to which issues of reproduction and sexuality dominated public debates and anxieties around modernization while sharing many of the general characteristics of the gendering of national identity outlined above are in the Irish case also powerfully linked to residual anxieties around race and Ireland's postcolonial position as white European nation.

The promulgation of the image of the Virgin Mary as 'Queen of Ireland'[17] is on one level just another permutation of the virgin/whore dichotomy at the heart of Western culture's representation of women. That dichotomy acquired a very particular paranoid intensity in twentieth-century Ireland, however, which is linked to both the history of colonialism and the compensatory urge to promote an essential Irishness which was purer – in effect whiter – than other European races. In this context, the relationship between images of the Blessed Virgin and Mother Ireland is important, not least because the veneration of the former was shadowed by disappointment in the latter. Tracing the evolution of 'visual Marianism' in Ireland, art historian John Turpin has argued that 'Marianism was a badge of national identity' sponsored by the post-independence southern state as well as the Catholic Church.[18] The influence of French Catholicism on the development of Marian devotion in Ireland is well documented;[19] in effect the image of the Virgin Mother imported from France in the nineteenth century was already highly politicized, anti-Marianne, and an instrument of anti-enlightenment, counter-revolutionary propaganda. Ultimately highly compatible with romantic nationalism, the cross-fertilization of this image with that of 'Mother Ireland' helped dislocate the traditions of radical republicanism from insurgent nationalism in nineteenth-century Ireland. In the post-independence southern state this fusion of national and religious iconography became a lynchpin of the ideology of race and gender.

The Disembodied Mother

In effect, the conflation of images of Mother Ireland and Virgin Mary deployed the Virgin Mother's status as epitome of whiteness as a guarantee of Irish (racial) purity. This function could only be performed if the maternal body was idealized out of existence, or at least out of representation. The peculiar stillness and singularly unmaternal figures of the Virgin Mary which predominate in Irish churches and grottoes only become apparent by contrast with the expressive faces and rounded bodies prevalent in, for example, Andalucian churches. Irish censorship was extraordinarily sensitive in excising all references to childbirth from the films it cut, including even comic scenes of fathers pacing hospital waiting rooms. Even the liberal journal, *The Bell*, found itself at the centre of a storm of controversy when it published Freda Laughton's poem 'The Woman with Child' in 1945. This refusal to countenance any representation of the mother's body as origin of life[20] was paralleled by the predominance of images of the Virgin Mary as mother of an adult son, usually Jesus in the mode of the Sacred Heart, and in general in visions, icons and statues which represented her after her assumption, that is to say after her disembodiment.

Most existing histories of Mariology focus on high art. For example, Kristeva suggests that in the Renaissance figures of the Madonna and child we see the emergence of a secular humanist sensibility, the new ego-centred, rational, masculine subject consecrated in the Christ child but also grounded in his very human relationship with his adoring mother. This is not the type of image of the Virgin Mary that predominated in popular Mariology in twentieth-century Ireland. The images that appear to have been most popular were, in statue form, Mary as apparition, with raised hands, sometimes standing on the stars, sometimes crushing the serpent and, particularly, the picture of the Immaculate Heart of Mary juxtaposed with the Sacred Heart of Jesus. This latter image is preserved in the names of numerous churches and religious institutions, including a religious order in both Ireland and the US. [21]

While the pictures of the disembodied mother as ideal may have disappeared, her cultural impact has not. An echo of this arose in the controversy over the EU-wide advertising campaign to promote voting in the last European Parliamentary elections. The advertisement naturalized the EU by embodying it as a nurturing woman, the good white mother offering herself freely (as opposed to impregnable Fortress Europe). The attempt to produce a transnational form of identity falls back here on the devices of the nation in order to attract affiliation. The opening image of a baby trying to choose between its mother's bare breasts was apparently considered offensive only by Ireland and Britain. The British response was to airbrush out the nipples, the Irish — initially at least — to simply not show the ad. (Irish exclusion of the maternal body in this instance reduced the English response to mere eccentricity.)

The popular reaction over-rode civil service squeamishness through sheer derision — though the laughter might have been more convincing did Ireland not have one of the lowest rates of breastfeeding in the world. The EU advertisement controversy and the low rates of breastfeeding are both indicative of residual unease around the maternal body in action. Indeed the willingness of women from other cultures to breastfeed at least in front of other women has been constructed as an intercultural 'problem', particularly in rural Ireland. The problem of the maternal body as a body has a very specific history in the construction of white, gendered, Irish identity.

The Virgin Mary, Queen of Ireland

A highly racialized discourse of nationality was prevalent in popular Catholic devotional literature in twentieth-century Ireland which promulgated the idea of a special link between Ireland and the Virgin mother. At the zenith of Catholic influence in the southern Irish State, Pope Pius XI's address to the Eucharistic Congess of 1932 spoke of the 'The Virgin Mary, Queen of Ireland'. [22] A survey of Mariological devotional literature, religious souvenirs and Episcopal pronouncements indicates that Pope Pius was not indulging in metaphorical flourishes. The concept of a special relationship between Ireland and the Virgin Mary was heavily promoted in the early decades of southern independence. Rev James Cassidy was a notable contributor to the genre of quasi-historical Mariological literature. In his book on *The Old Love of the Blessed Virgin Mary, Queen of Ireland*[23] he remarks on the prevalence of pictures of the Holy Family in Irish households of the time. In this devotion he finds 'an echo of what must have been a marked devotion of ancient Ireland, devotion of the family to the Mother of the Holy family'.[24] Cassidy's reasons for assuming that such a devotion 'must have been' widespread echo rather chillingly over the intervening decades: 'To such a devotion, Ireland would naturally lend itself, for the constant tribal scrutiny of family life encouraged the preservation of those domestic virtues which are the fundamental props of wholesome nationhood.'[25] The naturalization of tribal surveillance over the family is essential for Cassidy to 'the preservation of moral beauty',[26] but it is also an intrinsic part of Irish identity.[27]

The modernity of the dogma of the immaculate conception does not at all trouble Cassidy's identification of Mary's immaculacy with ancient, pure Irish identity: he suggests that a version of the doctrine could be found in the eighth-century writings of St Colgu. The circularity of Cassidy's mythmaking is an object lesson in the promulgation of ideology. Praising a 'typically Celtic tribute to Mary',[28] Cassidy remarks:

> The rugged humility of the tribesman and the chivalry of the holy warrior seek hand in hand the protection and ideal leadership of a great Queen in whom they see a fount of spiritual fortitude and a mighty inspiration. Its note of child-like familiarity and trustfulness tell of the ease with which the Irish have always lived in the world of the supernatural. What race could express to Mary the desire for eternal life in words of more trusting and loving simplicity than the writer uses here. Heaven for him meant the 'visit' of a child to its Mother. Of that 'visit' he felt assured, just because she was such a Mother and he had such a vivid sense of his child-like right to her maternal solicitude.[29]

A twentieth-century theological construction of Mary is rendered timeless by reference to an ancient Celtic past and the purity and continuity of the Irish nation validated by the attribution to it of devotion to a changeless icon of feminine purity. Cassidy's book is indicative of a strong trend in Irish Catholic publications where purported histories of devotion to Mary are also politically charged appropriations of Celticism for Catholic nationalism. 'The Irish people, too, have always seemed dowered with a genius for domesticity. In ancient Ireland, as in the Ireland of today, all roads seemed to lead to the hearth and the home. The result was an exceptionally wholesome family life that leavened the entire nation. This devotion to the principles of home life explains the unusual moral rectitude of Irish maid-enhood.'[30] In this formulation, Ireland was a nation which defined itself primarily in terms of its women precisely because they were scarcely there, immaterial; 'the true Gael saw a more fundamental support of national life in the luminous ideal of womanhood than in the more material service of the country's manhood'.[31]

Cassidy ends his book by calling Mary 'great Queen of Eire', 'the greatest queen Ireland ever knew, or ever can know, the Immaculate Mother of God'.[32] Not all accounts of Mariological devotion in ancient Ireland were quite so haphazard with historical fact as Cassidy. For example, Concan-non's *The Queen of Ireland: An Historical Account of Ireland's Devotion to the Blessed Virgin* praises the Irish role in the promulgation of the doctrine of the 'immaculate conception', thus at least acknowledging that both the doctrine and the Irish have a history that intervened between ancient Celts and 1922.[33]

The contemporary perception of Catholicism as an atavism that Ireland has outgrown ignores its specifically modernizing project in Ireland, promulgating regulation, bureaucracy and integration within the global/universal Church. This is modernization which understood itself in terms of achievement of an essential and ancient national destiny and iden-tity but relied on twentieth-century industrial and media production to promulgate that identity. John Turpin's work on visual Marianism in Ireland points out the importance of mass manufacture of objects of devotion in its popularization. The material culture of popular Catholic devotion in Ire-land was a point of intersection with the modern marketplace, not its antithesis. This is not so very different from the alliance of the GAA, Guin-ness, Bank of Ireland and ancient Irish myth in a series of recent sponsorship deals. The ensuing advertisement campaigns prove the endless plasticity of Cuchulainn in their promotion of the Celtic Tiger's trinity of questionable banking practice, beer and competitive sport in the holy spirit of high-end technical innovation as expressions of true Irish identity. The combination of the Giant's Causeway and CGI is the contemporary correl-ative of the industrialization of devotion. And both produce images of Ireland that are both racial and gendered.

Are We Post-Postcolonial Yet?

Irish critics sometimes react in hurt and bewilderment at the scepticism about Ireland's postcolonial status expressed by critics for whom the con-junction of postcolonial and white is highly suspect. The extent of Irish filiation to the late Edward Said's foundational model of postcolonial critique is in part accounted for by his understanding of Yeats and Joyce as paradigmatically postcolonial modernists. Vincent Cheng gives a highly illuminating account of the antipathy he experienced in the American academy for his work on a dead white male, no matter how colonized the Dublin of Joyce's upbringing. Cheng's use of Joyce as an emblem of inauthenticity and a useful resource for the construction of all sorts of cosmopolitan, migrant, hyphenated and intercultural identities is a highly attractive alternative to those elements in Irish cultural criticism that regard Irishness as some sort of privileged category for the understanding of Joyce's project. Cheng's warning that 'the search for genuine and authentic native voices will serve only to provide us with a feel-good liberal and multicultural glow – while in actuality merely recycling tokenism and nostalgia'[34] is salutary. Cheng's analysis draws heavily on Declan Kiberd's *Inventing Ireland*. Yet Kiberd's speculation, 'who is to say that the latest group of arriving Nigerians might not' become 'more Irish than the Irish themselves',[35] is predicated on the kind of 'authenticity without risk'[36] which Cheng critiques. Kiberd is very much to be commended for addressing the issue of racism directly in his recent work. However, there are limitations implicit in a paradigm where there still exists something called 'a people' which must be 'secure in its national philosophy' before it can deal confidently and fairly with others. Kiberd's essay lauds hybridity, not least because it assumes Irishness as the ultimate hybrid identity, infinitely capacious and assimilative and already so postcolonial that it need never be challenged and changed by the experience of Nigerian immigrants. The identification of Nigerian immigrants and Norman invaders hardly needs to be deconstructed: the sense of a foreign threat the nation must contain seriously threatens the liberal impulse. Kiberd's recruitment of the legacy of Irish missionaries and Bob Geldof to the argument (that argument again) that Ireland is not racist obfuscates completely the extent to which the discourse of missionary Ireland mimicked colonial stereotypes, this time casting the Irish as the bringers of civilization and salvation to the barbarian 'black babies'. (The assimilation of the lyricist of 'Banana Republic' to the postcolonial nation as inheritor of that tradition would, if it were tenable, certainly add weight to the argument that the 'Make Poverty History' campaign is more about assuaging the affluent world's guilt than solving Africa's problems.)

The danger to postcolonial critique now in Ireland is that it will be co-opted to a discourse of the authentic and native, sometimes called shared history. In short the danger is that the history of the nation will once again become an alibi for the depredations of the State. The relationship between nation and State is an unresolved tension within Irish postcolonial theory. As Colin Graham acutely observes, the case made by David Lloyd and

Carol Coulter for an affiliation between nationalism and feminism in the Irish context depends on the elimination of the hyphenated relation of the nation-state.[37] The economic disjunction between the two parts of the island of Ireland is the elephant in postcolonial theory's sitting room. In Sean O'Reilly's *The Swing of Things*,[38] the released republican prisoner and his Russian neighbour are (almost) equally marginal to contemporary Dublin. They sit silently over a pint, not talking about their past. Their status is of course different. One has an unquestioned right to stay, the possibility of a Trinity degree and of access to insider status, even if his history ultimately precludes achievement of this. The Derry labourers in the city's construction industry living like the other migrants in hostels, with the 'wife and wains' back home, are a closer parallel. O'Reilly's novel is interesting in that it marks one of the very few attempts to write a contemporary Dublin novel within the paradigms of Irish post/modernist fiction and it posits its northern protagonist (an odd amalgam of Leopold Bloom and Stephen Dedalus) as an insider/outsider. It is a position that might usefully be explored in contemporary theory, lest the north become the south's token of authentic historical trauma, another alibi.

The Postcolonial Girl

Of course, the position of the insider/outsider, of the bifurcated other within, is one that is already well articulated in Irish cultural theory. It is the position of feminist analysis, of queer theory, of groups whose marginality is romanticized into silence. Postcolonial theory in Ireland has been highly resistant to being 'differenced' from within. Declan Kiberd's *The Irish Writer and the World* quotes extensively from Julia Kristeva's *Strangers to Ourselves* in its concluding essay on multiculturalism, but includes no extended engagement with any Irish women writers. There are interesting parallels in the first issue of the *Field Day Review*, which reads almost as an elegy for the critical paradigms with which the key contributors to it have changed the face of Irish Studies in the last two decades. (The history of racism features fairly obliquely here in Cormac Ó Gráda's article on 'Dublin's Jewish Immigrants of a Century Ago'.) The text of the review essays is relatively familiar to anyone working in Irish Studies, with many essays based on lectures delivered to the Notre Dame summer seminar. It is significant that the only really paradigm-affecting piece is an elegy, Seamus Deane's essay on Edward Said, and that this is the only place where the radical shifts in cultural theory post 9/11 and the Afghan and Iraq invasions surface, however fleetingly.

As in *The Irish Writer and the World*, the literary writing of Irish women is absent, though there are a couple of scholarly essays. Images of women are not absent, however, and the inclusion of (one) woman artist's work is of particular significance. It is on the visual dimension of the volume that I want to concentrate, for it suggests the challenges that Irish Studies glimpses at its windows. The high production values of the review mark it as a product of a particularly well-endowed corner of the global academic marketplace. The first thing to strike the casual flicker-through is the contrasting preponderance of photographic images of past poverty. There is an emigrant narrative inscribed here, but it is too easy to dismiss it as an Irish-American narrative of sepia rags to well-designed riches. For the volume visually disrupts its own co-ordinates and it does so through the construction of a feminine gaze directed beyond its project. The front cover is folded over, with only one figure from Bert Hardy's original picture of Willie Cullen and his family apparent. This part is a little girl, her back to the photographer, who is looking out of the window. In the foldout, her younger sister becomes the centre of the composition, looking up at her father, who returns her look with great affection. The caption tells us this is a picture of Willie Cullen playing with his children, but it is only the smaller child who plays back. On the cover, the disengaged little girl is central but unreadable, her face turned in the opposite direction to our scrutiny.

The design offers the possibility of two overlapping interpretations. The most overt plane of meaning is that the new review, while representing the past, is conscious of another subject position, one oriented towards the future, the outside, the world beyond the little Cullen girl's window. This future-oriented Irish subject is constructed by the cover as feminine, nascent, yet to mature and still resistant to engagement and interpretation. It is the central enigma of the subject and critical perspective that this review celebrates and institutionalizes. The folding over of the photograph implies a further and autocritical impulse. The complete picture would place this feminine future within the framework of the domestic and the family. The design hides this possibility away, turning the picture of the nurturing father and the affectionate child into the lining of a carapace of feminine refusal. The review wears its unconscious on its sleeve, intensely desirous of an encounter with a feminine subject, insistent that such engagement is beyond its reach. But the little girls in the photograph would be women in their fifties now, women with lived lives beyond the photographic frame, their own mature perspective on the world beyond the window. The girls in the picture might be readable in terms of the definition of a (feminized) subaltern which Deane commends in Gayatri Spivak's writing, 'populations below the horizon for whom everything, even their liberation, had been already so spoken for that the effort was to enable these people – mostly women – to begin to speak and thereby create an alternative form of power to that which had silenced them'.[39] But what of the women the girls became and the generation they represent? Didn't they begin to speak, find their own alternative form of power? They belong to the generation of civil rights, women's liberation, of articulate women in all walks of life who engaged in a wide variety of political and artistic practices. They are far more than silent potential.

The rest of Bert Hardy's photographs of women, including a number where women and girls face directly to camera, form part of a sequence in the volume where they are heavily outnumbered by images of men engaged in work and politics. The female gaze continues to trouble the frame(work), however. Margaret Corcoran's series of paintings, *An Enquiry*, takes its title from Edmund Burke's *An Enquiry into the Origins of the Ideas of the Sublime and the Beautiful*. Two paintings from the series are included, both within the pages of Benedict Anderson's essay on globalization. The painting that figured prominently in Luke Gibbon's essay on the series, 'Engendering the Sublime: Margaret Corcoran's *An Enquiry*', *An Enquiry VIII*, is included in small format. *An Enquiry VIII* rhymes with the front cover illustration, showing a woman again with her back to us, her attention turned to the painting in front of her (George Barret's painting of Powerscourt Waterfall). The full-page and dominant illustration of Corcoran's work is *An Enquiry I*, which features a young woman looking towards the viewer, turned away from Thomas Hickey's orientalist painting of an Indian woman. All the paintings in *An Enquiry* are set in the Milltown Rooms of the National Gallery. These rooms contain the late eighteenth- and early nineteenth-century paintings of the Irish School, so that Corcoran's series is an interrogation of a canon of Irish painting as well as an exploration of Burke's aesthetics. Gibbons' reading of Corcoran's work in *Circa*[40] effectively reads it as a feminist extension of Burke's project, even suggesting that Burke's emphasis on anticipation and identification as elements of the sublime aesthetic experience prefigures Laura Mulvey's analysis of the gendered nature of spectatorship in cinema. Corcoran's identification of her painting technique with Degas and Monet certainly supports Gibbons' reading of her work in terms of modernist self-reflexive use of both framing and the gallery space. Yet this neat recruitment of *An Enquiry* to both Burkean aesthetics and modernist interrogations of tradition is undercut by *An Enquiry I*. The feminine subject here is not a good daughter who plays the game, nor simply a recalcitrant one who refuses to be read. Moreover, the differencing of the gaze in Corcoran's work exceeds the category of singular feminine intervention into an artistic practice and critical discourse conducted in exclusively masculine terms. The modern young woman who looks back at us from *An Enquiry I* does not block our gaze at the objectified 'oriental' woman behind her, but she does interrupt it. She looks back, challenging our secure spectatorship position, blocking the secure binary identifications of active gaze and agency on the one hand, and object of gaze and passivity on the other. In this painting to-be-looked-at is to challenge that look, at least if you are the white woman in the foreground of the canvas, not the 'other' woman in the background. The intervention of the female gazer poses a question before Hickey's portrait, 'what do you think you are looking at?' This painting is much harder than *An Enquiry VIII* to read as straightforwardly Burkean, for it insists on a pause before the onward rush of paint and emotion, forcing an internal dis-location in the position of subject and object rather than a synthesis of the two. *An Enquiry I* differences the role of painter and spectator and in the process differentiates itself from the Burkean sublime. There is a definite satirical edge to the portrayal of the female figure as art student, the painter framing her own position as copyist of the (minor) masters within the nar-rative of the series. That narrative is of course beyond the representational scope of selective reproductions. However, it is worth noting that what gets lost in the transposition is the sense of movement which all commentators (including Gibbons) have identified as a major component of Corcoran's technique. The foregrounding of *An Enquiry I* precludes any simplistic reading of this in terms of a transition from object to subject of painting, because the contemporary female figure is remarkably still and sharp, while it is the framed portrait behind that seems to promise movement and life. In this respect it echoes another woman's painting, one that thematically bears comparison with Corcoran's series. Moira Barry's *Self-Portrait in the Artist's Studio* (1920) is set within the privacy of the artist's studio rather than the national/public space of the National Gallery, but it also features a woman looking away from a variety of canvasses, over her shoulder, directly at the on-looker, in a pose which is uncannily close to the foregrounded young woman in *An Enquiry I*. The canvasses behind Barry are, however, blank, with one exception (which appears to be a still life), and only one is framed. Again the paintings are more fluid than the woman in front of them. Barry's self-portrait is a highly stylized work in a very traditional form, but it also uses the modernist techniques whose influence Corcoran acknowl-edges. *Self-Portrait in the Artist's Studio* is, like the paintings by Barret and Hickey, owned by the National Gallery, but not part of the canon config-ured by the Milltown rooms. It was, however, exhibited as part of the 1987 exhibition of Irish Women Artists at the gallery and featured prominently in the published catalogue of that exhibition.

Juxtaposing the two paintings suggests a genealogy of women artists' relationship with both modernist and postmodernist painting. Both challenge the opposition of subject–object, inside–outside, framed–framing. The woman in Barry's *Self-Portrait* is an artist surrounded by the potentiality of her own painting, the blank canvasses yet to be filled, and she reminds us that women have not only been part of the history of art, but have an artistic history of speaking, looking and painting 'for themselves'. In *An Enquiry I* there are two women, one an acute observer of a tradition of painting which leaves her below its framed horizon, overshadowed by a beautiful image of female otherness. The second woman seems almost to be flowing out of focus, her gaze directed at an object we cannot identify. The double framing of her image – within Corcoran's painting of Hickey's painting – in important respects de-mystifies her. She becomes less a token of the exotic, unknowable, to be exchanged for the authenticity of the sublime, and more a reminder of the structural limitations of the aesthetic.

An Enquiry suggests that the postmodern, feminist artist can keep on moving through and beyond the limitations of a national and patriarchal culture, but will never have the luxurious fiction of really blank canvasses to be filled. The Irish tradition behind her produces sublime and beautiful images of a romantic landscape and a racial stereotype, and Corcoran's series links the two in a way which exceeds Gibbon's description of its presentation of 'the image itself as an enquiry into its own making'.[41] The positioning of Corcoran's paintings in *Field Day Review* is highly significant, for it both cordons them off from the textual analysis of Ireland which dominates the volume and identifies them with the investigation of globalization in Benedict Anderson's essay. Irish Studies has been heavily invested in its particularity, a particularity that seeks exception from the global system that produces it. Ireland is produced in turn by this discourse as a beautiful and disturbing original, rather in the manner of a modernist work of art. Irish literary criticism has a brilliant history – brilliant in the mode of a moving searchlight, providing blindingly clear illuminations of particular texts and times without ever offering the larger view, which would show where exactly it itself is positioned. The inclusion of Corcoran's painting hints at a nascent awareness that race and gender will reconfigure the field. Perhaps it glimpses outside the window a landscape that includes Moira Barry, the adult women the Cullen girls became, the books written out there, the cultural maps the new immigrants will produce, the possibility of a very differenced Ireland in the world.

Common Interests

It is part of the function of Irish referenda to generate more crises than they resolve. The restrictions on citizenship were followed by the highly publicized deportation of Nigerian immigrants and asylum seekers and the equally highly publicized reversal of the deportation order on one individual, as if somehow this token could displace guilt for the enactment of what the referendum consensus had clearly mandated. Economic logic has very quickly superseded the legal fiction of a distinction between legitimate Irish citizens and mere economic migrants. The rapidity with which the trade union movement's efforts to extend protective employment legislation to migrant workers in the Irish Ferries dispute deteriorated into anxiety about immigrants taking Irish jobs was deeply alarming. Irish 'identity' is, it seems, poised between rational self-awareness and the deployment of historically produced paranoid localism in the interests of a highly accelerated techno-globalization. Feminist theory has an important role to play in countering the latter through excavation of the origins and persistent depths of the association of the body, maternity and the danger of the foreign. If we are to proceed to accept the strange and the migrant as no more nor less than our shared conditions of being, then we must begin with an acknowledgment of the history of difference, (m)othering the nation.

Notes and References

1 Gerardine Meaney, 'Sex and Nation', in Ailbhe Smyth (ed.), *The Irish Women's Studies Reader* (Dublin: Attic, 1993), p. 233. The essay was first published as part of the LIP series (Dublin: Attic, 1990).
2 Steve Garner, 'Guests of the Nation,' *Irish Review*, 33 (Spring 2005), 78–84.
3 Bryan Fanning, *Racism and Social Change in the Republic of Ireland* (Manchester: Manchester University Press, 2002).
4 Ronit Lentin, 'Black Bodies and Headless Hookers: Alternative Global Narratives for Twenty-First-Century Ireland', *Irish Review*, 33 (Spring 2005), 7.
5 Ibid., p. 9.
6 Anne McClintock, 'Family Feuds: Gender, Nationalism and the Family', *Feminist Review*, 44 (Summer 1993), 61.
7 Shelley Feldman, 'Feminist Interruptions: The Silence of East Bengal in the Story of Partition', *Interventions: International Journal of Postcolonial Studies*, 1:2 (1999), 177–8.
8 Miroslav Hroch, 'From National Movement to the Fully Formed Nation: The Nation-Building Process in Europe', *New Left Review*, 198 (March/April 1993), 15.
9 McClintock, 'Family Feuds', p. 62.
10 Peggy Watson, 'The Rise of Masculinism in Eastern Europe', *New Left Review*, 198 (March/April, 1993), 75.
11 Contributors to the 1999 special issue of *Interventions*, 2:1, consistently remarked on the process whereby, in the Indian context, relatively liberated women in the 1980s and 1990s became metaphors for secularism and modernity and a constituency to be targeted by the religious right.
12 Luke Gibbons, 'Race Against Time: Racial Discourse and Irish History', *Transformations in Irish Culture* (Cork: Cork University Press, 1996), p. 149.
13 Gerardine Meaney, 'Decadence, Degeneration and Revolting Aesthetics: The Fiction of

Emily Lawless and Katherine Cecil Thurston', *Colby Quarterly*, 36:2 (June 2000,) 157–76.

14 For an account of this process in the context of US immigration history, see Noel Ignatieve, *How the Irish Became White* (London: Routledge, 1997).

15 See, for example, Diane Negra (ed.), *The Irish in US: Irishness, Performativity and Popular Culture* (Durham: Duke University Press, 2006).

16 Richard Dyer, *White* (London: Routledge, 1997), p. 74.

17 See John Turpin, 'Visual Marianism and National Identity in Ireland: 1920–1960', in Tricia Cusack and Sighle Bhreathnach-Lynch (eds), *Art, Nation and Gender: Ethnic Landscapes, Myths and Mother-Figures* (Aldershot: Ashgate, 2003), p. 72.

18 Turpin, 'Visual Marianism,' p. 70.

19 See Turpin and, for a more historical reading, James S. Donnelly, Jr., 'A Church in Crisis: The Irish Catholic Church Today', *History Ireland*, 8:3 (2000), 12–17 and 'The Peak of Marianism in Ireland', in Stewart Brown and David Miller (eds), *Piety and Power in Ireland* (Indiana: University of Notre Dame Press, 2000), for an account of this relationship.

20 See Moynagh Sullivan, 'The Treachery of Wetness: Irish Studies, Seamus Heaney and the Politics of Parturition', *Irish Studies Review*, 13:4 (2005), 451–68, for an analysis of a parallel configuration in Irish literary criticism.

21 See Turpin, 'Visual Marianism'.

22 Ibid.

23 James F. Cassidy, *The Old Love of the Blessed Virgin Mary, Queen of Ireland* (Dublin: Gill, 1933), p. 17.

24 Ibid.

25 op. cit., p. 18.

26 Ibid.

27 op. cit., p. 35.

28 op. cit., p. 26.

29 op. cit., p. 28.

30 op. cit., p. 56.

31 op. cit., p. 56.

32 op. cit., pp. 60–1.

33 Mrs Thomas Concannon, *The Queen of Ireland: An Historical Account of Ireland's Devotion to the Blessed Virgin* (Dublin: M. H. Gill & Sons, 1938).

34 Vincent Cheng, *Inauthentic: The Anxiety Over Culture and Identity* (New Brunswick, New Jersey and London: Rutgers University Press, 2004), p. 27.

35 Declan Kiberd, *The Irish Writer and the World* (Cambridge: Cambridge University Press, 2005), p. 303.

36 Cheng, *Inauthentic*, p. 26.

37 Colin Graham, *Deconstructing Ireland: Identity, Theory, Culture* (Edinburgh: Edinburgh University Press, 2001), pp. 109–10.

38 Sean O'Reilly, *The Swing of Things* (London: Faber, 2004).

39 Seamus Deane, 'Edward Said (1935–2003): A Late Style of Humanism', *Field Day Review*, 1 (2005), 199.

40 Luke Gibbons, 'Engendering the Sublime: Margaret Corcoran's *An Enquiry*', *Circa*, 107 (Spring 2004), 32–8.

41 Ibid.

Still Changing Places:
Women's Paid Employment
and Gender Roles

PAT O'CONNOR

Introduction

In a timely discussion on Ireland and 'theory', the critic Claire Connolly suggested that there 'remains an almost reflex sense that, when "Ireland" is at issue, feminism is a tangential or subsidiary concern'.[1] The relationship between Irish Studies and Women's Studies has been described as tense,[2] arguably reflecting the fact that Irish Studies is uncomfortable with the idea that the majority of men in Ireland (albeit to varying degrees) enjoy a patriarchal dividend as men, in terms of 'honour, prestige or the right to command', including a 'material dividend'.[3] In this perspective gender is seen as related to privilege – with such privilege deriving from male power at a structural level. The sociologist R. W. Connell argues that, although only a minority of men actively subordinate women, the majority are comfortable with such a dividend when it appears to be given to them 'by an external force, by nature or convention, or even by women themselves, rather than by an active social subordination going on here and now'.[4] The most effective exercise of power of course is in situations where beliefs and practices are such that the exercise of power is seen as 'natural' and 'inevitable'.[5] It is because men wish to be men, within a society where being a man involves privileging, that patriarchy is perpetuated. Thus, for Connell, male privileging is maintained, not simply by individual or group attempts to intimidate, oppress and exclude, but by women and men's 'realistic' expectations. Their acceptance of the *status quo* effectively perpetuates 'a structure where different groups are rewarded unequally'.[6]

Such patterns are not of course peculiar to Ireland: the United Nations noted that 'no society treats its women as well as its men',[7] and indeed, Ireland's position in global gender gap indices gives little grounds for complacency.[8] For example, on an economic opportunity index which included type of work, maternity benefits, perceived discrimination and government-provided childcare, Ireland was ranked 51st out of 58 countries, its rank being broadly similar to Bangladesh (53rd) – and substantially lower than France (9th) or Thailand (39th). Thus, despite its rapid economic growth in the 1990s, to a large extent facilitated by a reserve labour force consisting of women,[9] Ireland is still very much a society in transition from its patriarchal roots.[10]

In this article, I look at change in Ireland on two levels: firstly, in terms of general changes in women's participation in paid employment, and in terms of specific changes in what Savage[11] has called positions of expertise and authority (focusing particularly on the university and the civil service respectively); secondly, I discuss cultural definitions of gender roles and constructions of the self, by drawing on European Values studies, as well as data on young people's constructions of themselves. The approach adopted can be seen as a response to Finlayson's exhortation to make use of 'a kind of radical empiricism' that seeks out the facts but at the same time goes beyond them.[12]

Women's Participation in Paid Employment

The changes in women's participation in paid employment in Ireland have occurred at two levels: firstly, the sheer proportion of women, particularly those with children, who are in paid employment; and secondly, the proportion of women who are in positions of expertise and/or authority. The extent of the change in women's participation in paid employment in Ireland can be illustrated by the fact that, in the thirty years between 1971 and 2001, the number of women in paid employment rose by 140 per cent, as compared to a rise of 27 per cent in the case of men.[13] This increase has been overwhelmingly due to married women's participation in paid employment. In the early 1970s, only 7 per cent of all married women were in the labour force, compared with roughly half of all married women in Ireland now. Indeed, by 2004, the highest labour force participation rate for women (76 per cent) was in the 25–34 years of age-group, precisely the group who are likely to be bearing and rearing children. At that time, just over half of mothers aged 20–44 whose youngest child was less than five years old were in paid employment. Overall, Irish women's participation in paid employment now is marginally above the average for the twenty-five countries in the EU – whereas even in 1997 it was significantly below it.[14] These dramatic changes in women's employment have come about despite very low levels of childcare provision. Average full-day childcare costs in Ireland are 20 per cent of average earnings,

while the average for other EU countries is 8 per cent.[15] Despite some limited attempts by the public and private sectors to facilitate the reconciliation of
work and family through arrangements such as job-sharing and flexitime,
individual families, and particularly women, have borne the brunt of the consequences of this dramatic increase in women's paid employment.[16]

Traditionally, although women's educational levels were higher than
men's in Ireland, the existence of the 'marriage bar' and related social and
cultural attitudes affected women's participation in paid employment in the
professions, associate professions and management.[17] Because of the increasingly service-oriented nature of the Irish economy, there have been
substantial increases in the size of these categories. Thus, even over the past
five years, the size of the professional category has increased by 33 per cent,
with more than half of that increase involving women. Similarly, the size of
the associate professional and technical category has increased by 28 per
cent, with more than three-fifths of that increase involving women. The size
of the executive and managerial category has increased by considerably less
over the five-year period (roughly 8 per cent), although almost 80 per cent
of that increase has consisted of women. Thus, roughly half of those in positions of 'expertise' (that is, professions and associate professions and
technical occupations) are women, but, despite this, just fewer than three
out of ten of those in positions of 'authority' (that is, managerial and
administrative positions) are women. This kind of imbalance between
expertise and authority, however, is not unique to Ireland.[18]

Even though there are now almost 300,000 women in these positions in
Ireland, comprising almost two-fifths of all women in paid employment, they
are rarely at the top of such structures. A large survey of managers and professionals showed that only at the lowest level was there a roughly equal
proportion of men and women. As one moved up the hierarchy, women disappeared, constituting less than one in ten of those at chief executive level – a
pattern not peculiar to Ireland.[19] Such women are arguably in positions of
cultural tension. On the one hand, they have symbolic capital – 'the esteem,
recognition, belief, credit, confidence of others' from participating at this level
in the occupational arena; yet, on the other hand, by virtue of their gender,
they find themselves less valued than their male counterparts.[20] We will now
look in more detail at the position of women in one professional and one
managerial area, the university and the civil service respectively.

University

Considerable concern has been expressed by the State and the media
about the feminization of education at primary level. However, there is no

corresponding concern about the continued masculinization of universities, especially at the higher levels. Indeed, it is not seen at all, since the equation of masculinity with authority continues to be seen as 'natural' and 'inevitable'. Even today only just less than two-fifths of faculty in universities are women. This does mark an increase – particularly over the past ten years (see Table 1 below).[21] Portugal and Finland are in a similar position to Ireland, with women constituting a similar proportion of faculty in these countries.[22] Such patterns cannot be explained by the level of economic development, by the proportion of women in the labour force, or by their educational levels.

TABLE 1

Comparisons over time in the proportion of women faculty (full-time) in the universities in Ireland

	Women as % of those at each level 1975/1976*	Women as % of those at each level 1984/1985**	Women as % of those at each level 1993/1994***	Women as % of those at each level 2002/2003****
Professor	5%	2%	4%	7%
Associate Professor	7%	5%	6%	12%
Senior Lecturer	3%	7%	12%	24%
College Lecturer	12%	23%	28%	39%
Assistant Lecturer/ Others	26%	34%	39%	53%
Overall	11%	15%	20%	39%

*HEA 1987; ** HEA 1987; *** Smyth 1996; ****HEA 2005

A very different picture emerges when we look at the proportion of women who are at the top of the educational hierarchy in universities. In Ireland the proportion of women in what are broadly synonymous with full professorial university posts is roughly half what it is in the EU, the United States and Australia (13–14 per cent, as compared with 7 per cent in Ireland).[23] The proportion of women at professorial level in Ireland is roughly one-third that in Finland, Portugal or Latvia. Perhaps even more revealingly, the proportion of women at full professorial level in Ireland has changed little over the past thirty years: rising from 5 per cent of such professors in 1975/6 to 7 per cent in 2002/3.[24] Furthermore, in Ireland the differential between men and women's chances of promotion was one of the largest in Europe, with Irish men having almost six times as much chance of getting to this level than Irish women.[25]

An increased proportion of women faculty in the universities, particularly at the higher levels, will help ensure that the production of knowledge is not the monopoly of (middle-class) men, that knowledge is not defined in a way which privileges their perspective and, hence, that a whole realm of experiences and representations is not marginalized. Since girls are now more likely than boys to attend university at both undergraduate and post-graduate levels, the under-representation of women, especially in senior faculty positions, raises issues related to cultural imperialism, indeed to colonialism.[26] Young women are deprived of a range of female role models, and, as American work has shown, such same-sex models are important in facilitating female students' career orientation, confidence and success.[27]

In summary then, Irish universities remain hierarchically male-dominated institutions with an increasingly female student population. These are the institutions that are involved in the creation and validation of particular kinds of knowledge. To anticipate that such structures would prioritize gender, problematize the patriarchal dividend, or facilitate the development of gendered constructions seems unrealistic, given Connell's observation that:

> A gender order where men dominate women cannot avoid constituting men as an interest group concerned with defence and women as an interest group concerned with change. This is a structural fact, independent of whether men as individuals love or hate women or believe in equality or abjection.[28]

Civil Service

Although it can be argued that policy direction is determined by the political leadership, the civil service is seen as particularly important, not least because it is an instrument for gender mainstreaming, that is, 'incorporating a gender equality perspective into mainstream policies as these are developed, implemented and evaluated'.[29] It is required to do this by the European Commission in the case of all policies and programmes funded through the National Development Plan. Potentially, it constitutes a driving force for a supportive focus on gender and its implications in the transformation of Irish society.

Over the past fifteen years, but particularly in the past six, there have been very substantial changes in the gender profile of the lower-middle level of the hierarchy (that is, the proportion of women at assistant principal and administrative officer level). Women now constitute between a third and a half of those at such levels (see Table 2 below). These patterns are all the more striking, since the proportion of women at these levels had not increased at all in the 1987–1995 period. Gender issues were prioritized at these levels of the civil service by the Co-ordinating Group of Secretaries in 1997, and were reflected in departmental and civil service-wide gender targets at the Assistant Principal level in the Strategic Management Initiative, which had the support of the civil service unions. Furthermore, specific measures such as term-time working, job-sharing and flexitime, which help individual women to reconcile work and family responsibilities, are more common in the Irish civil service than in the private sector.[30]

TABLE 2

Percentage of Women at each Grade in the Civil Service over time
1987, 1995, 1997 and 2003

Grades	1987*	1995*	1997**	2003***
General Secretary	0%	4%	5%	12%
Assistant Secretary	1%	6%	10%	10%
Principal Officer	5%	13%	12%	20%
Assistant Principal	23%	23%	24%	34%
Administrative Officer	26%	21%	37%	56%
Higher Executive Officer	34%	37%	39%	47%
Executive Officer	44%	51%	54%	64%
Staff Officer	67%	75%	75%	79%
Clerical Officer	68%	79%	79%	78%
Clerical Assistant	83%	82%	82%	

*Co-ordinating Group of Secretaries (1996:48), quoted in O'Connor (1998a: 221); ** Humphreys et al. (1999: 53 and 55); *** CSO (2004)

The continued dominance of men at senior levels in the civil service has been seen as an important factor in inhibiting the implementation of gender mainstreaming; McGauran noted that male 'champions' of gender equality did occasionally exist, but that, 'collectively, men seem to be better than women at defending their interests, particularly in relation to employment'.[31] The top echelons of the civil service remain overwhelmingly male, with 88–90 per cent of those at general secretary and assistant secretary level still being men. Humphreys et al. expressed concern about the unsatisfactory nature of promotion mechanisms, and affirmative action was recommended 'if women are not to be discouraged in their promotion prospects by the double burden of work and caring and the gender stereotyped attitudes of management'.[32] However, no such mechanisms seem to have been put in place to tackle the reliance on seniority or the promotional implications of differentially valued 'male'/'female' areas of work; nor have any targets been identified at these levels. The civil service is not of course unique: similar – and in some cases more male-dominated – trends exist in the private sector; studies show that between 3 per cent and 10 per cent of managing directors/chief executives are women.[33] With action plans and diversity targets, the civil service in the UK has increased the proportion of women in the most senior positions.[34] Such comparisons, however, need to be treated with caution, as they may reflect relative levels of pay and conditions inside and outside the civil service.

Overall then in Ireland, although the proportion of women at the lower-middle level of the civil service has dramatically increased in the past six years, the most senior positions (at general secretary and assistant secretary level) are still overwhelmingly held by men. This is particularly important, since it has had an impact not only on policies within the civil service, but more broadly on the failure to include a gender perspective in all mainstream policies, including those relating to the funding of research in the higher education sector, estimated at €422 million in 2003 and a projected €765 million in 2010.[35] Thus, for example, there seems to be little awareness that policies focusing research funding on areas such as information technology and biotechnology, which are of little or no interest to the high educational achievers who are girls, are inherently problematic.

Changing Gender Roles and Other Attitudes

Claire Connolly suggests that 'the sense that subjectivity is both scripted by and constitutive of ideology finds many echoes in Irish culture'.[36] It can thus be argued that Irish women's constructions of the self have been located within an overall context of gender roles that stress service, self-sacrifice and subordination.[37] In contrast, Breda Gray's work suggests that this is changing when she observes that 'the category "Irish women" . . . produced a martyred relationship to the self which they [the women in her study] identify with their mothers and refuse for themselves'.[38] In this section, drawing on data derived from various sources, the extent and kinds of changes that are occurring at a cultural level will be explored. This section will first look at changes in gender roles, particularly insofar as they relate to women's participation in paid employment; secondly, it will more specifically examine the extent to which cultural value is still seen as attached to women's activities within the domestic arena, while considering perceptions that women are discriminated against in the paid employment area; thirdly, it will weigh evidence as to whether a relational dimension continues to be important in women's construction of themselves; and finally, it will look at the extent to which gender is perceived as being irrelevant – an attitude which is at odds with the previous attitudes.

Firstly, when drawing on European Values data it is clear that positive attitudes to women's participation in paid employment increased amongst both men and women between 1990 and 2000 (see Table 3 below). In 2000 roughly three-quarters of the men and women in the Irish part of the European Values study saw a job as 'the best way for a woman to be an independent person'; and roughly four-fifths endorsed the view that 'husband and wife should contribute to household income'. The complexity of these attitudes was illustrated by the fact that, at that time, more than a third still agreed that 'A job is all right but what women really want is a home and children'. Furthermore, roughly a third also felt that 'a pre-school child suffers if mother works outside the home'. The implicit assumption that it is mothers who are the most important people in their children's lives was challenged when the majority of both agreed that fathers were 'as well suited to look after their children as mothers' (an indicator that was not included in the earlier study). [39]

TABLE 3
Support for Gender Roles by Gender in 2000★ (and 1990★★)

	Women	Men	Total
A job is the best way for a woman to be an independent person (% agree)	72% (59%)	75% (62%)	74% (61%)
Husband and wife should contribute to household income (% agree)	83% (73%)	79% (68%)	81% (71%)
A job is all right but what women really want is a home and children (% agree)	35% (55%)	39% (62%)	37% (59%)
A pre-school child suffers if mother works outside the home (% agree)	32% (46%)	39% (60%)	36% (53%)
Fathers are as well suited to looking after their children as mothers (% agree)	82% (n/a)	73% (n/a)	78% (n/a)
Being a housewife is just as fulfilling as working for pay (% agree)	62% (71%)	57% (73%)	60% (72%)

★ Fahey et al. (2005: 154) – source is European Values study 2000;   ★★ Whelan and Fahey (1994: 53) – source is European Values Study 1990

Secondly, there was a strong suggestion in the European Values data that cultural value was still seen as attached to women's activities in the domestic arena. Thus, even in 2000, and despite women's high levels of participation in paid employment, roughly three-fifths of both men and women agreed that 'Being a housewife is just as fulfilling as working for pay'. (These trends can be expected to vary by age and participation in paid employment.[40]) Since a focus on culinary expertise has never been a part of Irish culture, it seems plausible to suggest that such trends may reflect a yearning after women's traditional levels of authority in the domestic area and their role in maintaining personal relationships there; or the difficulty of being promoted in the paid employment setting and/or of combining paid work and family responsibilities in a societal context that is deeply unhelpful.

The accounts of young people aged between 18 and 30 arguably help make sense of the high value attached to 'being a housewife' in the European Values study.[41] They suggested that the gendered patterns of housework and childcare were seen as reflecting women's greater competence and responsibility. Thus, the idea of role reversal (with the man being responsible for the home and family) was greeted with incredulity: 'He'd have them [children] killed. He'd be bankrupt. He wouldn't be able to [cope].'[42] In anticipating the perceived difficulty of combining paid work and family responsibilities, these young women, the majority of whom were not parents, advocated deferring having children, juggling these responsibilities and (reflecting their perception of the value of work in the home) some kind of payment by the State for such work, whether or not the woman was married.[43] The Irish State currently provides such payments only to lone mothers on condition that they are not co-habiting (effectively replacing a male breadwinner in these situations). Amongst the young men there was ambivalence about such payments even to lone mothers – such attitudes reflecting their conception of breadwinning as a key element in men's role in the family.

The perceived cultural value of women's activities in the domestic area is possibly not unrelated to the perceived discriminatory attitudes to women in the paid employment area. Amongst those aged between 18 and 30, both men and women suggested that women had to be more qualified and to work harder than men in Ireland to get promoted. Most of the young men did not see men as more competent than women but 'that's just the way things are'. Although at one level the young men accepted that the system was unfair to women, at another level they felt no responsibility to change it and in certain contexts did not see it as an issue at all:

> I think most women are [able to do anything] . . . But men are still looked at as more dominant, even though they are not . . . the men are looked for in the management positions . . . You just have to look at top executives of any company . . . and they are all men. So I presume there must be some disadvantage for women. But I wouldn't see it.[44]

Such attitudes were not peculiar to Ireland, although they were particularly strong here. Indeed Bjerrum Nielsen showed that, whether societies purported to endorse gender equality or complementarity, a positive valuation of womanhood did not exist nor a positive male role *vis-à-vis* women.[45]

Thirdly, there was a suggestion that women's constructions of themselves remained strongly relational. Drawing on texts written by 10–12 year-olds and 14–17 year-olds in a school context, and reflecting a 'weak cultural feminist tradition',[46] gender was seen as a repressed but crucially important framework in the construction of young people's sense of self.[47] Building on a traditional cultural validation of relational strength, it is evident that girls reflexively constructed their identity in terms of relational discourses. For these young women such discourses mainly revolved around same-sex best friends with whom relationships were intimate and long-standing. In addition, and arguably reflecting an enhanced sense of their categorical identity as women, they also described side-by-side activity-based categorical friendships (the only type of friendships the boys mentioned, if they mentioned any). Furthermore, girls aged between 14 and 17 were also more likely to refer to family in general, and extended family in particular, arguably reflecting their greater relational orientation. In contrast to the importance of the relational dimension for girls, boys constructed their idea of themselves hierarchically: this was reflected in accounts of attempts to establish hierarchical dominance competitively through football, physically through fighting, and/or through their presentation of themselves as authoritative interpreters of a wide range of economic, political and social phenomena.

The relational dimension was also evident in girls' subject choices at university level. In a context where roughly one in two of those who do the Leaving Certificate go on to higher education, the areas where women constitute at least three-quarters of the students were in the broadly person-oriented 'caring' areas, such as education, medical science and social science. In contrast, the area where men constitute a clear majority (that is, more than three-quarters) is technology.[48]

Fourthly, despite these trends, the educational institutions and the State frequently depict society as gender neutral. Perhaps not surprisingly then, when the 18–30 year-olds were asked if they saw gender as making any difference to their future lives, overwhelmingly they said that it would not do so.[49] Similarly, the 10–12-year olds and the 14–17 year-olds did not think of themselves as boys/girls and suggested that consumer society was eroding gender differences in specific areas (with references to part-time jobs, clothes and consumption of alcohol not being gender differentiated).[50] In addition, there seemed to be a rhetorical degendering of occupational choices, which in fact concealed a valuing of male career choices. Thus, women formed the majority of the students choosing to study stereotypically male areas such as law, science, and commerce at university.[51]

It seems plausible to conclude that gender roles and constructions of the self are confused and complex in Ireland today. The Irish element of the

European Values study suggested that paid work was increasingly seen as desirable for women. In this context a residual attachment to being a house-wife emerged – arguably because it potentially avoided the difficulties of combining paid work with family responsibilities, and offered greater possi-bilities than paid employment as regards authority and the facilitation of relationships in the domestic area. These attitudes might not be unrelated to the fact that women were seen by these young men and women as less like-ly to be promoted in the paid employment arena because of discriminatory attitudes to them as women. Young women's constructions of themselves continued to revolve around relationships and caring, while young men's revolved around technology and hierarchy. Finally, there were some indica-tions of the adoption by girls of what purported to be gender-neutral patterns, but for the most part these seemed to be traditionally male ones, with gender in certain contexts being presented as having no relevance to their lives. Nevertheless, gender seemed overall to be a repressed but crucial-ly important framework in their constructions of themselves and their lives.

Summary and Conclusions

Ireland, in some ways, is changing rapidly. The extent of that change is most vividly illustrated by the increase in women's participation in the labour force in general, and their occupancy of positions of expertise and/or authority in particular (that is, in the professions, associate professions and technical occupations; and in managerial and administrative occupations respectively). Furthermore, not only has the number of these positions grown, but also, even over the last five years, women's access to such posi-tions has dramatically increased. Almost two-fifths of the women in paid employment in 2004 were in these positions. These general patterns are reflected, for example, in the universities, where just under two-fifths of faculty are now women, and in the civil service, where women constitute between one-third and a half of those at administrative officer and assistant principal level. However, a rather different picture emerges when one looks at the proportion of women at the top of these structures. The proportion of women at professorial level (at 7 per cent) in Ireland is little different to what it was thirty years ago when the marriage bar had just been lifted. Similarly, men continue to dominate the top of the civil service, where only 12 per cent of those at general secretary level are women.

Gender roles, particularly in relation to women's participation in paid employment, have also changed. Nevertheless, a residual attachment to being a housewife persisted in the European Values study, possibly owing to the difficulty of combining paid work with family responsibilities and/or because being a housewife offered the possibility of greater authority than paid employment as a result of perceived attitudes to women's promotion. There was some evidence of a denial of the relevance of gender to young people's future lives – arguably reflecting an institutional rejection of the importance of gender – one which often concealed an implicit positive valuation of male patterns. The young women, however, in their subject choices and their constructions of the self, continued to valorize female relatedness.

The male-dominated universities and civil service seem unable or unwilling to grasp the implications of gendered patterns – not only as regards combining paid work and family responsibilities, but also insofar as such gendered patterns impact on the strategic planning of the economy. Both of these institutions (and the OECD[52]) have prioritized research into information technology and biotechnology and are investing very substantial amounts of public money in these areas. They have failed to recognize that girls, who have the highest levels of educational participation and success, are not interested in such programmes: the calibre of the (predominantly male) students who are interested in these areas is thus a major long-term but unrecognized constraint.[53] For high-achieving young women, the areas which offer some hope of making sense of their gendered constructions of the self in the occupational area are those areas which involve human well-being, such as medicine, therapies, social sciences. Such choices are subverting this national educational and economic project, and they are not even perceived by the male-dominated power hierarchies of the civil service, the universities and other established and decision-making institutions.

Notes and References

1 Claire Connolly, 'Theorizing Ireland', *Irish Studies Review*, 9:3(2001), 309.
2 Linda Connolly, 'The Limits of "Irish Studies": Historicism, Culturalism, Paternalism', *Irish Studies Review*, 12: 2 (2004), 139–62.
3 R. W. Connell, *Masculinities* (Cambridge: Polity, 1995), p. 82. For evidence as regards the existence of such dividends in Ireland, see Pat O'Connor, 'Ireland: A Man's World?', *The Economic and Social Review*, 31:1 (2000), 81–102; Augusto Lopez-Claros and Saadia Zahidi, *Women's Empowerment: Measuring the Global Gender Gap* (Geneva: World Economic Forum, 2005).
4 R. W. Connell, *Gender and Power: Society, the Person and Sexual Politics* (Oxford: Blackwell, 1987), p. 215.
5 Steven Lukes, *Power: A Radical View* (London: Macmillan, 1974).
6 R. W. Connell, *Masculinities*, p. 82.
7 *UN Human Development Report* (Oxford: Oxford University Press, 1995), p. 75. A similar conclusion was reached by Lopez-Claros and Zahidi, op. cit.

8 Lopez–Claros and Zahidi, op. cit.

9 See Philip O'Connell, 'Sick Man or Tigress? The Labour Market in the Republic of Ireland', in A. Heath, R. Breen and C. T. Whelan (eds), *Ireland North and South: Perspectives from Social Science* (Oxford: Oxford University Press, 1999).

10 See for example Evelyn Mahon, 'Ireland: A Private Patriarchy', *Environment and Planning*, 26 (1994) 1277–96; and Pat O'Connor, *Emerging Voices: Women in Contemporary Irish Society* (Dublin: IPA, 1998).

11 Michael Savage, 'Women's Expertise: Men's Authority', in M. Savage and A. Witz (eds), *Gender and Bureaucracy* (Oxford: Blackwell/*Sociological Review* Monographs, vol. 40, 1992).

12 Alan Finlayson, 'Towards a Radical Empiricism', *Irish Review*, 28:4 (2001), 139.

13 Anne Coughlan, *Women in Management in Business* (Dublin: Irish Business and Employers' Confederation [IBEC], 2002).

14 CSO [Central Statistics Office Ireland], *Women and Men in Ireland* (Dublin: Government Publications, 2004).

15 Clare O. O'Hagan, 'Family or Economy Friendly?', Paper presented at Sociological Association of Ireland Annual Conference, Nenagh, 2005, p. 11.

16 See Philip J. O'Connell and Helen Russell, *Equality at Work?* (Dublin: The Economic and Social Research Institute, 2005); B. Fynes, T. Morrissey, W. K. Roche, B. J. Whelan and J. Williams, *Flexible Working Lives: The Changing Nature of Working Time Arrangements in Ireland* (Cork: Oak Tree, 1996).

17 The marriage bar obliged women to retire on marriage from a variety of jobs, including the Civil Service, second level teaching and other related professions. See Pat O'Connor, *Emerging Voices*.

18 *UN Human Development Report* (Oxford: Oxford University Press, 2003).

19 Anne Coughlan, op. cit.

20 Pierre Bourdieu, *Pascalian Meditations* (Cambridge: Polity, 1999), p. 166.

21 HEA [Higher Education Authority], *'Gender by Level in Ireland'*, *Unpublished data 2003* (Dublin: HEA, 2005); *Women Academics in Ireland: Report of the Committee on the Position of Women in Third Level Education in Ireland* (Dublin: HEA, 1987); Ailbhe Smyth, 'Reviewing Breaking the Circle', in O. Egan (ed.), *Women Staff in Irish Colleges* (Cork: Higher Education Equality Unit, 1996).

22 The overall percentage of women in such academic positions across the EU in 2000 was 31%: 'She Figures', *Women and Science: Statistics and Indicators*, http://www.cordis.lu/improving/women/home.htm (Luxembourg: European Commission, 2003).

23 ETAN [European Technology Assessment Network], http://www.cordis.lu/ Table 2.1 (Luxembourg: European Commission, 2003).

24 Ailbhe Smyth, op. cit., and HEA, *'Gender by Level in Ireland'*.

25 'She Figures', op. cit.

26 Almost three-quarters of eighteen-year-old girls are in full-time education, as compared with just over half of the boys of the same age. Just under three-fifths of the undergraduates and more than half of the postgraduates are women. Such patterns reflect the fact that admission to universities is competitive and girls are out-performing boys in State examinations. This pattern has existed since the 1980s, although it has only recently become part of the public consciousness. See Pat Clancy, *College Entry in Focus: A Fourth National Survey of Access to Higher Education* (Dublin: HEA, 2001).

27 See Pat O'Connor, 'Women in the Academy: A Problematic Issue?', in A. B. Connolly and A. Ryan (eds), *Women and Education* (Maynooth: MACE, 1999), pp. 17–48.

28 R. W. Connell, *Masculinities*, p. 82.

29 Anne Marie McGauran, *Plus Ca Change . . .? Gender Mainstreaming of the Irish National Development Plan* (Dublin: The Policy Institute, Trinity College, 2005), p. 1.

30 See Philip J. O'Connell and Helen Russell, op. cit.; B. Fynes et al., op. cit. For the limitations of such arrangements as an instrument for transforming the work setting, see for example Sue Lewis, 'Family Friendly Employment Policies: A Route to Changing Organisational Culture – or Playing About at the Margins?', *Gender, Work and Organisation*, 4:1 (1997), 13–23.

31 Anne Marie McGauran, op. cit., p. 84.

32 P. Humphreys, E. Drew and C. Murphy, *Gender Equality in the Civil Service* (Dublin: Institute of Public Administration, 1999), pp. 190–1.

33 NWCI [National Women's Council of Ireland], *Irish Politics – Jobs for the Boys? Recommendations on Increasing the Number of Women in Decision Making* (National Women's Council of Ireland, 2002); Anne Coughlan, op. cit.

34 WEU [Women and Equality Unit], *Gender Briefing*, www.womenandequalityunit.gov.uk/publications/ (London: Women and Equality Unit, 2002).

35 See OECD [Organisation for Economic Co-operation and Development], *Review of Higher Education in Ireland: Examiner's Report* (Paris: OECD, 2005); and for a critique see, for example, John Sheehan, 'Review of National Policies for Education: Review of Higher Education in Ireland: Examiner's Report', *Economic and Social Review*, 36:1 (2005), 67–75.

36 Claire Connolly, op. cit., p. 305.

37 See Liam O'Dowd, 'Church, State and Women: The Aftermath of Partition', in Chris Curtin, Pauline Jackson and Barbara O'Connor (eds), *Gender and Society* (Galway: Galway University Press, 1987); Pat O'Connor, *Emerging Voices*.

38 Breda Gray, *Women and the Irish Diaspora* (London and New York: Routledge, 2004), p. 42.

39 Chris Whelan and Tony Fahey, 'Marriage and the Family', in C. Whelan (ed.), *Values and Social Change in Ireland* (Dublin: Gill & Macmillan, 1994), and Tony Fahey, Bernadette C. Hayes and Richard Sinnott, *Conflict and Consensus* (Dublin: IPA, 2005).

40 Chris Whelan and Tony Fahey, op. cit.

41 Pat O'Connor, 'Criacao social de problemas e solucoes', *Sociolologia: Problemas e Practicas*, 27 (1998), 79–96; and Pat O'Connor, Janet Smithson and Maria Das Dores Guerreiro, 'Young People's Awareness of Gendered Realities', in J. Brannen, S. Lewis, A. Nilsen and J. Smithson (eds) *Young Europeans, Work and Family* (London: Routledge, 2002), pp. 89–115.

42 Pat O'Connor et al., 'Young People's Awareness of Gendered Realities', p. 98.

43 In the context of deferring having children it is worth noting that the age at which women give birth to their first child inside marriage has steadily risen in Ireland since 1975 and is now at almost 31 years (Central Statistics Office Ireland, 2004).

44 Pat O'Connor et al., 'Young People's Awareness of Gendered Realities', p. 105.

45 H. Bjerrum Nielsen, 'European Gender Lessons: Girls and Boys at Scout Camps in Denmark, Portugal, Russia and Slovenia', *Childhood: Global Journal of Child Research*, 11:2 (2004), 207–26.

46 Judith Evans, *Feminist Theory Today: An Introduction to Second-Wave Feminism* (London: Sage, 1995).

47 Pat O'Connor, Amanda Haynes and Ciara Cane, 'Relational Discourses: Social Ties with Family and Friends', *Childhood: Global Journal of Child Research*, 11: 3 (2004), 361-82; Pat O'Connor, 'Young People's Constructions of the Self: Late Modern Constructs and Gender Differences', *Sociology*, 40:1 (2006), 107–24.

48 Pat Clancy, *College Entry in Focus.*
49 Pat O'Connor et al., 'Young People's Awareness of Gendered Realities'.
50 Pat O'Connor et al., 'Relational Discourses'.
51 Pat Clancy, *College Entry in Focus.*
52 OECD, *Review of Higher Education in Ireland.*
53 John Sheehan, 'Review of National Policies for Education'.

Sex and the Single Girl in 1920s and 1930s Ireland

MARIA LUDDY

The writing of Irish women's history has made huge strides over the last two decades. A range of subjects, including work, politics, education, emigration, domesticity and the symbolic meanings of the place of women in Irish society, have begun to be explored. Of particular interest to a number of writers has been the ways in which women were treated in the new State, established in 1922. There have been valuable studies of the depiction of women in the Irish press, their campaign to retain the right to sit on juries and their role as mothers.[1] In this article I want to concentrate on another aspect of Irish women's lives in this period – the ways in which the State and the Church shaped the function and place of women in the new State through issues relating to sexuality.

There is ample evidence to show that there was considerable discussion on sexuality in Ireland in the 1920s and '30s. Within the sphere of government the printed but unpublished 'Report of the Interdepartmental Committee of Inquiry Regarding Venereal Disease' (1926) and the 'Report of the Committee on the Criminal Law Amendment Acts (1880–1885) and Juvenile Prostitution (1931)', known as the Carrigan Committee report, offer extensive and complex accounts of perceived sexual activity throughout the country and the fears raised by that activity. Other publications include *The Report of the Committee on Evil Literature* (1927) and the *Report of the Commission on the Relief of the Sick and Destitute Poor* (1927). The work of the Inter-Departmental Ad-Hoc Committee on the Suppression of Prostitution (1947–1948), which was again unpublished, provides much information on the 1920s and 1930s.[2] Through these reports and investigative committees concerns were raised about illegitimacy, unmarried mothers, the apparent spread of venereal diseases, prostitution, levels of sexual crime, deviancy, and the dangers of sociability, particularly reflected in dance halls and the motor car, which appeared to offer possibilities for unrestricted mixing of the sexes. Throughout the period earthy newspaper accounts of sexual crime[3] and the extensive publication of clerical sermons and pamphlets about immorality and the dangers of sex reinforced public concern about sexual morality. Despite the reticence of a number of TDs and Senators, some of these issues even found public expression in the Dáil and Seanad. Both the State and the Church emphatically presented women's place as being in the home and the ideal role of the Irish woman was as mother. The idealization of motherhood was a significant feature of the rhetoric of politicians in the new Irish State; the female body and the maternal body, particularly in its unmarried condition, became a central focus of concern to the State and the Catholic Church.

While the politicization of sexual behaviour had been a feature of Irish nationalism from the late nineteenth century, evident most strongly in the equation of the British garrison as a source of moral and physical contagion for Irish women, problems were to arise when the British garrison was gone but levels of sexual immorality appeared to rise rather than decrease in the new State. Regarding one form of vice, prostitution, Richard S. Devane, S.J., evangelical in his concern with sexual immorality, observed in 1924 that as long as the British garrison was 'in Dublin it was impossible to deal with prostitution effectively. Now a new order has opened up, and things can be done with comparative ease, quite impossible before.'[4] However, what was to emerge from the early 1920s was a belief, strongly evident in the various reports mentioned above and in clerical and public discussion of sexuality, that the real threat to chastity and sexual morality resided in the bodies of women. Thus moral regulation, by Church and State, attempted to impose, particularly on women, standards of idealized conduct that would return the nation to purity.

Sermons – many reprinted in the press – and pamphlets abounded with views on how women should express or repress their sexuality. The Bishop of Limerick, Dr Denis Hallinan, in a 1919 letter to the press, noted that the Pope had recently dwelt on 'one of the great evils of the time – the immodest fashions in women's dress'.[5] A 1926 sermon by the Rev Dr Gilmartin, Archbishop of Tuam, noted that 'there was a time in Ireland when the prevailing type of woman was the sister of Mary Immaculate, but, unfortunately, in recent times there has been a kind of falling off. There was a time in Ireland when the dress was modest. In recent times, however, there is a bordering on the indecent.' He was further to note that the 'future of the country is bound up with the dignity and purity of the women of Ireland'. Gilmartin prayed for the return of 'a holy and Catholic Ireland – an Ireland of brave, manly boys, an Ireland of pure, modest girls – an Ireland of honest toil, an Ireland of happy marriages'.[6] The Jesuit Michael Garahy published as a pamphlet a series of Lenten lectures that he had delivered in the church of St Francis Xavier in Upper Gardiner Street, Dublin, in 1922. The title of his sermons was 'Idols of Modern Society', where he explored the 'menace of materialism', the 'collapse of chastity' and 'godless education', among other issues.[7] Where materialism triumphs, Garahy noted, 'sexual vice, with all the evils that follow in its train, is spreading like a prairie fire . . . in the great centres of progress the streets swarm with harlots'.[8] Expressions of concern about women's place in public life were also evident in this period. Issues relating to women and work, and their role in politics, caused uneasiness in government and Church circles. The *Irish Independent* noted in 1925 that there were 'mothers who preferred the fashionable and crowded thorough-fare to their own quiet home; there were mothers who preferred talking on a platform or in a crowded council chamber to chatting to their children in a nursery'.[9] It was evident that such pursuits were 'unnatural' and unsuited to the role of women as wives and mothers.

While such concerns – particularly over clothing – might appear trivial, what is evident from the early 1920s is a focus on women, their appearance and presence in public life that is deemed to have upset the moral order or has the potential to continue to upset that order. The danger to Irish survival and renewal becomes centred in the form of debased womanhood. Some women are debased through sexual immorality, others through their desire to have public careers. The redemption of chaste reproductive sexuality is prescribed as the antidote to moral bankruptcy: women must return to the home, to the domestic sphere. While England and its culture might be the source of moral corruption, once independence is achieved the focus on women, and their moral regenerative powers, becomes central to the idea of the Irish nation.

Evidence of this concern was particularly clear in one aspect of 'immorality' that caused anxiety in the government and the Catholic Church, the unmarried mother. Both the State and the Church emphatical-ly presented women's place as being in the home and the ideal role of the Irish woman was as mother. Throughout the 1920s, and later, conflicting representations of unmarried mothers abounded. They were seen as inno-cent victims or corrupting agents, they were 'poor girls' or potential blackmailers. They brought 'shame' to the nation and to their families. Uneasiness about the apparent rise in the numbers of unmarried mothers forced the State and the Catholic Church to implement policies to stem illegitimacy and attempt to control behaviour. While the State and the Church chose to care for unmarried mothers and their children, they consistently evoked the obligation of the mother to support her child.

The issue of unmarried mothers came to light primarily through levels of illegitimacy, although official statistics for illegitimate births were low throughout the period of the Irish Free State. In 1922, the birth rate of illegitimate children was officially described as 'less than that recorded for most other countries'[10] and, for 1921–1923, such births amounted to 2.6 per cent of all births in the twenty-six counties.[11] The average illegitimate birth rate per annum between 1920 and 1930 was deemed to be 1,706.[12] Between 1926 and 1929, the numbers of such births had risen from 1,716 to 1,853, revealing a gradual increase in each intervening year. The members of the Committee on the Criminal Law Amendment Act, reflecting the voices of 'concerned citizens' and some members of the government, found this rise worrying and believed that illegitimacy was increasing throughout the country at an 'unprecedented rate'.[13] In 1926 the secretary of the Committee for the Reform of the Laws Relating to the Protection of Women and Young Girls alerted the Minister for Justice to the fact that the rescue societies were almost overwhelmed, 'so much has the number of unmarried mothers increased during the last few years'.[14] What was more worrying to the members of the committee was the fact that illegitimacy levels were rising in social conditions that had stabilized after a period of civil strife. There was also a strong belief that unregistered births of illegitimate children possibly exceeded those registered.

The rise in illegitimacy levels was attributed to a loss of parental control and responsibility during the period of the war of independence and civil war. That parental control, it was argued, had never been restored. Moral laxity was seen to be a result of the prevalence of 'commercialised dance-halls, picture houses . . . and the opportunities afforded by the misuse of motor cars for luring girls'.[15] From the mid-1920s and throughout the early 1930s there were constant references in the newspapers to the problems of dance halls and motor cars. In 1931 Cardinal McRory combined the two and saw a growing evil in 'the parking of cars close to dancehalls in badly lighted village streets or on dark country roads. Cars so placed are used . . . by young people for sitting out in the intervals between dances.'[16] 'Joy-riding' had a very different connotation in that period than it does now. Reporting on a sermon by the Bishop of Galway, the *Irish Independent* noted that 'joy-riding' was conducted by 'Evil men – demons in human form come from outside the parish and outside the city – to indulge in this practice. They lure girls from the town to go for motor drives into the country, and you know what happens . . . it is not for the benefit of the motor drive. It is for something infinitely worse.'[17] The Report of the Committee on the Criminal Law Amendment Acts noted that solicitation was an 'offence very rife in Dublin . . . being practiced by men in motor cars who patrol the streets, stopping here and there to invite young women to whom they are unknown to accompany them for a drive'.[18]

Dance halls were clearly sites of corruption, dancing could be sexually charged, and the presence of alcohol made the possibilities more frightening. In 1925, the Irish hierarchy issued 'a grave and solemn warning to the people with regard to the spiritual dangers associated with dancing'.[19] Dangers lurked in cars, in dance halls, in country lanes, in city streets, even in newspaper reports themselves. Providing the full address of a 'refreshment house' in Dublin where 'women of loose character' were allowed to assemble might very well have been good for the proprietor's business.[20] The legal regulation of recreation and recreational spaces was deemed, together with supervisory vigilance, to be the means by which appropriate behaviour at such venues could be ensured. For the Church, the State and many welfare workers, the way forward was to introduce legislation that would, for instance, raise the age of consent, or introduce harsher punishments for solicitation, or regulate the dance halls in a stricter way. Much of this type of legislation found its way onto the statute books by the mid-1930s.[21]

The State and the Church identified unmarried mothers as a particular danger. Such women belonged to one of the following categories: those who were redeemable and those who were not. Such distinctions refer back to the rescue homes that existed for 'fallen' women in nineteenth-century Ireland, which separated their inmates into the same categories. Attitudes to 'first' offenders were not necessarily harsh. They were depicted as unfortunate rather than immoral. One report noted that

> the problem of unmarried mothers should be dealt with from the standpoint that they are entitled to take their place in ordinary life without any disability attaching to them as a result of their offence: and any child should get every opportunity to understand and appreciate the family life.[22]

One writer, noting the availability of birth control methods or 'scientific vices' suggested that it was only the 'frail, ignorant girl, often mentally deficient, and always weak-willed who finds herself pregnant'. The lack of sexual knowledge revealed by a woman who became pregnant showed that she was 'not bad'. This was someone who needed to be taken in hand immediately to ensure a successful recovery of virtue.[23] Both the State and the Church approved of the 'hopeful cases' being cared for in institutions set aside for that purpose and, ideally, these were to be managed by nuns. For this group treatment was to be

> in the nature of moral upbringing and, while requiring firmness and discipline, must be characterised by and blended with a certain amount of

individual charity and sympathy which can only be given when a true estimate of the character of each girl or young woman has been made by those in charge.[24]

The fear expressed for these 'first' offenders was that they might fall into prostitution. Early intervention was the best way of rescuing them from such a fate.

How were the 'less hopeful cases' to be dealt with? The authorities and experts in the field believed it essential to separate the 'first offenders' from the 'less hopeful cases'. The issue of the 'second' or 'third' fall posed particular difficulties for a sympathetic representation of unmarried motherhood. The Commission on the Relief of the Sick and Destitute Poor provided very clear recommendations about what was to happen to these 'intractable' girls, suggesting that where an unmarried mother applied for relief during or after a first pregnancy it should be possible to detain her for up to one year. If the woman was to be admitted on a second pregnancy, she should be retained for two years; if she was being admitted for a third or subsequent pregnancy, she should be detained until it was considered suitable for her to return to society.[25] This stance, though not intended to be penal, allowed for the development of an attitude that accepted detention as a means of protecting society from these reoffending women. Such 'reoffenders' were also deemed to be 'mentally defective'. The inspector of boarded-out children noted in her annual report of 1932 that many of these reoffenders were

> of weak intellect and completely lacking in moral fibre . . . A grave wrong is done to their children by maintaining them in the county homes, but retention is the only means of securing their mothers from the danger which freedom spells upon them. It is a question of whether a graver social wrong is not committed by allowing these women their freedom, since freedom, to them, will undoubtedly mean the birth of another child whose chances of average health and intelligence are small. I have no solution to offer except one which is repugnant to me, that is, the power of detention in special cases, which would allow boarding out of the children and at the same time keeping their mothers under control and discipline.[26]

The less hopeful cases presented images of contagion. Those unmarried mothers who 'offended' more than once offered tangible evidence of sexual transgression. It seemed imperative to categorize these women according to their level of sexual experience or knowledge, in order to protect more innocent girls from corruption. These were women whose sexuality had to be managed and contained. The Commission on the Relief of the Sick and

Destitute Poor did recommend terms of detention for repeat 'offenders'. The purpose of the recommendation was to 'regulate control according to individual requirements, or in the most degraded cases to segregate those who have become sources of evil, danger, and expense to the community'.[27] What appears to have happened is that some of these 'repeat offenders' found themselves admitted to Magdalen Asylums, which proved difficult to leave.[28] Much more could be said about unmarried motherhood in Ireland. But what we need to note here is that unmarried mothers were stigmatized. Unmarried mothers and illegitimate children were symbols of moral and particularly of sexual failure.

One of the concerns to re-emerge in the 1920s was the incidence of venereal diseases. This had been a significant issue in Ireland during the period of the first world war, especially with the ending of the war in 1918, when there was the prospect of thousands of allegedly syphilitic troops returning to Ireland. Concern with venereal disease became muted after the crisis of 1918 had passed. With the withdrawal of the British garrison, it was believed that the danger to Irish survival, to the future of the race, had passed. However, the subject of venereal disease was to become problematic in the Irish Free State in the early 1920s. Logically the sexual danger evident in the presence of the British soldier in Ireland should have disappeared in 1922. The immorality associated by nationalist propagandists with the British presence could no longer exist. How then was the State to acknowledge the rising rates of illegitimacy, venereal diseases and sexual assault in the first years of independence? If the contaminant had been eliminated, had the new State essentially failed, since sexual immorality seemed to be rife in the country?

The Inter-Departmental Committee of Inquiry regarding Venereal Disease was established in 1924 to 'make inquiries as to the steps necessary, if any, which are desirable to secure that the extent of venereal disease may be diminished'. The report, which was not made public, revealed that 'venereal disease was widespread throughout the country, and that it was disseminated largely by a class of girl who could not be regarded as a prostitute'[29] and suggested that venereal diseases were a serious health problem in Ireland. The soldiers who contracted VD were obliged to identify the place and source of infection and it was suggested that, rather than being confined to urban areas, VD was to be found 'in every parish in Ireland'. It was also noted that prostitutes constituted the source of infection in only 30 per cent of cases. To some extent, it can be argued that the VD inquiry was an evaluation of sexual behaviour and revealed a promiscuous nation. What was now becoming evident was that all women, not only prostitutes, were possible sites of venereal infection. Disease and moral corruption had made their way momentously into the preserves of respectability. Women had the ability to destroy or recreate, to foster sterility or to make fertile, to be the agent of contamination. There was still a way out for those who believed that it was impossible for Irish women to have such varied power and that England was still to blame. Fr Devane suggested to the committee of inquiry that the original source of the disease was the British soldiers stationed in Ireland and, in particular, the Black and Tans, who had travelled around the country. He wrote: 'In the past few years we have had wave after wave of men passing over the country . . . It will be found that, *in many cases*, the girls who acted as camp followers to Black and Tans, etc., were the same who pursued the Free State troops, conveying in not a few cases infection.'[30]

The shadow of the prostitute looms large in discussions of unmarried mothers and venereal disease. The prostitute was seen as 'a force of moral pestilence to the public', and Devane noted that on the route to prostitution the unmarried mother was 'an intermediary place'.[31] Frank Duff, founder of the Legion of Mary, was to note that unmarried mothers formed a major recruiting group for prostitution.[32] For Devane, an unmarried mother left without support could easily fall into prostitution; another recruit to the ranks of the prostitute was the 'semi-imbecile and mentally deficient' woman; a third recruit was the woman over 21 who was 'of normal mentality, who, through some perversity of nature, take[s] up this life by preference'.[33] The worst offender, however, was the 'amateur', identified as a young woman who engaged in sexual activity without looking for monetary gain. The 'amateur' was the figure identified in the Inter-Departmental Committee of Inquiry regarding Venereal Disease as the source of infection. Though named as a prostitute by the inquiry, the 'amateur' was clearly not a prostitute. However, the focus on the 'amateur' allied the sexuality of young women with that of the stigmatized prostitute. 'Amateurs' could and did come from the 'respectable classes'. The context of venereal disease in which the sexual activity of young women was placed saw them as a threat to national health and morals.

Frank Duff, together with Devane, both witnesses to the inquiry, agreed that it was the prostitute who was the primary source of venereal infection. For them, the brothel system which both sustained and was sustained by prostitution was the main site of contamination. Devane noted that Dublin 'seems to me to be the G.H.Q. of venereal disease as it is of the prostitute and the brothel'.[34] Something then needed to be done about the brothel system in that city. Dublin's red light district was the site of both physical and moral contagion. The 'Monto' district, Joyce's 'Nighttown', had long had a reputation. A Fr Creedon, who began to be involved in rescue work in the area from 1922, noted that women who worked as prostitutes were 'not pariahs'. 'They appear', he noted, 'to penetrate freely into the homes of the respectable poor, and are on familiar terms with the growing boys and girls in the neighbourhood'.[35] What was even more significant was that these women appeared to be accepted within the community. Creedon noted that 'half the natural disgust and fear at the idea of a depraved life is gone if those who we know and like are leading it. The boys and young men are not the better enabled to be good by the fact that immorality is locally so easy and attractive, and the effect on the young girls may be as bad'.[36] What was evident in the area was the fact that female sexuality went unregulated, and that this was a dangerous and disruptive force to society at large.

In March 1923, the Legion of Mary began to visit brothels in the Monto district to persuade the women to attend a retreat at the Legion's Sancta Maria hostel. Over the next eighteen months the Legion continued in this work and Duff claimed that so successful was its work that only forty prostitutes were operating in the district by 1925. Then he organized a major assault on the area. The campaign to close the Monto brothels, in which the Legion of Mary, the St Vincent de Paul Society, Jesuit missionaries, including Fr Devane, and the police cooperated, a true alliance of Church and State, began in earnest in February 1925 during a Lenten mission in the Marlborough Street Pro-Cathedral. Initially, representatives of the Legion and the Jesuits approached the brothel owners and pressurized them to close. This did not elicit the desired response, and the campaigners appealed to the police for assistance. A raid was organized on 12 March 1925 and more than one hundred people were arrested. Further raids were led by the police, and the 1926 report of the Inter-Departmental Committee regarding Venereal Disease accepted that, as a result of the 1925 actions, the problem of the 'open brothel' no longer existed in Dublin.[37]

By 1925, Monto had been under assault as an area where prostitution was rife, and also as an area where the forces of disorder – and particularly political disorder – reigned. (It was believed to be the location of many Irregulars.) Why was the assault on Monto apparently successful? There were some practical reasons for this success. Since the withdrawal of British forces, the area had declined in terms of business. Once the women agreed to attend a religious retreat over a number of days, respectable poor families who were living in tenement accommodation were moved into the former brothel premises to ensure that they would not reopen, leaving the women little option but to take shelter in the hostel provided by the Legion of Mary.[38] The assault on the brothels also reshaped the relationships the women had with the brothel keepers. As exploitative as brothel life might be, it had provided these women with a stable environment. Once that relationship had been broken, the Legion of Mary attempted to form new, more appropriate and stable relationships for the women. The reform process in the hostel was intense: 'Every entrant is made the object of a special and individual attention, directed in the first place to the creation of moral fibre.' Many of the women were married off; between 1922 and 1923, sixty-one of the entrants were married.[39] Marrying off the women quickly provided them with another form of stability, replacing the brothel keeper with a more respectable husband. Within the hostel, the women were domesticated, given housework to do and trained in neatness, tidiness and cleanliness. They were being taught the same virtues of domesticity that were advocated for all Irish women at this time. Through routine and the assumption of domesticity, the behaviour of the women was modified. The hostel and retreat work was declared a great success by the Legion. By 1930, fewer than one hundred women were classified as common prostitutes by the police. This does not mean that prostitution declined further or was eliminated by the State – a fact evidenced by yet another inquiry into prostitution in the 1940s.

The Committee of Inquiry regarding Venereal Disease, the Report of the Committee on the Criminal Law Amendment Acts (1880–1885) and Juvenile Prostitution (1931), and the Inter-Departmental Ad-Hoc Committee on the Suppression of Prostitution (1947–1948) provide key information on prostitution and sexual crime in the early decades of the State. None of these reports was published. While the government had considered publishing an edited version of the VD inquiry, Archbishop Byrne, who was shown a copy of the report, suggested it be delayed until it became evident that the incidence of VD had actually declined.[40] The Department of Justice opposed the publication of the Carrigan Committee report, noting that:

> it contains numerous sweeping charges against the State of morality in the Saorstát and even if these statements were true, there would be little point in giving them currency. The obvious conclusion to be drawn is that the ordinary feelings of decency and the influence of religion have failed in this country and that the only remedy is police action. It is clearly undesirable that such a view of conditions in the Saorstát should be given wide circulation.[41]

The gap between ideal and practice was too much for the State to bear. While much more can be said about all of these reports, and the nature of sexuality in the first decades of the Free State, it is enough to note at present that making these reports public would make evident a suggestion that sexual chaos and sexual immorality were rife in the State. It is clear that unmarried mothers, venereal disease and prostitution formed a significant focus of concern in these various enquiries and reports. The need to control venereal disease was used as a rationale for moral regulation. Unmarried mothers and prostitutes were particularly targeted as sites of contagion. Women were central to understanding how both disease and immorality became so evident in society. Much of the moral legislation imposed, such as the Criminal Law Act of 1935, reveals an attempt by the State and Church to curtail sexual autonomy, particularly that of women. Clear also is an attempt to curtail any expression of sexuality and to curb, for instance through censorship, the assault on the Monto district, the regulation of dance halls and the consumption of sexuality. Moral judgement had social power in Ireland, seen particularly in the condemnation of unmarried motherhood. Intervention into the lives of unmarried mothers saw the State and the Church concur in creating a system that kept these women incarcerated, at best, in mother and baby homes and, at worse, in Magdalen Asylums. The policing of sexual activities was to become a feature of Irish life for much of the twentieth century. This, allied with familial and community surveillance, exerted its greatest force on women.

Notes and References

1 For an overview of writings on women in Ireland in the nineteenth century, see Maria Luddy, 'Women's History', in Larry Geary and Margaret Kelleher (eds), *Nineteenth-Century Ireland: A Research Guide* (Dublin: University College Dublin Press, 2005), pp. 43–60. For the contribution of women to Irish society and culture, see Angela Bourke et al. (eds), *The Field Day Anthology: Irish Women's Writings and Traditions* (Cork: Cork University Press, 2002). For histories of women in Ireland in the twentieth century, see Caitriona Clear, *Women of the House: Women's Household Work in Ireland, 1922–1961* (Dublin: Irish Academic Press, 2000); Louise Ryan, *Gender, Identity and the Irish Press, 1922–1937: Embodying the Nation* (Lampeter: Edwin Mellen Press, 2002); Joan Hoff and Moureen Coulter (eds), *Irish Women's Voices: Past and Present* (Bloomington: Indiana University Press, 1995); Myrtle Hill, *Women in Ireland: A Century of Change* (Belfast: Blackstaff, 2003).

2 *The Report of the Committee on Evil Literature* (Dublin: Stationery Office, 1927); *The Report of the Commission on the Relief of the Sick and Destitute Poor, Including the Insane Poor* (Dublin: Stationery Office, 1928). The 'Report of the Committee on the Criminal Law Amendment Acts (1880–1885) and Juvenile Prostitution' (1931) can be found in Department of the Taoiseach File, S 5998, National Archives of Ireland, Dublin [hereafter NAI]; 'Suppression of Prostitution Inquiry' can be found in Department of Justice File DJ 72/94A, NAI; the unpublished Report of the Inter-Departmental Committee of Inquiry Regarding Venereal Disease can be found in the file 'VD in the Irish Free State', Department of the Taoiseach File, S4183, NAI.

3 See, for instance, *Irish Times*, 23 April 1931; *Irish Independent*, 24 March 1931; *Evening Herald*, 3 March 1931.

4 Evidence of R. S. Devane, in 'VD in the Irish Free State', Department of the Taoiseach File, S4183, p. 30.

5 *Irish Catholic Directory and Almanac, 1920* (Dublin: James Duffy & Co., 1920), p. 514.

6 *Irish Independent*, 12 May 1926. See also *Irish Catholic Directory and Almanac, 1927* (Dublin: James Duffy and Son, 1927), p. 569.

7 Rev. M. Garaghy S.J., *Idols of Modern Society* (Dublin: Office of the Irish Messenger, 1922).

8 Ibid., p. 9.

9 *Irish Independent*, 4 September 1925.

10 *Annual Report of the Registrar-General for Saorstát Éireann* (Dublin: Stationery Office, 1924).

11 J. H. Whyte, *Church and State in Modern Ireland* (Dublin: Gill & Macmillan, 1971), p. 31.

12 Memorandum from the Adoption Society of Ireland, 9 February 1950, in Department of the Taoiseach File, S 10815A. Adoption of Children: General File, NAI. For numbers of illegitimate and legitimate births from 1864 to 1945, see appendix 1 in E. W. McCabe, 'The Need for a Law of Adoption', Statistical and Social Inquiry Society of Ireland, p. 11, in the same file.

13 Report of the Committee on the Criminal Law Amendment Acts, p. 8.

14 Mrs J. McKean to An Runaidhe, Roinn Dli agus Cirt, 22 November 1926, in Department of Justice File, H 171/1, NAI.

15 Ibid., pp. 12–14.

16 *Irish Independent*, 7 March 1931.

17 *Irish Independent*, 7 May 1931.

18 Report of the Committee on the Criminal Law Amendment Acts (1880–5) and Juvenile Prostitution (1931), p. 32.

19 *Irish Independent*, 7 October 1925.

20 *Irish Times*, 11 March 1931.

21 The Committee on the Criminal Law Amendment Acts suggested a series of legislation that might be enacted. Similar proposals for legislative action were made by the Committee for the Reform of the Laws Relating to the Protection of Women and Girls, the Dublin Christian Citizenship Council, and other organizations.

22 Typescript report entitled 'Unmarried Mothers', unsigned, undated but circa 1924. Dr Bernard Hackett Papers, Waterford Diocesan Archives, Bishop's House, Waterford.

23 Joseph A. Glynn, 'The Unmarried Mother', *Irish Ecclesiastical Record*, 18 (1921), 463.

24 *Relief of the Sick and Destitute Poor, Including the Insane Poor* (Dublin: Stationery Office, 1927), p. 68.

25 Ibid., p. 69.

26 *Department of Local Government and Public Health, Annual Report* (Dublin: Stationery Office, 1932), p. 29.

27 *Relief of Sick and Destitute Poor*, p. 69.

28 We have no detailed history of the functioning of Magdalen Asylums in twentieth-century Ireland. However, they appear to have retained their inmates for long numbers of years.

29 Report of the Inter-Departmental Committee of Inquiry Regarding Venereal Disease, p. 3. 'VD in the Irish Free State', Department of the Taoiseach File, S 4183. NAI.

30 Ibid., p. 29. Emphasis in the original.

31 Ibid.

32 Ibid., p. 33.

33 R. S. Devane, 'The Unmarried Mother: Some Legal Aspects of the Problem – the Legal Position of the Unmarried Mother in the Irish Free State', *Irish Ecclesiastical Record*, 23 (1924), 180–3.

34 Inter-Departmental Committee of Inquiry Regarding Venereal Disease, 'VD in the Irish Free State', Department of the Taoiseach File, S 4183, p. 30, NAI.

35 'Report on the Rescue Work in Harcourt Street, Dublin, 15 July to 15 October 1922, by Rev. M. Creedon', in Department of Justice, File H266/40, NAI.

36 Ibid.

37 Inter-Departmental Committee of Inquiry Regarding Venereal Disease, pp. 31, 33.

38 Ibid., p. 33.

39 Report on the St Vincent de Paul Society and miscellaneous papers in Byrne Papers, Dublin Diocesan Archives.

40 'Dr McDonnell's Report on His Interview with Archbishop' and a memo, 13 May 1927, in Department of the Taoiseach File, S 4183, NAI.

41 Unsigned memorandum, 27 October 1932, Department of Justice, H247/41C, NAI. See also, Mark Finnane, 'The Carrigan Committee of 1930–31 and the "Moral" Condition of the Saorstát', *Irish Historical Studies*, 32:128 (November 2001), 519–36.

Ireland and Rape Crises

SUSAN McKAY

I

'You were up against a strange hostility that gave you a shock each time you encountered it.' This was Gemma Hussey's recollection of what it was like to raise the subject of rape in Ireland at the end of the 1970s. This was at a time when the first Women's Aid refuge, a rented Dublin house with four bedrooms, was sheltering 117 women and children. 'Rape was just not spoken about.'

A quarter of a century later, there has been outrage, grief, anger and, from the Catholic Church, much hand-wringing since the publication in autumn 2005 of the Ferns Report into clerical abuse in Wexford. Further reports are to follow, including, notably, one for the Dublin diocese, which will undoubtedly also present a litany of outrageous child abuse and equally outrageous cover-ups by the hierarchy.

When these scandals break, those in authority always say: 'We must ensure it never happens again.' However, there is a question which needs to be asked at every level of Irish society: Why do we keep on acting as if we didn't know it was happening?

Child abuse has flourished in Ireland. It has done so in a context of widespread and extreme sexual and physical violence, largely carried out by men, against women. There is growing evidence that much child abuse happens in families in which there is also domestic violence against the children's mother. The Church has colluded with these abusers, too. Patsy McColgan, whose husband Joseph was jailed in 1995 for decades of sexual and physical violence against their children, told me that a priest in whom she had confided that her husband was violent had told her she must stay in her marriage. When I was writing my first book, *Sophia's Story*, Sophia

McColgan was insistent that those reading the book must be made to understand: 'My mother couldn't protect us – she was one of us.'

Those who have tried to speak out against these crimes have been derided, and strenuous efforts have been made to silence them. My book, *Without Fear*, on the history of the Dublin Rape Crisis Centre (DRCC), was published in October 2005. Researching it, I was constantly appalled by the extent and depravity of the violence. There is nowhere in Ireland, it seems, free of rape. A young woman was even raped on the grave of the poet W. B. Yeats. Every imaginable cruelty has been inflicted.

I was also shocked by the way the women running the centre, despite presenting evidence of the need for the services they were offering and the growing demand for them, had to struggle every inch of the way. They had to struggle for recognition and they had to struggle for every penny of the funds they needed. They were accused of propaganda and lying. They were often given too little, too late, while victims of horrific crimes remained on waiting lists for counselling. Several times, the centre came very close to having to shut down.

In 1979, the Pope came to Ireland and the DRCC published its first report. Mná na hÉireann took 'strong exception'. The self-styled champions of traditional Irish Catholic values declared that the reprehensible women of the DRCC had 'implied that the men of this nation, our husbands, our brothers, our sons, are guilty on a national scale of incest and child molestation' and that this was a 'downright lie'. The DRCC provocatively quoted US author Susan Brownmiller: 'All men are potential rapists.'

In the 1980s, the DRCC stated that 'the majority of rapes probably occur in marriage'. Bishop Jeremiah Newman declared that 'extremist feminists' were leading an 'anti-family revolution'. In 1996, the organization Victims of Child Abuse Laws was still denouncing those who ran the 'child sex abuse industry'. In 2007, various organizations are still attempting to deny the extent and ferocity of domestic violence by men, and to claim that women are just as violent. (It is harder for them to claim that women are just as likely to commit rape.) The 'strange hostility' Gemma Hussey described still exists and harsh old attitudes have been slow to change.

However, change has come. In the law, in provision of services and in attitudes. 'We were considered off the wall,' said Anne O'Donnell, the DRCC's first director. 'People say to me now in 2005, "Your views have moderated." But they haven't. What has happened is that society has caught up with us – almost. But back in the dark old days of 1978, Ireland was completely not ready for us.'

II

'The more you learned, the more incensed you got', says writer Evelyn Conlon, recalling the educational process which she and the other women who set up the DRCC had entered into back in the mid- to late-1970s. They found out that women were suffering in silence because they felt shame about what had been done to them and blamed themselves. They found that the view that women were to blame was deeply embedded in Irish cultural values. Rape was shrouded in myths which were still being perpetuated. 'She must have been asking for it' was the most pervasive of these. Women who did report rape were liable not to be believed. Trials were rare and rarely led to rapists being convicted.

In 1969 the legendary Irish agony aunt, Angela MacNamara, had warned in the *Sunday Press* that 'it is in the nature of a man to be the aggressor – the one who initiates' and that if a girl allowed a man to 'fondle and embrace her . . . she cannot blame him if his nature propels him in passion to seek the ultimate closeness of sexual intercourse'. The DRCC challenged the notion that men were subject to uncontrollable sexual urges and that it was a woman's responsibility not to awaken these. Most rape was planned, and anyway, it wasn't about desire: 'Rape is a crime of violence using sex as a weapon.'

The ignorance was shocking. 'The fear of parental rebuke and the fear of pregnancy are the two outstanding reasons why so many willing partners, later on reflection, decide to report their case as one of rape', declared Dr Percy Patton, who in the 1970s and '80s carried out most of the medical examinations of women in Dublin who had gone to the Gardaí alleging rape. Medical textbooks advised student doctors that probably ten out of twelve rape allegations were false, and that the doctor needed to single out 'the chaste from the wanton . . . the shy and bewildered from the brazen and affectedly hurt'.

The DRCC women heard staff from a Dublin hospital tell them that it should not be assumed that incest was entirely bad, because, for some children, it might be their only experience of physical affection. They learned that many social workers and other professionals who came into contact with children who had been subjected to incestuous child abuse believed that incest was just a fact of life in some working-class communities. They learned that women, who had only recently got the right to sit on juries, were routinely objected to because it was considered that they might be biased against defendants. Some women who had gone through the courts told them it had been 'like being raped all over again'.

III

The DRCC opened its phoneline in 1979. 'We were shocked to find that women were contacting us who had been raped maybe 10 or 20 years previously', said Conlon. 'A lot of them would say they had never, ever spoken about it before, to anyone. We were an organization that believed people. We didn't at first really understand how monumental it was that these women had been given this right, by us, to speak. And it was hard, at times, to listen to what you had to listen to.' By the early 1980s, the women working in the centre had understood that child abuse was Ireland's most appalling secret. They were inundated with calls. While the DRCC was arguing that provision must be made to rescue children from abusive families, some health boards continued to make decisions based on the idea that keeping the family together was the most important principle of social work.

'The Rape Crisis Centre has raised a great rumpus about the prevalence of rape', claimed Family Solidarity, and the Catholic pressure group went on to argue that the DRCC 'used public aversion to rape as a lever to serve its own ideologies', which were 'radical feminist and anti-life'. They demanded to know why the DRCC was getting public funds to 'pass out abortifacients'. Rape Crisis counsellors were called abortionists and murderers. In this climate, the centre's decision to oppose the so-called Abortion Referendum was brave. This was designed to outlaw abortion through a constitutional amendment. The campaign was rancorous, divisive and violent. I recall being told while handing out anti-amendment leaflets in Donegal: 'You should all be put up against a wall and screwed and screwed and made to get pregnant.'

The DRCC's policy was to support a woman's right to make her own decisions in the aftermath of rape. Having an abortion might be one of them. Right-wing groups, which had become highly influential because of the cowardly attitude of both Fianna Fáil and Fine Gael over the amendment, made a concerted effort to get the centre's funding stopped. There were just 11 women to 155 men in the Dáil at this time. As Monica Barnes, who supported the DRCC, said: 'It was just wall-to-wall men. Women had no power.'

Despite this, the DRCC, and the other Rape Crisis centres which began to be set up from the 1980s on, continued to struggle, with the ambitious aim of eradicating rape from Irish society. In 1986, the DRCC led a campaign to change the law on rape. This led in 1990 to the criminalization of rape in marriage, heavier penalties for oral and anal rape (though they were not defined in law as rape), and the extension of the law to include the rape of men.

It campaigned for treatment programmes in prisons, arguing that locking men up without challenging their attitudes to women meant that there was every likelihood they would rape again on their release. It campaigned for and got the Sexual Assault and Treatment Unit to be set up in the Rotunda Hospital, and it pressured the government into setting up units in the children's hospitals at Crumlin and Temple Street. It campaigned for sex education in schools and supported the introduction of the Stay Safe programme for national school children. 'Resistance to Stay Safe was concentrated in areas with a very strong Catholic ethos', said psychiatrist Deirdre McIntyre, one of those who designed it. 'It demonstrably worked.' She said the DRCC had played a pivotal role. 'Our awareness about the sexual abuse of children came out of our awareness of the sexual abuse of women and our awareness of that came from the Rape Crisis Centre. They woke the country up.'

Now that the taboo on speaking about sexual violence had been broken, radio and TV programmes were dealing with the subject. The DRCC regularly ran helplines late into the night after such programmes, and the lines were often jammed with callers. After one programme, an eighty-year-old man rang to talk about abuse he had suffered as a ten-year-old boy. He had told no one in the interim.

In 1993, in the aftermath of the rape of Lavinia Kerwick by her boyfriend, the Irish Family League claimed that the 'natural order' had been rejected. In the past, it said, 'boys and girls were warned not to go to lonely places together. If they were foolish enough to do so, they were ashamed to talk about it. This folly has been raised to heroine status by the feminists.' The young man who raped Lavinia was not jailed. But the climate had changed, had been changed – by the Rape Crisis centres and other feminist campaigners.

Lavinia forfeited her anonymity and spoke out on RTÉ about what had happened and how she felt. There had been no opportunity for her to do this in court. There was outrage on her behalf. One journalist wrote that 'the country was dizzy with shock and anger'. The DRCC had made it possible for women and men to protest about rape. The Kerwick case led to a new law in 1993 allowing the DPP to appeal lenient sentences and for victim impact reports to be presented in court. The Department of Justice organized a conference and a newspaper reported that 'the heavyweight women's organizations were powerfully represented'.

By 1994, the DRCC was already dealing with about four calls a month about clerical sex abuse. In the month that the Father Brendan Smyth scandal broke, it took sixty-eight such calls, along with hundreds of others, most of them about child sex abuse. The Catholic bishops asked the DRCC to advise the committee they had set up to look into clerical abuse. The centre agreed, though director Olive Braiden stressed that the centre's first obligation would always be to the victims of such abuse. It would insist that its independence from the bishops be respected. 'We cannot give them answers to their problems.'

<h1 style="text-align:center">IV</h1>

Joanne Hayes was accused of murdering a baby which could not have been hers. An all-male tribunal put it to her that she might have been having sex with more than one man so that she had two babies by different fathers in her womb. 'What sort of ladies are we dealing with here?' asked the judge. Eileen Flynn was sacked for being pregnant by a man she loved but couldn't marry because he had been married before and (pre-1996) there was no divorce. Ann Lovett died, aged fifteen, giving birth in a grotto to the Blessed Virgin. No one admitted to knowing she had been pregnant. Her sister committed suicide soon afterwards. The young woman in the Kilkenny incest case suffered rape and brutality for years from her father and gave birth to his baby, all without anyone rescuing her.

The fourteen-year-old girl in the 'X' case was raped by a neighbour and, when she got pregnant, the State tried to stop her going to England for an abortion. Father Michael Cleary said the case was a fake. The rapist got his sentence reduced, obtained a taxi licence and attacked another girl. The girl in the 'C' case similarly had her private trauma turned into a frenzied national debate about abortion. Sorcha McKenna revealed that her father, who claimed to be a campaigner for human rights, was actually a vicious child abuser. Sophia, Michelle, Keith and Gerry McColgan got their brutal father jailed, then took the State to court for failing to protect them. There had been ample evidence for years that he was a child abuser, but nothing was done.

The DRCC commented on all of these cases, and on others which reached the public eye. It always insisted that Ireland needed to wake up to the fact that the high-profile cases were not isolated ones, that they were representative of many others. It defined sexual harassment as a serious and destructive crime in the workplace. It trained Gardaí, teachers, social workers, counsellors and employers – and it offered to train judges, but they have so far declined. Blasts of Victorian values still emanate from some of them, though some, by now, are more enlightened. The DRCC also carried out training programmes in Bosnia and Kosovo after it emerged that mass rape had been carried out there as an act of war.

In 1998, the DRCC published the results of an ambitious piece of research carried out by Professor Ivana Bacik of Trinity College Law

School and others. This was a comparative study of legal procedures on rape in fifteen European states. It found that Irish rape victims felt that the State Prosecutor had poorly represented them in court. They felt that they were the ones on trial. At present, the rape victim in Ireland is regarded in our adversarial system as merely a witness to the crime. The study made several important recommendations, including a broadening of the definition of rape and a change in the interpretation of consent. The DRCC continues to campaign for legal change, notably for separate legal representation for rape victims. Ireland still has the lowest rate of conviction for rape in the EU.

The Sexual Abuse and Violence in Ireland (SAVI) report of 2002 is a powerful retort to those who deny the prevalence of sexual violence in Irish society. Forty-two per cent of women and 28 per cent of men in this country have experienced some degree of sexual abuse. Ten per cent of women have been raped, as have 3 per cent of men. Six per cent of women were raped as children, as were 3 per cent of boys. Only 12 per cent of victims had told a counsellor and just 10 per cent of women and 6 per cent of men had told the Gardaí. Forty seven per cent of those who had suffered rape or sexual abuse had never told one single other person about it.

The survey was carried out by Professor Hannah McGee of the Royal College of Surgeons at the request of the DRCC. The centre had been raising funds and planning this project for several years. 'We knew we'd be faced with people who were unwilling to believe our findings', said McGee. 'We were extremely careful. The information we got is very explicit.' The survey was conducted anonymously by telephone. Support structures were put in place for those taking part.

'Irish society is not as open and liberal as it likes to think it is', said Olive Braiden in 2000, after announcing her retirement as director of the centre (she had joined it in 1983). 'While it has moved on in leaps and bounds, the narrowness and conservatism is still there. When a woman is raped, people still persist in asking incriminating questions [implying] that the victim was in some way responsible for what happened to them. Attitudinal change doesn't happen quickly. It is the area that disappoints me most. There is a fundamental lack of understanding.' She said fundamental work still remained to be done. Children needed to be educated in how to express anger and frustration in non-violent ways, so that they do not grow up to be abusive or to rape.

There is also an urgent need for those in positions of power to end their denial. After RTÉ's 'States of Fear' programmes at the turn of the twenty-first century, the floodgates were opened and the DRCC and other services were inundated with calls from victims of institutional abuse.

Brave people like Colm O'Gorman have spoken out about their experience of rape at the hands of squalid priests who were entrusted with the moral guidance of society.

In 1979, 79 people sought help from the DRCC. In 2003, nearly 16,000 did. There is now a thriving network of Rape Crisis centres around the country, all of them extremely busy and under-funded still. Women's Aid is likewise starved of funds. There are other counselling services, too, like One in Four, set up by survivors of clerical abuse, and they, too, struggle on inadequate budgets. A plethora of private counselling services is also available for those who can afford to pay.

The DRCC was the catalyst. It has saved lives and helped to make unbearable lives good and fulfilling. It has changed laws and minds. As Mary Robinson states in her preface to *Without Fear*, 'this is a proud history'. It is also a history of defiance – and this is an attitude which is just as necessary today as it was in the 1970s. There are rapists operating with impunity all over Ireland. How dare they say they didn't know it was happening.

From Virgins and Mothers to Popstars and Presidents:

Changing Roles of Women in Ireland

IVANA BACIK

This article seeks to examine how particular stereotypes of Irish woman-hood have changed over time, developed and shaped through history and mythology – by the law, the Catholic Church and the media – to emerge as post-independence 'ideal types' of virgin and mother. It also considers how these stereotypes are now being supplanted by what are apparently more powerful role models for younger women in Ireland.

Women in post-independence Ireland

In the struggle for independence up to 1922, the image of woman as warrior was borrowed from the Celtic mythology of Queen Medhbh and Grainuaile and invoked to describe real-life leaders such as Constance Markiewicz and Maud Gonne. After independence, however, these 'unmanageable revolutionaries' were suppressed by the emergence of conservative nationalism. As Margaret Ward writes, the 1922 legislation giving women over the age of twenty-one the vote was the last progressive law reform for women until a new generation of Irish feminists became politically active fifty years later.[1]

Indeed, over the five decades from 1922 to 1970, women lacked visibility in the public arena. Their tradition of 'external opposition', so vibrant pre-independence, occasionally twitched and revived, as with the Irish Women Workers' Union laundry workers' strike, but generally remained 'buried deeply, though not dead'.[2] Carol Coulter emphasizes that campaigning women's organizations did exist during this time, most notably the Irish Countrywomen's Association and the Irish Housewives' Association. Hilda Tweedy has described, for example, how the IHA actively supported Noel

Browne's Mother and Child Scheme in 1951.[3] However, the members of community-based women's groups of the time were generally organized around their domestic roles as wives and mothers; while the other mass women's movement, the nuns, organized themselves around their role as virgins, symbols of Mary.

The roles of wife/mother or virgin/nun therefore remained the accepted social functions for Irish women for many years, expressed through Church teaching and the law, most notably in certain fundamental rights Articles of the 1937 Constitution, which was strongly influenced by Catholic doctrine. When these provisions were being debated in the Dáil, women's groups protested outside the chamber about their depiction of women's function as located in the home. However, of the 152 TDs taking part in the debate within, only 3 were women, and they have been described as the 'silent sisters', since they made no meaningful comment on the text.[4]

The most objectionable provision from a feminist perspective is Article 41.2 of the Constitution. Article 41 guarantees the rights of the 'family'. Article 41.2 recognizes woman's natural role to be 'her life within the home' and guarantees that mothers should not be obliged to engage in labour 'to the neglect of their duties within the home'. There is no mention of fathers. The image of woman as mother was clearly uppermost in the minds of the draftsmen who formulated these clauses, which remain part of the Constitution to this day, despite numerous calls for their removal.[5]

The organized Church had a large part to play in the construction of the virgin/mother identity for women. Mary Condren[6] writes that patriarchal theology was consolidated in Ireland when the power of the Goddess Brigit, the supreme lawmaker in Brehon law times, gave way to Mary the Virgin Mother with the coming of Christianity. Long after the cult of virginity first took hold within the Catholic Church, idealized images of the virgin persisted in Irish art and literature. Lorna Reynolds provides an apposite description of the 'sentimental, nineteenth-century Irish colleen, with the shawl over her head and the limpid, trusting eyes, a notion perpetuated by the figure on our pound notes'.[7] But the colleen of Irish currency was an artificial creation: the English Lady Lavery in rural fancy dress. The idealized image of woman as virgin may be less powerful in contemporary writing now we are aware of its artifice, but it remains pernicious, with the continued stigmatization of sexually active single women as 'sluts'.

The construction of Irish woman as mother has been even more problematic. First, there is the notion of 'Mother Ireland', symbol of the nation, the figure of Mother Éire so dominant in nationalist iconography. Both the motherland and the stereotypical self-sacrificing 'Irish mother' exercise power over their children, and are ultimately demanding of them. Yet these images of mother are fundamentally disempowering of women. First, the demanding mother has a sinister aspect, that of the 'monstrous maternal', like the figure of the 'monstrous feminine' which has endured, from the Medusa of ancient mythology to the deranged villain of Hollywood films such as *Fatal Attraction*.[8] Similarly, the 'monstrous maternal' means that woman as mother/land is seen paradoxically as both nurturer and destroyer, demanding the ultimate blood sacrifice from her sons.

The concept of the monstrous maternal is present implicitly and often explicitly in contemporary debate about abortion: when anti-choice campaigners claim that women are not to be trusted as mothers; that they are liable to turn on their unborn children. The concept was central to the infamous 1980s Kerry Babies case, where a young woman, Joanne Hayes, was cast by the State in the role of murderous mother.[9] And it remains present in the law, particularly in family and criminal law, where judges tend to penalize women more harshly if they are seen to have transgressed their 'natural' maternal role, for example by abandoning or assaulting their children.

Secondly, the notion of 'motherland' itself is disempowering because it renders women as 'the territory over which power is exercised'.[10] The image of the feminine as a colonized territory may have become somewhat banal, but the construction of the colonized feminine as maternal is particularly striking in an Irish context, where women's maternal role is especially emphasized. If a woman, especially a married woman, does not want a child, then she must be 'unnatural'. This construction is strongly reinforced by the Catholic Church, through its ban on contraception and the excommunication of women who have abortions.

Other powerful forces, such as laws, also reinforce the 'maternalization' of women's bodies. Mary-Joe Frug[11] has described how the law compels women into bearing and caring for children, explicitly in regard to laws dealing with reproductive control and more implicitly through family law. In an Irish context, this description is particularly apt. In 1983, when the lives of women and the unborn were expressly declared constitutionally equal,[12] it appeared that women existed only as a function of their reproductive capacity in the dominant discourses of law and politics. During the 1992 X case,[13] and in the many constitutional referenda about abortion since, the discourse has remained the same.[14] Further, in a legal culture where the (marital) 'Family' is constitutionally revered as the 'natural primary and fundamental unit group of Society',[15] and in which single mothers do not have any rights as part of that constitutional family unit, the law is especially maternalizing of women in a very narrow way, through the creation of a State-sanctioned model of married motherhood, which ignores the fact that one-third of births now take place outside marriage.[16]

The other side of this maternalization is that women who do not conform to the Church/State model of married motherhood are subject to legal and societal sanction. This is demonstrated by revelations about the extent of infanticide in Ireland in the 1940s and 1950s, the routine incarceration of children of unmarried mothers in industrial schools for many decades, and the phenomenon of Magdalen Laundries for 'fallen women'. Some women have paid the ultimate price for their perceived transgression, like Ann Lovett, aged fifteen, who concealed her pregnancy from her peers and died alongside her stillborn baby in a field in front of a shrine to the Virgin Mother in Granard, Co. Longford, in 1984. What a tragic irony in that most poignant image.

This maternalization of women continued into the 1980s and the 1990s, in the way in which the laws and ethics of our State have imposed motherhood upon women in the most brutal way. In 1983, Sheila Hodgers, a pregnant woman with cancer who was denied medical treatment because she was pregnant, died in hospital along with her prematurely born baby. In 1992, a fourteen-year-old suicidal pregnant rape victim was initially denied the right to travel to England to terminate her pregnancy; and three years later a thirteen-year-old girl in similar circumstances had to go to court in order to vindicate her right to travel abroad for an abortion.[17] The virgin/mother stereotypes so embedded in Irish law and culture portray women as de-sexualized, monstrous, colonized and maternalized, yet they represented the visible identity of Irish women for most of the twentieth century. How then have things changed more recently, and what are the roles to which a younger generation of women aspire?

Recent Changes in Women's Roles

In the last two decades, women's voices have at last become audible in the public arena, as women have moved in from the margins, no longer content to organize only at community level as housewives or countrywomen nor to retire from fulfilling jobs upon marriage. Ailbhe Smyth has documented the different phases of the Women's Movement in Ireland after 1970, from growing politicization in the 1970s, to the years between 1983 and 1990, where feminist activism was repressed through a succession of political and legal defeats.[18] During what Nell McCafferty has called the 'amendment years',[19] the Eighth Amendment was passed, giving the foetus the right to life in 1983; the divorce referendum was defeated in 1986; a series of cases against women's centres and students' unions prohibited the provision of information on abortion; and a series of personal tragedies occurred, involving individual women and girls like Ann Lovett.

Yet, during this time, new and exciting developments were taking place internationally, with the deconstruction of the very idea of 'woman' as a single entity. Issues of class, race and sexuality began to be addressed within feminism. Slowly, lesbianism came out of the closet and the accepted notion of 'fixed' sexual identity was challenged publicly. Popstars such as Morrissey and Madonna gave cultural expression to this idea of sexual ambiguity and had an immense influence on an emerging generation of young Irish women and men.

The 1980s can be seen therefore as a decade of contradictions in Ireland, politically repressive and economically stagnant, but culturally exciting with signs of change to come. Although thousands of young women and men continued to emigrate to find work, things began to change in the early 1990s. A critical turning-point occurred with the election of feminist lawyer Mary Robinson as President in 1990. Another such point occurred in November 1992, when the people voted in a referendum to give women the right to travel to access abortions abroad. Yet another occurred in 1995, with the introduction of divorce. In 1998, comprehensive workplace equality legislation was passed.[20] In 2000 came the Equal Status Act, prohibiting discrimination in the provision of goods and services on a range of grounds, including gender. Perhaps most importantly, with increased economic prosperity from the early 1990s onwards, greater numbers of women have now entered the paid labour force to take on new roles very different to those of wife or mother.

Undoubtedly, women have made many advances in a very short time. Just over thirty years ago, women still had to retire from the civil service upon marriage; twenty years ago, it would have been unthinkable to have one Irish woman President, let alone two. The years since 1990 may thus be seen as having marked a further stage in the development of feminism in Ireland; a time of legal gain, and immense economic and social progress.

Despite this undoubted progress, the majority of women in Ireland remain unequal economically and socially. Some may now have achieved positions of power, but the substantive gender inequalities remain. After over thirty years of equal pay legislation, we still have a significant pay differential between men and women[21] – the majority of low-paid workers are women – and the Republic of Ireland has a rate of women in its national parliament that, at just 13 per cent, is among the lowest in Europe.[22] The victims of rape and domestic violence are overwhelmingly female; contraception remains inaccessible for many women and abortion unavailable. Ireland remains the only EU country in which the 'life' of the foetus is given equal constitutional protection to the life of the pregnant woman. Women continue to have to travel to England in their thousands every year to obtain abortions there. Yet a State that appears to value the foetus so highly places no value on the work of those who care for children. Parental leave remains unpaid; fathers have no entitlement to paid paternity leave. The lack of State provision of childcare services and the lack of tax relief for childcare payments mean that many mothers are forced out of the workplace and back into the home.

Although evidence of continued gender inequality abounds, it is surprising that no identifiable 'women's movement' exists in Ireland. This absence is often attributed to the failure of younger women to identify themselves as feminist, and to their tendency to view feminist ideology as a relic of the past, outdated and irrelevant. This view has been fostered to a great extent by a media-generated 'backlash', which has created the impression that women have now gained not only equality but dominance; that downtrodden men must fight back against aggressive hordes of 'feminazis'.[23] The media technique of 'recuperation' has co-opted the subversive discourse of feminism and hijacked its terminology, but not its ideology, in a manner designed to mislead: 'Not only do the oppositional ideas and practices lose their bite, but they can function to make it appear as if change has been effected.'[24] The effect of this co-option of language is, as Myra Macdonald believes, that 'for many women, feminism is now thought of as a historical rather than a current ideology; their primary contact with its objectives may often be through the discourses of consumerism'.[25]

This may explain why, for many younger women, feminism is seen as irrelevant and outdated. Yet powerful female singers dominate pop culture as never before (in Ireland, women such as Sinéad O'Connor, Dolores O'Riordan or Samantha Mumba). They represent successful cultural and commercial role models for young women, just as two successive women Presidents, Mary Robinson and Mary McAleese, represent powerful political role models. However, in the Irish political system a president represents power that is more symbolic than substantive, like the power of a popstar; not reflective of a substantive empowerment developed through an independent feminist discourse. Young women and girls may now aspire to becoming popstars or presidents, and that heightened aspiration is itself a sign of great progress, but change for the majority of women cannot be achieved no matter how many women take on those roles alone.

The truth is that, despite the emergence of powerful individual role models for young women, the campaign for women's rights is far from over. Real gender equality remains only an aspiration, like the Celtic Tiger itself, that myth of universal national wealth exposed by UN reports (that Ireland has the highest levels of poverty and economic inequality in any OECD country except the US).[26] A reinvigorated feminist campaign, aimed at achieving substantive change for women, is necessary in order to ensure that the roles aspired to by younger women today do not become 'Celtic Tigers' tomorrow: empty symbols of power and success that hide deep-rooted economic and social gender inequalities in society.

Notes and References

1 Margaret Ward, *In Their Own Voice: Women and Irish Nationalism* (Dublin: Attic, 1995) and *Unmanageable Revolutionaries: Women and Irish Nationalism* (London: Pluto, 1995).

2 Carol Coulter, *The Hidden Tradition: Feminism, Women and Nationalism in Ireland* (Cork: Cork University Press, 1993), p. 59.

3 Hilda Tweedy, *A Link in the Chain: The Story of the Irish Housewives Association, 1942–1992* (Dublin: Attic, 1992), p. 73.

4 Yvonne Scannell, 'The Constitution and the Role of Women', in Brian Farrell (ed.), *De Valera's Constitution and Ours* (Dublin: Gill & Macmillan, 1988), p. 123.

5 Most recently, the Constitution Review Group recommended its replacement with a revised gender-neutral provision recognizing the importance of persons who perform a caring function within the home: *Report of the Constitution Review Group* (Dublin: Government Publications, 1996), p. 333.

6 Mary Condren, *The Serpent and the Goddess: Women, Religion and Power in Celtic Ireland* (Dublin: New Island, 2002).

7 Lorna Reynolds, 'Irish Women in Legend, Literature and Life', in Sean Gallagher (ed.), *Woman in Irish Legend, Life and Literature* (Gerrard's Cross: Colin Smythe, 1983).

8 Barbara Creed, *The Monstrous-Feminine: Film, Feminism, Psychoanalysis* (London: Routledge, 1993).

9 See Nell McCafferty, *A Woman to Blame: The Kerry Babies Case* (Dublin: Attic, 1985).

10 Gerardine Meaney, 'Sex and Nation: Women in Irish Culture and Politics', in Ailbhe Smyth (ed.), *Irish Women's Studies Reader* (Dublin: Attic, 1993).

11 Mary Joe Frug, *Postmodern Legal Feminism* (London: Routledge, 1992).

12 This was effected by the Eighth Amendment to the Constitution, which inserted a new Article 40.3.3 into the text, reading: 'The State acknowledges the right to life of the unborn and, with due regard to the equal right to life of the mother, guarantees in its laws to respect, and, as far as practicable, by its laws to defend and vindicate that right.'

13 *Attorney General v. X* [1992] 1 IR 1. In February 1992, the High Court granted a court order preventing X, a pregnant fourteen-year-old rape victim, from leaving Ireland to have an abortion in England. Amid public outcry, the Supreme Court overturned this decision two weeks later to allow her to travel, because there was a 'real and substantial risk' that she would commit suicide if the pregnancy continued. This case established that, where the rights to life of the pregnant woman and the foetus are in conflict, the right to life of the pregnant woman prevails, with the result that abortion is legal in Ireland where necessary to save a woman's life, but for no other reason.

14 Three referenda concerning abortion were put to the Irish people in November 1992. Two were passed and these amended Article 40.3.3 to safeguard the rights of pregnant women to travel and the right to information about abortion. A third was defeated. If passed, it would have limited the effect of the X case, by restricting its effect to cases

where the risk to the pregnant woman's life was a risk other than suicide. In March 2002, a further referendum, also aimed at removing suicide risk as a ground for legal abortion, was again defeated – a victory for the pro-choice campaign.

15 Article 41.1.1 of the Constitution provides that: 'The State recognises the Family as the natural primary and fundamental unit group of Society, and as a moral institution possessing inalienable and imprescriptible rights, antecedent and superior to all positive law.' The word 'Family' has been interpreted by the courts as being limited to the family based upon marriage.

16 CSO figures, 2002.

17 *A and B v. Eastern Health Board* [1998] 1 IR 464, otherwise known as the 'C' case. C was a young girl in the care of her local health board, which sought permission from the court to take her to England for an abortion. Permission was granted on the basis of medical evidence showing that she was suicidal and that the continuation of her pregnancy would pose a 'real and substantial risk' to her life.

18 See *Irish Women's Studies Reader* (Dublin: Attic, 1993).

19 Nell McCafferty, *Nell* (Dublin: Penguin Ireland, 2004).

20 The Employment Equality Act, 1998.

21 *Gender and Pay* (Dublin: Irish Council of Trade Unions, 2004). This report found that a gender pay gap of 15 per cent existed.

22 *Women's Manifesto* (Dublin: National Women's Council of Ireland, 2004).

23 See Susan Faludi, *Backlash: The Undeclared War Against Women* (London: Chatto & Windus, 1992).

24 Charlotte Brunsdon (ed.), *Films for Women* (London: British Film Institute, 1986), quoted in Myra Macdonald, *Representing Women: Myths of Femininity in the Popular Media* (London: Arnold, 1995), p. 92.

25 Ibid., p. 92.

26 *UN Human Development Report*, 2003.

Men in No-Man's Land:

Performing Urban Liminal Spaces
in Two Plays by Mark O'Rowe

CATHY LEENEY

'Adventures happen to those who know how to tell them.' (Henry James)

I

Despite the economic success of the 'Celtic Tiger' economy of Ireland over the past ten years, the country is deeply riven by poverty and inequality. As Fintan O'Toole has observed, Irish governmental policy systematically discriminates against the poor.[1] The OECD places Ireland sixteenth in its Human Development Index (just ahead of the United States), which ranks countries according to a combination of poverty and inequality, showing how Ireland's socially unjust society is 'sustained quite deliberately by a political policy of keeping both taxes and social spending low'.[2]

What is at issue here is equal access to education, healthcare and participation in society's structures and functions, not to mention participation in recent prosperity. Inequality of access and opportunity, over generations, creates social groupings which have no stake in governmental decision-making at either national or European levels, or in civic or social futures. Ghettos develop around cities and towns, where the rule of law is replaced by male gang control. While many Irish people never had it so good, others are alienated, displaced and disempowered. Theatre has a number of potential roles in this context. It may work to naturalize social divisions, reflecting hierarchies outside the performance in such a way as to represent them as fated, beyond the power of change. It can also work to represent these hierarchies and contests for social power as historical and mutable. Theatre has the potential to explore the unstable relationship between the story of Ireland now and how ways of telling that story will open or close possibilities in our imagined future.

As Ireland becomes more and more materialistic, identity revolves increasingly around wealth, possessions and consumer power. Narratives of self are dominated by images of consumption and ownership: lifestyle choices, financial futures, branding, body choices, image and, overarching all of these, shopping. Ways in which geography (city, town, village, townland, parish, locale) defines the self, and is defined by those who inhabit it, are threatened by the demands of distant, globalized, industrial, commercial and infrastructural interests. Carparks, shopping centres, warehouses and motorways cut across the locales of people's lives. The flow of information and persons through these spaces works to destabilize them as places. Mark O'Rowe has written several plays which expose such locales and attempt to dramatize the imagined lives of some of their inhabitants. This is the context for an examination of productions of two plays by Mark O'Rowe, *Howie the Rookie* (1999) and *Crestfall* (2003).

In its relatively new prosperity, Ireland illustrates a widening gap between class divisions in material terms. Consumer power becomes synonymous with social power, and wealth and possessions define identity while place and values are destabilized. Both of O'Rowe's plays are about people on the margins of the recent bonanza. Both plays work through serial monologues, and both rely on narrative and linguistic fireworks rather than action. Lives are described, performed through language, but no action is dramatized. Both plays work to create an imagined landscape, the no-man's-land at the edges of cities or large towns, 'new places' created by urban expansion, amidst shopping centres, motorways, industrial estates, warehouses. Since the audience come to know the geography of the narration as described by the performers, both plays inherently explore the relationship between the identity of the person, their sense of themselves and their community, and the locale they inhabit. Finally, both plays exploit the paradoxical attraction of the local, even when it is embedded in a dramatic form that fails to represent identity in agency.

On stage, in performance, the notion of 'locale' is binary. It is created, on the one hand, by the narratives spoken. On the other hand, the scenographer has created a stage locale, which frames the geographies and identities being performed. O'Rowe's stage language was not performed, in these productions, in a metatheatrical, fluid stage space (in the way that Shakespeare's words may be imagined to have come from the stage of the Globe Theatre). In the cases of both *Howie the Rookie* and *Crestfall* the stage space was expressive. It therefore impacted powerfully on the audience's reception of O'Rowe's language, the persons speaking it, and the world they together create for an audience.

II

My argument is that *Howie the Rookie*, although linguistically exciting and rich, is, theatrically, deeply conservative in its form and dramaturgy. It represents an aspect of life in the Irish underclass in such a way as to close off a dynamic which might acknowledge the possibility of, indeed the necessity for, change. While it appears to refer to a social, liminal reality rarely represented in contemporary Irish theatre, the play mythologizes violence and sacrifice, which it contains within a closed dramatic structure. Although this approach has many points of contact with Eamonn Jordan's analysis of the play (also in this issue of *The Irish Review*), one point of contrast is that, where Jordan reads doubleness, I read a gradual development from doubleness towards the sealed triangulation of need and desire, as identified by René Girard.[3]

In relation to both *Howie the Rookie* and *Crestfall*, the scenography of their respective productions plays a central part in the process of mythologizing the situations of the speakers, and this is carried to a greater extreme in the 2003 Gate Theatre production of *Crestfall*. In this production, three women's monologues describe a nightmare which they narrate to the audience from a symbolic, imaginary location; a nightmare in which they are, like the audience, passive voyeurs.

Howie the Rookie and *Crestfall* conjure life at the edge of Irish cities – landscapes which contrast with tourist images of Ireland; landscapes which might be found on the edge of any city anywhere in the world. Jordan makes both links and contrasts between O'Rowe's dramatization of violence and masculinity in *From Both Hips* and *Made in China*, and his work in *Howie the Rookie* and *Crestfall*; this analysis is focused on the latter two plays in performance, and their reception, from the space of performance as designed by the scenographer, by the audience.

Howie the Rookie was first produced by the Bush Theatre in London in 1999, designed by Es Devlin and directed by Mike Bradwell. It is a play in two halves. First we meet The Howie Lee, a young man living with his parents in an outer suburb of Dublin. He is unemployed and spends his time hanging out with his friends and drinking. Through his irresponsibility, he contributes to the death of his infant brother Mousie. Howie's parents blame him. Howie blames himself. In part two we meet The Rookie Lee, a womanizer who owes money to a dangerous criminal. In a desperate attempt to regain his honour, Howie sacrifices himself to save Rookie. He represents an absurd Christ figure at the end of the play, crucified on railings, the victim of the fates which have shadowed him and Rookie from the start. Rookie finds himself returning to Howie's house to tell Howie's parents that their second son is now dead too.

The title of the play is significant, as it points to the overlapping identities of Howie and Rookie: both persons share only one definite article. Both characters are versions of the type character in Roman comedy, the *miles gloriosus*, or braggart soldier.[4] The play's subtext concerns the possibility of brotherhood. It places women as aliens, as 'use value'; their presence is mediated through the misogynist descriptions of Howie and Rookie. The social value system represented works on patriarchal tribal principles of kinship, revenge, scapegoating and the intervention of the fates. Howie is as doomed as Oedipus, pursued by vengeful gods, not in a chariot, but in a Hiace van. Beneath the images of doubleness between Howie and Rookie, there is another, shadowy presence – The Mouse, the sacrificial victim. The narrative tension of the play, however, is sustained after The Mouse's death by the possibility of further victims. In Girard's terms, this proliferation of victims signals violence run riot. The play is about the possibility of brotherhood. Howie, Rookie and The Mouse are all Lees. They are all brothers in the sense that Howie's and Rookie's identities overlap, and in the sense that Howie atones for his responsibility for Mousie's death by saving Rookie. In performance, we see, through a lens that is powerfully ironic, Howie's vision of Rookie as a replacement for his lost infant brother. Unlike the audience, Rookie is unaware of the meaning of Howie's gesture:

> ROOKIE: Then he reaches out an' touches me bruised eye. Gently. Gently. Not gay, like, just . . . And then he puts his hand once through me hair, like that, starin' at me like he's thinkin' 'bout somethin' else.[5]

In the Bush Theatre production Es Devlin chose to create three planes, representing dark-grey shiny, graffitied surfaces, floor, back wall and side wall, pierced by barbed wire, and ripped through the centre by a luminous stripe representing the centre marking of a roadway.[6] Each plane was edged with green, as Devlin describes it, 'the immodest green grass of Tallaght, an estate in concrete outside Dublin'. The visual image reinforced images in the narratives of Howie and Rookie of urban wastelands, dreary housing estates and sinister derelict sites.

> HOWIE: Smoke. Black smoke ahead there, north end of the field. Thick billowin', curlin' up. Something burnin'. Me, the Howie, south end, amblin'. Approachin'. A figure. A man ahead, some fuck standin' there, stick in his hand, proddin' whatever's burnin'. Makin' sure it all goes up.'[7]

Es Devlin's image of the roadway works to identify the world created through narrative, without commenting on it. It is sufficiently cold, unspecific and spatially open to communicate a sense of placelessness, of *anomie*.

III

Crestfall was premièred at the Gate Theatre, Dublin, in May 2003, designed by Francis O'Connor and directed by Garry Hynes. It consists of three monologues by three women. Crestfall is the town they live in. It could be anywhere. It is Ireland now. The women use terms which remind the audience of our voyeuristic relationship with them and with the experiences they relate to us: 'Stop. Scope. Behold. Describe.'[8] Jordan identifies O'Rowe's awareness of the relationship of complicity between audience and action, but this sensitivity on the playwright's part does not exonerate him from responsibility for the coerciveness of his dramaturgy, which excludes anything but passive reception of a nightmarish illusion.

As the three women, Olive, Alison and Tilly, plot the locale of their lives, they reveal the brutal individuality, violence and misogyny endemic around them.[9] In turn, they describe the same night from three different points of view. They are all abused and at the mercy of violent men. They tell varying versions of a savage taking of revenge through the torture and death of a horse.

There is little division between public and private in the world of *Crestfall*. The familial sphere, usually dominated by female values of connection and nurture, is narrated as intruded upon and shattered. As in *Howie the Rookie*, familial bonds are meaningless. Children are not safe in this world. The public sphere is dominated by tribal struggles for glory and honour, and by savage assaults on images of the feminine or the natural. Destructiveness is turned inward, against the community itself. There is a deep sense of self-victimization, and of violence run riot, breaking the bounds of kinship rivalries.

Francis O'Connor's design created a cavernous obsessive space, like a deep cave, constructed in dark but reflective material. The floor was also a shadowy distorting mirror. Each performer wore black. The only object representing 'real life' was a tiny child's toy, which, at a crucial point, is fished out of a small pool of water in the floor of the set. This image of underworld was accompanied by a soundscape by Paul Arditti which created an atmosphere of tense anxiety in the audience. The stage image framed the narratives of the three women as coming from hell. The women occupy the space magically – they enter and exit in blackout. The dark mirrors all around them twist and distort their shapes. They are suspended in an unreachable space, beyond history, beyond change.

The soundscape tells us at once that we are in for a deeply serious and upsetting experience, that we will be confronted with obscenity and outrage. The scene frames the play with a moral interpretation. With the exception of the toy, no representation of the world described appears on stage. The women themselves become icons of the savagery they describe, and icons of their defeat by that savagery. O'Rowe attempts an image of redemption at the end of the play, but it comes so late, and is so pat, that it is prey to sentimentality.

In these two plays, O'Rowe creates a landscape made up of dramatic language. This language asserts a geography in the imagination of the audience. It is an act of dark creation rooted in the extremities of urban existence on the social periphery. O'Rowe's work expresses a crisis in location, a crisis in the sense of place, of being in place. *Crestfall*, like *Howie the Rookie*, occupies an uneasy territory between social realism and mythic representation.[10] This crisis connects with crises of identity and control. In cultural psychology, place is seen to play a central part in the construction of human identity, followed closely by language. This issue of the link between place, narrative and self informs Ciaran Benson's analysis in his book *The Cultural Psychology of Self*, where he describes self as a locative system.[11] He quotes E. S. Casey, who asserts that '[w]here we are – the place we occupy, however briefly – has everything to do with what and who we are (and finally, that we are)'.[12] Persons transform spaces into places through the meshing of their experience of location as community, and identity becomes wrapped and interleaved with geography, with locale and with the language used to describe and define identity and community. Here Benson refers to the ideas of Jerome Bruner on how lives are constructed by texts, at least as much as texts are constructed by lives.[13] Bruner talks about self as narrative. 'This notion of identity as a woven narrative has focused attention on the nature and processes of autobiography and on the ways in which the shape of a life is made and remade by the stories a person tells of herself or himself.'[14]

IV

In plays where dialogue is replaced by monologue, as in *Howie the Rookie* and *Crestfall*, the relationship between staged identity and narrative is crucial. But the playwright is powerfully present in this relationship, since the audience have access only to the narrative as defined by the writer; they have no opportunity to see identity defined by action, in relationship with others on stage. In a monologic play, identity is defined by language – the language of narrated action – and by scenography. The scenographer has the opportunity to comment on the narrative of the speaker, to frame the identity of the speaker as received by the audience. To return to cultural psychology for a moment, Benson conceives of the idea of 'reticences'; that is, the defences employed by the unconscious to protect the individual from overstepping what is sayable in particular cultural contexts. The person checks their expression 'as a way of negotiating meaning with a specific social context'.[15] I want to apply this idea to theatre, and to suggest that scenography can function as a system of 'reticences'; that scenography may work to frame an intense and shocking stage narrative, so that it is received by the audience as part of the conversation that defines society and our places in it; that scenography is part of how we speak to ourselves about ourselves through theatrical performance.

My argument is that the designs for O'Rowe's two plays work very differently from each other. In the case of *Howie the Rookie*, the design by Es Devlin reflects the world of the play, but, as it were, without judgement. The semiotics of transitoriness, of open spaces and roadways, is held in balance with a representation of the tentative marking of public spaces by graffiti. Francis O'Connor's design for *Crestfall*, in contrast, assigns a singular meaning to the narratives of the three women – they come out of the mouth of hell. There is a central gender aspect to this crisis of identity and hence of responsibility in *Crestfall*, signalled by violence and rituals of male kinship, and the placing of women as powerless voyeurs. In *Crestfall*, the town, the women can only suffer, watch and wait.

I hope that, through this brief examination of two productions of two plays, two broader questions might be explored. Firstly, how do design decisions impact on our perceptions of theatrical representations of urban *anomie*, and the normalization of class and gender division in a highly materialistic and globalized world? Secondly, what does a playwright's choice of monologue tell the audience about crises in social formations and in individual identities, and how do the scenographer's design choices relate to this crisis in representation of what used to be called character? In other words, how may scenography in theatre relate to, define, or inhibit representations of agency and change in social and cultural formations?

V

In *Howie the Rookie*, and in *Crestfall*, 'place' works in a complex way. The personae in each play occupy a narrated space, created by their speech, their stories. They also occupy a conceptual space, which, in these two cases, works to dislocate, to assert placelessness, and to interrogate ideas of environment and locale. In this sense, place betrays the personae of O'Rowe's plays; it challenges them rather than helps them to be social subjects. The characters cannot control the physical spaces they live in. They turn to language to root their existence, to assert their presence and their identity and values. They speak in monologue so as to be sole creators of their own histories, so as to *have* histories. They work to remake place through language.

But in *Howie the Rookie*, the fates overtake this linguistic enterprise and The Rookie Lee is finally confronted by a flickering video image, an unreliable simulacrum. In *Crestfall*, the three women are trapped in a geography of patriarchal destructiveness, tribal ritual and misogyny. Their role as voyeurs makes them complicit with the terrible events they describe. The setting they speak from asserts their entrappedness and mythologizes their suffering and tragedy.

Agency and subjectivity are radically corrupted in this representation. Power is defined as violence and language is the only field available for resistance or denial, the only field in which a person might, tenuously, try to think otherwise. Only Alison, in *Crestfall*, succeeds in creating an image of being otherwise, an image of connection and love.

Both plays are saturated by notions of geography. The minutiae of dreary despoiled urban environments is created through language. Both plays dramatize the crisis in identity arising from placelessness. Both plays naturalize violence as part of patriarchal social formations. *Crestfall* places women as helpless accomplices in a hellish social reality, yet also as moral measures of the corruption of spirit, of family, of nurture. 'Reticences' (as Benson has defined them) that surround the relationship between women and representations of violence were visible in Francis O'Connor's setting for *Crestfall* and signal anxieties in our culture about the stories women may have to tell, and how they reflect male realities and everybody's nightmares.

Jerome Bruner reflects on how the narrative of autobiography is a two-way affair, 'just as art imitates life in Aristotle's sense, so, in Oscar Wilde's, life imitates art'.[16] In these two plays by Mark O'Rowe, the 'reflexivity of self-narrative',[17] identified by Bruner as posing problems of verification and profound instability, is disguised in performance, where each monologuist controls the experience of the audience and their participation in making meaning in the theatre. The narratives of Howie and Rookie are those of agent protagonists who are, nevertheless, subject to theatrical models of fateful tragedy and sacrifice through scapegoating. In *Crestfall*, Olive, Alison and Tilly report their own victimization, their 'perpetual crestfall'.[18] Where the only possible agency is participation in savage, meaningless brutality, passivity is the only expression of resistance. If life imitates art, these plays signal a crisis in the articulation of resistance to normalized violence, and the patriarchal structures that support it, where conservative theatrical forms such as monologic narrative and illusionist scenography frame that violence as inevitable, fateful and immutable. As

Bruner remarks, '[w]ays of telling and the ways of conceptualising that go with them . . . become recipes for structuring experience itself'.[19]

Notes and References

1 Fintan O'Toole, *After the Ball* (Dublin: New Island, 2003), pp. 60-81.
2 O'Toole, p. 61.
3 René Girard, *Violence and the Sacred* (Baltimore: Johns Hopkins University Press, 1983).
4 Mic Moroney, 'The Twisted Mirror: Landscapes, Mindscapes, Politics and Language on the Irish Stage' in Dermot Bolger (ed.), *Druids, Dudes and Beauty Queens: The Changing Face of Irish Theatre* (Dublin: New Island, 2001), p. 257.
5 Mark O'Rowe, *Howie the Rookie* (London: Nick Hern, 1999), p. 41.
6 See images of Devlin's design for the Bush Theatre production at www.esdevlin.com.
7 O'Rowe, *Howie the Rookie*, p. 7.
8 Mark O'Rowe, *Crestfall* (unpublished manuscript).
9 In the programme for the Gate Theatre production a map of the locale of the play, as drawn by the actor Aisling O'Sullivan, was reproduced, in addition to drawings illustrating impressionistic portraits of characters, and of moments in the narrative by artist Joanna Hayden. See Programme for Crestfall at the Gate Theatre, Dublin, premiered 20 May 2003.
10 Spokespersons for the British organisation Mothers Against Violence articulate the pain and loss of situations parallel with those narrated in *Crestfall*. Those women are not disempowered by their catastrophic loss, but are active agents in resisting the macho posturing that destroys their locales. The aims of Mothers Against Violence were represented by a photographic exhibition of work by Paula Keenen at the Imperial War Museum of the North in December 2004.
11 Ciaran Benson, *The Cultural Psychology of Self: Place, Morality, and Art in Human Worlds* (London: Routledge, 2001), p. 3.
12 E.S. Casey, *Getting Back Into Place: Toward a Renewed Understanding of the Place-World* (Bloomington: Indiana University Press, 1993), p. xiii.
13 See Jerome Bruner, 'The Autobiographical Process', in *Current Sociology*, 43: 2/3 (Autumn 1995), quoted in Benson, 'Life as Narrative', *Social Research*, 54: 1 (Spring 1987), p. 1.
14 Benson, *The Cultural Psychology of Self*, p. 46.
15 Benson, *The Cultural Psychology of Self*, p. 48.
16 Bruner, 'The Autobiographical Process', p. 13.
17 Bruner, 'The Autobiographical Process', p. 13.
18 O'Rowe, *Crestfall* (unpublished manuscript).
19 Bruner, 'The Autobiographical Process', p. 31.

Project Mayhem:
Mark O'Rowe's *Howie the Rookie*

EAMONN JORDAN

I

Patriarchy has both prescribed and fictionalized societal, gender, class and race relations, and it has also, to a considerable extent, fashioned and fabricated the dramaturgical practices of Irish theatre in terms of how plays are written, programmed, directed, produced, marketed and consumed. Moreover, the imaginations of Irish theatre practitioners, and playwrights especially, have been seriously ideologically loaded, not only in the specific prioritization of primarily male values, references and aspirations, and in their general scrutiny of and obsession with masculinity, but also in their consistent subjugation of the feminine. Gendered relationships have been subjected to critical enquiry in terms of power, authority, the body, space, transgression, and execution of subjectivities, while post-colonial theory has expounded specific relationships between split subjectivities, patterns of imperial oppression and the dynamics of play. In relation to Mark O'Rowe's *Howie the Rookie* (1999), I want to look particularly at issues of masculinity, trauma, violence, working-class suburbia, and how popular culture shapes a performative identity.

During the 1980s, Irish theatre witnessed a series of plays that attempted to deal with male trauma, from Tom Murphy's *The Gigli Concert* (1983) and *Conversations on a Homecoming* (1985), and Dermot Bolger's *The Lament for Arthur Cleary* (1989), to Frank McGuinness's *Innocence* (1986) and *The Breadman* (1990). Occasionally in these plays, either narratives or monologues were used to address disturbance or distress, or to give particular expression to an array of complex interlocking and, often, contradictory emotions. Michael, in *Conversations*, reveals his inability to succeed in New York and his attempt to kill himself. The Sinner Courtney in *The Breadman* tells of his failure to save his drowning brother and expresses the near madness and dysfunctionality that follow this incident. In *The Gigli Concert* masculinity is in the grip of fantasy and despair, and, ultimately, it is the delusion of magic that offers release and transformation. Put simply, potentially these plays take place in public, shared spaces, amongst characters in conflict, where opposing values are articulated, scrutinized and debated.

Since the mid-1990s, characters in Irish plays increasingly do not interact, even when some shared trauma exists between them. The spectator seldom witnesses the characters negotiating their way with or through upset; they may share a stage, as with Billy and Breda in Eugene O'Brien's *Eden* (*2001*), they may offer different versions of the same story while delivering a sequential narrative, as in Conor McPherson's *This Lime Street Bower* (1995), or they may follow on from each other, as in Mark O'Rowe's *Howie the Rookie* or *Crestfall* (2003), but there is an absence of interpersonal relating that is dominating dramaturgical practices. This accounts, in part, for the closing down of the broader communal, public spaces and the emergence of the more isolated interior ones. Tension is generated between the conscious awareness displayed by the narrator and the unconscious, subtextual and physical betrayals that suggest something else. The teller often wants to be liked or accepted. As such, the narrative is an elaborate fantasy, a self-constituting tale as to how the character makes sense of the world.[1] In the contemporary Irish theatre monologue, the fearful inability of male characters to commit to their traumas outside the frame of performance has become increasingly evident. (That is to make this point without discounting the public nature of the monologue in performance before an audience, and not confusing introspection with the extrovert nature of the monologue in theatre.)

II

Fintan O'Toole has written extensively about the use of doubles and doubleness in Irish theatre, arguing that:

> with the emergence of Brian Friel, the doubleness begins to be internalised, to infiltrate the borders of personality itself. In Friel, doubleness is characteristically located in the notion of exile, but equally characteristically, even that very notion of exile itself is double . . . This doubleness of exile leads to a kind of theatre in which character, personality, and language itself become slippery, and constantly threaten to divide . . .[2]

We can track doubleness back to Oscar Wilde's *The Importance of Being Earnest* (1895) and a range of Sean O'Casey's comic duos, through Frank

McGuinness's pairing of characters in *Observe the Sons of Ulster Marching Towards the Somme* (1985) (and of course the split of Pyper into his younger and elder self) and to Marina Carr's twins in *Portia Coughlan* (1996). There are many other examples, including the interactions between Brendan Bracken (Minister for Information in the Churchill government during the second world war) and William Joyce (Lord Haw-Haw) in Thomas Kilroy's *Double Cross* (1986)[3] and the connection between the public and private aspects of Gar O'Donnell in Brian Friel's *Philadelphia, Here I Come!* (1964). Kilroy juxtaposes Bracken and Joyce, palimpsest-like, through innovative staging techniques and has the same actor play both characters in order to make a comment on the radical lives of both of his protagonists, thereby suggesting that imperial rule had been the driving force behind the obsessions, manias and disturbances of both. Their need to disguise fundamental anxieties and fears shaped who and what they were. Likewise with Friel's Gar O'Donnell: his split subjectivity is the result of a repressive inability to give expression and release to a complex self and to the trauma surrounding the loss of his mother.

Initially, the link between The Howie Lee and The Rookie Lee in *Howie the Rookie* (and not *The Howie and The Rookie*) is not inordinately complex, but the characters do form part of that tradition. Part One is narrated by The Howie and Part Two by The Rookie – played brilliantly by Aidan Kelly and Karl Shiels, respectively, in the first production of the play, directed by Mike Bradwell. Part Two is a continuation of the first narrative, albeit from a different point of view. O'Rowe's characters do not share the same space. The Howie Lee and The Rookie Lee are doubles, not in the sense of the doppelganger or of a fractured subjectivity, but in terms of layering and superimposition. Their connection is not then imperial rule, as in *Double Cross*, Irishness, or the twin-deep, doubled relationship between Charlie and Jake in Marie Jones's *Stones in his Pockets* (1999). Rather, The Rookie is The Howie's 'namesake in Lee-ness'. The link is the dead, mythologized film actor Bruce Lee, star of martial arts movies – 'You me an' The Bruce Lee' (p. 18), as The Howie remarks to The Rookie.[4] Identity thus has spatial, imaginative and popular cultural co-ordinates, as well as genetic, psychological and social determinants.

I have suggested elsewhere that Irish theatre has maintained fundamental distinctions between pain and pleasure, and violation and innocence, thereby finding articulation that was beyond a simple morality, and that these distinctions were thus a rejection of an empty postmodern tendency to refuse to prioritize any value system or point of view. In addition, an increasing emphasis on the eroticization of violence and on despoiled, desecrated innocence have put pressure on contemporary writers to go to extremes. Sexual deviance, torture, mutilation and paedophilia became the heightened subjects of theatre practice at times.[5] Increasingly, however, the fundamental distinction is between two opposing types of pain: one that is articulated through dialectical or opposing perspectives, generated by a split self somewhat grounded in the real, and one that is fundamentally performative in such a way that male trauma is never actively authentic. At its heart are a fear and dread that there is not so much general indifference to male trauma in contemporary culture, but rather an increasing inability to place such trauma or give it some substance. In order to elevate that pain to any significant level, two things become obvious in many plays and in this play specifically. These are the deployment of the death of children as the emotional springboard, and the templating of performative violence, which mimics the frame of the real, but is a world whose discernible parameters are furiously contested as fantasy and fabrication are increasingly prioritized. Performance can contest the real or it can fundamentally disengage with it, and violence, when it is almost utterly performative, is very difficult to contextualize. It is the monologue format that both stabilizes the relationship between stage and performance and attests to the internalization of play that ultimately drives inward the focus of male characters. The result is not to deliver some blatant confessional configuration, but to release an expression of violence that can be suicidal or self-destructive.

III

O'Rowe is part of the trend to offer an Irish theatre based more in urban settings. Some critics suggest Tallaght, Dublin 24, close to the Springfield area where O'Rowe grew up, as the locale for the play, but any close scrutiny makes it somewhat difficult to say that. Es Devlin's design for the first production was highly abstract. Cathy Leeney, in this issue of *The Irish Review*, describes Es Devlin's set as being 'sufficiently cold, unspecific and spatially open to communicate a sense of placelessness, of anomie'. Dublin serves both as text, but also as symbolic landscape. Yvonne Whelan argues for an understanding of Dublin from the perspective of postmodern iconography. For her, '[much] more than an areal [sic] container of culture, landscape is now conceived as being actively shaped and reshaped, created and destroyed, by people. It acts as a social and cultural production, which both represents and is constitutive of past, present and future political ideologies and power relations.'[6]

Cathy Leeney reflects on Marc Augé's notion of the 'non-place', 'a space which does not affirm sociological or cultural identities as they have been defined by social and psychological sciences'.[7] In that way, the characters in

Howie the Rookie are dislodged non-bodies and not specifically located by the urban realism of Tallaght.[8] O'Rowe blurs the co-ordinates of the space, and specific references to Dublin are intentionally scattered, something which in turn maps onto the disorientation of character. Deborah Stevenson argues that at one point 'City life (as *gesellschaft*) was regarded as superficial and impersonal while life in the country (*gemeinschaft*) was celebrated as fostering positive and enduring relationships between close friends and kinship groups.'[9] However, the village, as Declan Hughes states, 'is no longer the objective correlative for Ireland: the city is, or to be more precise, *between* cities is'.[10] Mythologically, the village 'doesn't resonate any more', Hughes claims.[11] While it is clear that suburbia can never grip the imagination in the way that the sensibility of a village may do, the more important question is, can suburbia resonate? Maybe it can, but with little or no postcolonial resonance at any rate. Today, imperial intent is not as blatant; it is more invisible, woven as it is by first-world capitalism's drive for material profit. The land and resource acquisition of early imperial projects are replaced by psychological co-option within a set of notionally shared values, those of the freedom, progress and acquisition dictated by the marketplace. O'Rowe generates a space that is also like an urban village, given the connections between people and how the characters operate within the parameters of space. (In *Postmetropolis*, Edward W. Soja identifies 'the spatiality of human life' and also the 'spatial specificity of urbanism'.[12])

Not only does the performativity of the monologue complicate the relationship between space and time, but, additionally, The Howie Lee narrates a story in the present tense, one which only The Rookie Lee can complete. The Howie's later absence denies corporeality, and thus the only realm of existence available is narrative-identity as a hypertext. Lee's martial arts movies emphasize self-defence as personal expression, but also combat as a way of seeking justice. There are often vicious fights, exaggerated by sound effects and unbelievable moves and blows. It is often a combat situation with no holds barred. There is not only an anti-authoritarian sentiment, but also an anti-police one. Further, there is a general denial of justice following on from normal police investigations into the murder of innocent parties. So, in a sense they become revenge dramas as they quest for justice that is not available to the dispossessed.

For many young men, violence is a form of self-validation and Bruce Lee (famed as much for his ability to commingle different martial arts styles as for the one-inch punch of immense power) is a heroic figure amongst some young working-class men, in particular. In Lee's early work, a teacher or a mother places restraints on vengeance. Here, in *Howie the Rookie*, there is no figure of restraint. As Rookie gets ready for Dave's party, he tells himself that he 'looks like a warrior' (p. 42). In this play there is a community of urban warriors, without a classical class grievance. Thus, the citation of Bruce Lee is not so much one of intertextual echo, but one of disassociative imperson- ation, the enactment of the sensation of supremacy through false allegiance. Really, it is not about dominance or patriarchal subjugation, but rather about acts of invisibility (non-entity), hiding behind the myth of the macho mas- culinity of Bruce. Also, the use of the Bruce Lee figure here calls attention to the 'free floating' nature of identity, one without substance and one funda- mentally grounded in artifice.[13] Melissa Sihra raises the important issue of the 'conflictual resonances of the body and the "non-body"'[14] in the work of Marina Carr. So, to the categories of 'non-body', 'non-space', or non-Dublin we can add the concept of non-time or cultural timelessness, in order to understand how the figure of Bruce Lee becomes a dominant, symbolic non-presence and an instructive and conscriptive text.[15] Among many working-class communities, violent behaviour can be a reflex response to or caused by socio-political dynamics. Leeney claims that the 'social value sys- tem represented works on patriarchal tribal principles of kinship, revenge, scapegoating and the intervention of the fates'. Class differences in terms of health, crime (joyriding, drug-taking, burglary), school performance and employment success are blatantly palpable in contemporary Ireland and the emergence of the Celtic Tiger made that obvious.

IV

Not only does O'Rowe invent eloquent phrases, but also his characters com- municate in very strange ways, often deploying slang, key words or action words as unfinished sentences. He does so in order to reflect on a mindset that is blatant and focused in such a way that linguistic coherence is not nec- essarily beyond them, but that the characters are indifferent to it.[16] When they communicate in fragments, an audience must do the rest. Likewise, the naming of characters The Howie, The Rookie, The Mousey, The Peaches (only occasionally) and The Bruce adds something to the quest for distinc- tiveness and individuality within a social class. (Dave McGee gets a full name. Ladyboy, the inter-sex character, is described in vivid terms – 'his oul' dear threw away the body an' raised the afterbirth' some say, others say 'cos of his ingrown flute' [pp. 32–3].) The language is reminiscent of *A Clockwork Orange* and the destructive violence of that particular piece as much as of the urban rhythms of contemporary rap music, something which codifies sexist, anti-law, macho and materially aspirational lyrics.[17] Leeney contends that 'this language asserts a geography in the imagination of the audience' and goes on to argue that people 'transform spaces into places through the meshing of their experience of location as community, and identity becomes wrapped and interleaved with geography, with locale, and with the language used to describe and define identity and community'.

The linguistic exuberance and pop values of the urban gothic world of this play[18] come from videos (Video Vendetta) and, for a slightly younger generation, from video games. (*Street Fighter* and *Mortal Combat* are obvious examples.) In an interview with Fiachra Gibbons, O'Rowe states that video came out when he was about thirteen:

> so he grew up on video nasties, cannibal movies and kung-fu flicks – *I Spit on Your Grave* and all that stuff. Really we only watched them for the goriness of the special effects. *Nightmare in a Damaged Brain* was so chopped to pieces by the censors that we would have to sit there and imagine what happened in the cut-out bits. I suppose they got our brains going.[19]

As the play begins, Ollie and Peaches seek The Rookie's help to beat someone up – they are 'after someone' (p. 9), both having contracted scabies (*Sarcoptes scabiei)* from the mattress in Ollie's place. (The infestation can be transmitted by either sexual contact or from shared bedding, towels or clothing.) Peaches had to shave his body and was given cream by a 'doctor, this packie dirtbird', which burned him up (p. 15). His trauma is added to when his father discovers him 'on the jacks floor in his nip, bollox shaved to bits' (p. 15). 'But [as] straight Rookie, *hetero* Rookie, chose the mat', and not Ollie's bed, he is regarded as the source of the contamination (p. 15). Lady-boy is also after The Rookie because he stood on his Siamese fighting-fish – 'Betas . . . Chink fightin' fish. Chink meanin' Oriental' (p. 33). The Howie likes confrontation: 'I enjoy bein' after people . . . Specially cunts like The Rookie Lee. Handsome cunts. Specially cunts with the same last name as me' (p. 11). The Rookie states that 'The Howie has a bit of a rep himself' and 'he's a goer goes all the way' (p. 46), suggesting he is a serial fighter of sorts. The Rookie admits that he has 'No mates, I've only the birds I shagged . . . Birds think I'm it' (p. 34). (THE ROOKIE: 'Break hearts an' hymens, I do' [p. 30].) In terms of illegality, while neither The Howie nor The Rookie Lee displays any strong associations with criminal gangs or illegal activities (apart from aggression and joyriding), they do experience violence in their everyday lives. (Some recent critics of the play overstate their criminality, simply because they align working-class violence with criminality in an all-pervading manner.)

The Howie Lee's relationship with his parents is deeply dysfunctional. The Howie's parents just roll through life, operating at a general level of numbness. His father has a bad heart, saves for a car, but blows it on a handicam, so he persists in cycling fifteen miles to work and back each day – 'HOWIE: . . . Now, has the handicam, fuck the car. Fuck the ticker, fuck his life, full fuckin' stop' (p. 10). The exchanges between the son and his parents are noted for their aggression and avoidance. The Rookie's parents are separated. His father believed that having a younger woman made him 'virile' (p. 30). The Rookie regards her as a 'dirty jezebel, stole the oul' fella from us' (p. 30). Rookie slept with his father's new girlfriend, a 'ten years younger hooer could slicken up better than the oul' one' (p. 30), and showed him what a real 'stud' is. After that, The Rookie had not seen his father in twenty months, having presented him with his girlfriend's underwear as evidence of their dalliance. Now, as the Rookie is desperate for money, he calls around to meet his father and asks for help. They exchange pleasantries: 'Have you started seein' them pitbulls yet' (p. 31), his father asks, based on the notion that the 'Mayan Indians' are visited by an animal that foretells their deaths.

The Howie sees in Ollie 'the scabies' pain' (p. 19), and thus volunteers to be part of the avenging party. The Rookie is duly beaten up and 'Vengeance [is] extracted' (p. 21). Up to this point, The Howie Lee displays a great degree of arrogance and distance. His desperation is only made conscious through the accidental death of his brother, for which he is part responsible. He had refused to baby-sit his brother and the coins The Mousey Lee died trying to retrieve had fallen from The Rookie's pockets earlier when he rejected and fled his mother's requests to stay at home and take care of his younger brother. We get a strong sense of The Howie's vulnerability after he steps in to rescue The Rookie from Bernie's son – who is described as being 'built like a human white puddin', looks inbred' (p. 38). Howie cries after beating him up. He moves in a different emotional direction again when he asks The Rookie: 'Tell me your woes 'bout the fishes an' I will help you' (p. 41). Further, he buys The Rookie some cream to ease the scabies itching: the cream The Rookie regards as a 'gift' (p. 41). Now The Rookie can state: 'So I kind of believe in him' (p. 43).

The changing connection between the two males is also significant, because the degree of violence also shifts, from a somewhat casual beating that The Rookie initially receives, through the brawl involving Bernie's son, to the more sinister fight in 'Dave McGee's gaff' between Ladyboy and The Howie Lee. (Matt Dillon, the actor, is supposedly in attendance at the annual bash.) Ladyboy wants to damage The Rookie's knees and 'turn him into a gammy boy', because he had not handed over the money to replace the dead fish (p. 45). This fight takes on the detail and sensibility of the final fight sequence to so many Kung Fu movies,[20] a battle to the death between hero and villain – ''Cos it's not normal fisticuffs any more, not Marquis of

Queensberry. It's blood an' bone' (p. 47). In some perverse way violation becomes the code of conduct. It is a scene of horrific confrontation. Both fighters are crying. The Rookie's description of the fight is complex, revealing a range of responses from awe and fear to exhilaration and trauma. He states: 'Both cryin'', I think, a weird kinda keenin' sound' (p. 48). It ends with The Howie being victorious, only for Peaches and Ollie to attack him. The Howie is thrown out a window and is impaled on the railing. O'Rowe pushes things a bit further. The Hi-ace, with Flann Dingle driving and Ginger Boy surfing on the roof, pursued by the police, slams into the railing where the The Howie is impaled – 'The Howie's body comes apart by itself, just before the two tons of metal slams into him, me mate, me new, me impaled mate, me namesake the name of Lee, me saviour' (p. 51). (This calls to mind some paintings of the martyrdom of Christian saints, which display a significant degree of sexual imagery.)

It is worthwhile considering the concept of impalement, because it can be argued that there is a strong sexual overtone to such an action. Proof of this is to be found in O'Rowe's *Made in China* (2001). Not only is this play full of references to same-sex sexual abuse, but the rape of Kilby – rectal penetration by means of a pool cue – and the damage to bowel and organs that followed, became the means by which a policeman (Copper Dolan) and a gang leader (Puppacat) establish a binding agreement:

PADDY: They shook in your shite?!
KILBY: Shook symbolic, they did, all ceremonial, made the pact legit an'
bindin' on the sufferin', the martyrdom of Kilby. (p. 77)

Late in the play Kilby tries to re-enact his own assault, attempting to rape Hughie with an umbrella. Kilby describes his experience as that of being a 'cue stick's whore' (p. 79), but also sees the pain that he suffered during his violation as something that gives him the status and distancing of a Shaolin monk, practised in martial arts fighting. Further, when Kilby threatens Hughie he speaks of 'impalin'' him (p. 79). (Kilby's fantasy of revenge against Copper Dolan is to rape him.) *Made in China* offers a far darker vision of the perverted, retributive justice of street gangs with their rule of law, punishment beatings, and twisted codes of honour. Instead of narrating the violence, as in *Howie the Rookie*, the spectator experiences sequences of violence on-stage. (Ollie's sexuality in *Howie the Rookie* is accepted and makes it very different to the rampant homophobia throughout *Made in China*.) In Bruce Lee's films *Fist of Fury* and *Enter the Dragon*, concluding or near final fight sequences offer impalements. In the latter, during a memorable hall of mirrors sequence, the evil leader, pierced by a spear coming through a mirror, dies impaled on a rotating, revolving panel, and in the former, one enemy is held in place while a sword falling from the air pierces through his body.

If violence controls the dynamics of *Howie the Rookie*, its connection to sex is just as provocative. Throughout the drama there is an ongoing sense of sex without purpose or passion. If the scabies disease is the initial kick-start or the excuse for violence, then the death of The Howie comes about because of his rejection of Avalanche, Peaches' sister. She is referred to by Howie as being sixteen stone (p. 11), and that 'her grotesque arse [is] bet into a pair of ski pants . . . see her piss-flaps an' everything' (p. 13). (On another occasion he describes her as a 'Dirty fat cunt' [p. 27].) Peaches accuses The Rookie of 'Makin' her think someone loved her when she was unlovable? Givin' her hope' (p. 49). Nicholas Grene suggests that in the early monologues of Conor McPherson the male characters are noted for 'their abuse of, obsessions with, and dependence on women'.[21] Likewise, Karen Fricker argues that Irish male characters on television and screen are 'useless with women' and 'inept at love'.[22] There is nothing chivalrous about The Howie's behaviour towards either Bernie or Avalanche. O'Rowe shifts male relationships with the opposite sex towards indifference and rejection. Bernie is attracted to Howie's 'machoness' (p. 22), as he sees it. Sexual attraction is on this level only. Bernie would have liked to observe the earlier fight involving The Rookie and The Howie and Peaches, as she 'likes watchin' blokes scrappin'' (p. 23). Those gathered at the McGee party share a similar fascination. Sex and violence are fundamentally interconnected and nothing else seems to generate a value system. There is no alternative to that and nothing that could be equated with intimacy. Both sex and violence are just transactions. Ultimately, Howie's death is a form of self-destruction. (*Fight Club* also ends with the death of the narrator.)

The spectator's expectation of grief is superbly shattered when, after The Howie's death, The Rookie calls to his parents in order to 'Let them know he was good at the end' (p. 51). On the television, there is a video of the dead Mousey Lee, being held steady in order to pose for the camera: 'The boy's face is grey. His eyes are on mine. His expression doesn't change' (p. 51). The Rookie sits in the same seat from which the first recording was made, invited to do so by The Howie's father because he is photogenic. In the double image of the living and the dead, an audience is challenged to consider the dynamics of violence and violation. This scene captures the desensitization of a family to trauma. While obviously real, their pain is distanced and eschewed through a recording, in a way that violent films can manage to both satisfy a need to address an injustice and also ratify social immobility without getting to its root cause, inequality. Initially, the scabies was the initial source of violation. Then Peaches and Ollie murder The

Howie in order to defend the dignity of Avalanche. What kind of dignity are we talking about being available to that society? The notion of empathy arises many times in O'Rowe's work. The Rookie gets double whiskey for the price of a single from a barman, as he 'feels' for him, 'gives' him 'empathy' (p. 32). (There are echoes here of Conor McPherson's *The Weir* [1997].) But, like dignity, the empathy has little substance, because it is a society cut off substantially from grief, not capable of acknowledging fully its own traumas.

In lieu of a cash-down payment, The Rookie offers to teach Bernie's son 'manly things of how to survive in a world of pain, made doubly worse 'cos he's slow' (p. 37). Bernie's reply to The Rookie's invitation is to tell him that he knows 'nothing of manly things'. The Rookie's response is telling: 'Sore point, me lack of manliness, so it slips out. Cunt' (p. 37). Agency is not an available word, for almost the only thing active about these males is their violence, in that they are 'self-made', through the disciplining of the body. To be macho is not so much about expression, more about cultural compensation. Violence is a way of gaining respect and a way of marking out territory. The play is in part about men on the rampage, set loose on themselves.

The play text *Howie the Rookie*, published by Nick Hern, offers an image of a face with teeth sharpened to look like those of fighting fish or Ladyboy's. The back cover's blurb describes the script as 'a bizarre feud of honour' and a play 'where the most brutal events take on a mythic significance'. This drama never gets into that territory; it escorts an audience potentially into the terrorism of a world where actions have no significance beyond the immediate, because it is a world without resonance or connection. There is little or no honour to be found. What the novel, *Fight Club*, and later the film version of it achieve is that they both reflect an anarchic sensibility, along with the sheer desperation for which contemporary consumer culture is, in part, accountable. *Fight Club* offers developmental phases of rebellion, unlike in O'Rowe's play, where the social system is just a given. American society offers the myth of progress and improvement, though here it is self-destruction and self-laceration in O'Rowe's urban landscape. What makes it different from O'Rowe's work is that the anarchic tendencies of *Fight Club* become expressed publicly as attacks on social institutions, thus violation is more like spurious revenge, whereas O'Rowe's characters seem to have all but internalized such rage.

V

In some monologue-driven dramas, as in Tom Murphy's *Bailegangaire* (1985), through the telling of story, some level of acceptance is not only achieved, but revelation and release are transformative. This O'Rowe play has strayed very far from the optimism of Murphy. These monologues offer no sense of recovery or closure, no sense of placing oneself through story-telling, no hint of an ingrained narrative that is a life story of sorts which must be betrayed. In general, with this current crop of monologues in Irish theatre we get a displaced, dispersed masculinity, not only one that is decentred and split. It is especially vital to distinguish between the general crisis of masculinity in Ireland today and that which is specific to the working classes.[23]

While the play is not in the territory of the romanticized working class-es, neither is it set in an underclass, with all the pejorative ideas and implications associated with the term. In this play there is none of the defi-ant intimacy of the working classes that is to be found in plays of a previous generation of writers. Likewise, the spectator experiences none of the com-munal supports and levels of care nominally associated with that community. The play maps how disadvantage is perpetuated. The endeav-our, commitment and strong work ethic as well as strong community spirit once associated with the working classes have shifted. For the characters, stoicism has become withdrawal; there is a huge absence of resistance and the levels of acceptance and tolerance are frightening. There is no protest and no political agitation. A true absence of connection and real impover-ishment in terms of the imagination are visible. (Social and community groups in working-class areas would reject such an observation.) What intrigues about this play is not the basic dysfunctionality that it creates; more, it is the misplaced emphasis on redemption. The play struggles with the status of virility, with testimony to little other than emasculation. The primal urgency of fighting, something that *Fight Club* establishes, is clearly attested. Masculinity will forever remain in process and will always be unre-solved. Here the rehearsals of masculinity are off key.

In an interview with Eileen Battersby, O'Rowe comments: 'When I heard the actors I realised they spoke to the audience, they make the audi-ence complicit.'[24] It is that sense of complicity that strains and complicates the relationship between audience and stage, for it is as if only terror can generate a 'near-life' experience as in *Fight Club*. In the novel, pain func-tions as a form of attestation. 'Tyler's kiss', which is a chemical burn administered with flakes of lye and saliva, is the mark of belonging. In this work of O'Rowe, emotion and pain are accessible only when they are rout-ed through a performative frame.

The reality of the Lees is one without tragic purpose; the discipline and self-defence of martial arts become self-destruction and carnage. It is a world that becomes locked into a performative hermeneutic of sorts. The initial connection between the Lees is tentative. Later, The Howie seeks to protect The Rookie. But The Howie dies, like his hero Bruce Lee, prematurely. Bruce Lee serves as both a cultural artefact and a motivating artifice. It is a world enveloping upon itself, as is the monologue – which has swapped metaphysical debate for the intertextuality of popular culture, martial arts movies and the meta-physicality or metro-corporeality of aggressively narrated, doubled (and dubbed, perhaps), urbanised language. The characters are caught between the fabricated impersonality of suburbia and the impracticality of an increasingly performative, globalized popular culture, wedged between the absence of physical amenities and the convenience and vicariousness of urban myth, jammed between open spaces of the edge of the suburban sprawl and the partitioned and relatively immobile nature of socially ranked relationships. The generation and ingestion of popular culture, which is an urbanized phenomenon in most respects, maps onto the production and consumption of a dystopic urban sprawl. Cities consume spaces, eating into the countryside, as Tallaght itself has done. The festering notions of nation and post-colonialism seem increasingly remote and obsolete. The overlaid personae of the two Lees are not only mobilized by popular culture and repositories of it, but are identities that are also mass-produced. It is no longer nation; rather, it is popular culture, which is the more influential and ideologically priming 'imagined community'.[25]

Notes and References

1 See Ciarán Benson, *The Cultural Psychology of Self: Place, Morality and Art in Human Worlds* (London: Routledge, 2001), p. 45.
2 Fintan O'Toole, 'Irish Theatre: The State of the Art', in Eamonn Jordan (ed.), *Theatre Stuff: Critical Essays on Contemporary Irish Theatre* (Dublin: Carysfort, 2000), p. 52.
3 See Eamonn Jordan, 'Thomas Kilroy's *Double Cross*: Mediatized Realities and Sites of Multiple, Projected Selves', *Focus: Studies in English Literature* (Winter 2004), 101–15.
4 Bruce Lee was the San Francisco-born but Hong Kong-raised martial arts actor. He is well known for the TV series *The Green Hornet* and guest appearances in *Batman*, before he went on to make a series of cult martial arts films comprising *The Big Boss*, *Fist of Fury*, *Way of the Dragon* and *Enter the Dragon*. He died at thirty-two with a brain aneurysm on 20 July 1973 while working on *The Game of Death*.
5 Fintan O'Toole argues that: 'If *Crestfall* was indeed a movie, it would probably be banned . . . [having a] climax of such extreme violence that it makes *Reservoir Dogs* seem like a Hallmark Mother's Day card'. See *Irish Times*, 22 May 2003.
6 Yvonne Whelan, *Reinventing Modern Dublin: Streetscape, Iconography and the Politics of Identity* (Dublin: University College Dublin Press), p. 12.
7 Cathy Leeney, 'Hard wired/tender bodies: Power, Loneliness, the Machine and the Person in the Work of Desperate Optimists', in Brian Singleton and Anna McMullan (eds), *Performing Ireland*, *Australasian Drama Studies Special Issue*, 43 (October 2003), 78.
8 Gerry Smyth notes that 'the impression of space that emerges most strongly from postmodern geography is one of incompleteness, contingency and partiality. The

sequentiality of time is always mitigated by the simultaneity of space'; *Space and the Irish Cultural Imagination* (Basingstoke: Palgrave, 2001), pp. 14–15.

9　Deborah Stevenson, *Cities and Urban Cultures* (London: Open University Press, 2003), p. 7.

10　Declan Hughes, 'Reflections on Irish Theatre and Identity', in *Theatre Stuff*, p. 12.

11　Ibid.

12　Edward W. Soja, *Postmetropolis: Critical Studies of Cities and Regions* (London: Blackwell, 2000), p. 6. Soja also argues for distinctions between '*perceived* space (prompted by Henri Lefebvre)', that is the 'concrete forms and specific patternings of urbanism as a way of life', '*conceived* space of the imagination (urban imaginary)' and a third space, '*lived* space', which is 'simultaneously real-and-imagined, actual-and-virtual, locus of structured individual and collective experience and agency', pp. 7–10.

13　Judith Butler argues that gender is a 'free floating artifice' and that, as a 'shifting and contextual phenomenon, gender does not denote a substantive being, but a relative point of convergence among culturally and historically specific relations'. See *Gender Trouble: Feminism and the Subversion of Identity* (New York: Routledge, 1990), pp. 6 and 10, cited by Robin Roberts in 'Gendered Media Rivalry: Irish Drama and American Film', in *Performing Ireland*, p. 109.

14　Melissa Sihra, 'Renegotiating Landscapes of the Female: Voices, Topographies and Corporealities of Alterity in Marina Carr's *Portia Coughlan*'. See *Performing Ireland*, p. 24.

15　In *From Both Hips* (*Two Plays: From Both Hips* and *The Aspidistra Code* [London: Nick Hern Books, 1999]), O'Rowe uses Don Johnson from the *Miami Vice* television series as a point of popular cultural connection, reference and identification, and in *Made in China* (London: Nick Hern, 2001) it is action movie hero Chuck Norris, who also starred opposite Bruce Lee in *The Way of the Dragon*.

16　We get no sense of the occupations of most of the characters. In the main, money is in short supply. And the day after he is beaten up, The Rookie does not seem to have work commitments.

17　The actors in the first production of the play performed with distinctly working-class Dublin accents. But, apart from the local references, it would be interesting to consider the appropriateness of the play to any major urban centre.

18　Likewise the ability of popular culture to permeate a consciousness is fastidiously articulated, namely, John Woo's *Last Hurrah for Chivalry* (1978), the *Tarzan* movies ('fuckin' Weismuller' [p. 20]), and the athlete (The) Linford Christie, John Wayne, *Gladiators* (the television show) and *The High Chaparral*.

19　Fiachra Gibbons, 'The Dark Stuff', 24 November, 2003, *Guardian* (http://film.guardian.co.uk/interview/interviewpages/0,,1091907,00.html).

20　Leon Hunt argues that 'Kung fu is a genre *of* bodies: extraordinary, expressive, spectacular, sometimes even grotesque bodies . . . This ecstatic excess extends to the aural dimension; Bruce Lee's panoply of shrieks and roars, rhythmically orchestrated thuds and swishes, the reverberative (orgasmic?) aftershocks that follow definitive strikes'. See Leon Hunt, *Kung Fu Cult Masters* (London and New York: Wallflower, 2004), p. 2. Hunt also identifies Kung Fu's 'corporeal exhilaration' (p. 3).

21　Nicholas Grene, 'Stories in Shallow Space: *Port Authority*', *Irish Review*, 29 (2002), 71.

22　Karen Fricker argues that the 'Irish male is becoming increasingly introspective, insecure and immobile. We see this crisis manifest itself across Irish culture through the representation of men who are consumed by self-examination and self-doubt.' See 'Same Old Show: The Performance of Masculinity in Conor McPherson's *Port Authority* and Mark O'Rowe's *Made in China*', *Irish Review*, 29 (2002), 84.

23 The three female characters in O'Rowe's *Crestfall* (2003) in a way test that trajectory. The amount of monologues involving male characters I think invites the speculation that there is a cultural fear, with some exceptions, of the female as performative. Women may deliver personal narratives occasionally, but seldom perform multiple roles.

24 Eileen Battersby, 'The Eloquence of Rage and Fear', *Irish Times*, 18 March 1999.

25 See Benedict Anderson, *Imagined Communities: Reflections on the Origins and Spread of Nationalism* (London: Verso, 1983).

Belfast, Boys and Books:
The Friendship Between Forrest Reid and Knox Cunningham

GRAHAM WALKER

I

In his second volume of autobiography, *The Middle of My Journey*, the playwright John Boyd sketched his impressions of his fellow Belfastman, the esteemed novelist Forrest Reid.[1] Boyd got to know Reid during the four to five years preceding the latter's death in January 1947, when Reid was 71. Boyd at the time was a young schoolteacher with aspirations to become a writer, and he was aware of the high regard in which Reid was held by other writers in Britain and Ireland (including Reid's long-standing friends E. M. Forster and Walter de la Mare). 'In E. M. Forster's opinion', wrote Boyd, 'Forrest was the most important person in Belfast. This was an opinion I shared and I was not likely to forget that it was a privilege to belong to his small circle.' Boyd went on to qualify this by acknowledging that he did not know all of Reid's friends, and that there was one of whom he disapproved.[2]

This was Samuel Knox Cunningham, known as 'Knox', who belonged to one of Ulster's great dynasties. His father was Samuel Cunningham, a fierce opponent of Irish Home Rule who helped organize and finance the original Ulster Volunteer Force and permitted the local battalion to train on the family estate of Glencairn in West Belfast. Folklore has it that he signed the cheques for the guns smuggled to Ulster on board 'The Clydevalley' ship in 1913.[3] Samuel became a member of the Northern Ireland Senate in 1921 and was a powerful voice in the ruling Ulster Unionist Party until his death in 1946. More recently, Josias, a grandson of Samuel, was President of the Ulster Unionist Council and a crucial party 'fixer' for David Trimble during the Peace Process, until his death in a car crash in 2000. The Cunningham family also had extensive local business interests, including the *Northern*

Whig newspaper. Knox, born in 1909, went to Cambridge, where he became a champion boxer and, after dabbling in the family businesses and becoming a barrister, entered Westminster, after earlier failed attempts, as an Ulster Unionist in 1955. After passing his South Antrim seat on to James Molyneaux in 1970 he retired from politics, notwithstanding some rabble-rousing interventions of an extreme Loyalist variety as the Troubles took a grip on Northern Ireland. He died suddenly in 1976.[4]

Boyd found the friendship between Reid and Cunningham 'incomprehensible' and imagined that a 'liberal' like Forster would have had little time for a 'reactionary' like Cunningham.[5] Other eyebrows have been similarly raised since.[6] Drawing on the evidence of a collection of Reid's letters to Cunningham covering the period 1934–46, this article will try to explain this friendship and also offer pointers to Forster's relationship with Cunningham.[7] Moreover, it will attempt to assess the significance of the Reid–Cunningham friendship in the context of Reid's preoccupation, literary or otherwise, with boys and of Cunningham's alleged links to those convicted of abusing boys at the Kincora care home in Belfast during the1960s and 1970s.[8] In another Belfast writer's autobiography, Robin Bryans' *The Dust Has Never Settled*, Reid's predilection for boys is a matter of sexual innuendo, and Cunningham is 'outed' as homosexual and accused of being part of a cover-up of the abuse at Kincora. In Bryans' recollections, Cunningham is also linked to his Cambridge contemporary Anthony Blunt, who in turn is connected with homosexual circles in Northern Ireland.[9] These allegations were aired subsequently in books by the journalists Chris Moore and Martin Dillon.[10]

II

Reid's letters to Cunningham were by turns affectionate, tender, frank, humorous, waspish, sarcastic and truculent. They cover various aspects of Reid's domestic life in his council house in East Belfast, and contain observations, some of them personally revealing, on relationships, as well as critical reflections on literature and ideas. At regular intervals they also rhapsodize about boys. Reid clearly took Cunningham into his confidence, and the correspondence constitutes strong evidence of a friendship based on trust and shared intimacies and interests.

The friendship seems to have begun in 1934. Within two years it was significant enough for Reid to dedicate his novel *The Retreat* to Cunningham. This book was the second in what would become a trilogy about boyhood, the first, *Uncle Stephen*, having been published in 1931 and the third, *Young Tom*, to arrive in 1944. Cunningham's enthusiasm for *Uncle Stephen*, a variation on the Greek ideal of the teacher–pupil relationship, was reputedly the basis for the friendship.[11] By 1937 Reid's letters to the now married Cunningham – his wife was bizarrely referred to in the correspondence as 'Bob' – contain comments on the relative attractiveness of different male youths, and are marked by the rather arch tone with which he would convey his gossipy and mischievous observations on other friends and on young male callers to his house. Among the latter were future writers Robin Perry, Robert Greacen and Hugh Shearman, all then in their late teens. Shearman, a 'prig' in the estimation of Reid, was to become Ulster unionism's most reliably sympathetic historian as well as a novelist; in 1942 Reid ruefully compared the popular impact of Shearman's *Not an Inch: Northern Ireland under Lord Craigavon* with the indifference accorded by the book-buying public to his own novels. The early letters also reveal that Reid wasted little time in putting Cunningham in touch with Forster, who appears to have been quite taken with the tall, well-built Ulsterman; Reid described with evident relish Forster's anxiety to arrange meetings with Cunningham.[12]

Forster may have warmed to Cunningham in spite of the latter's politics. However, Reid was temperamentally conservative and disinclined to take politics very seriously, as Boyd found to his annoyance when he attempted to interest him in socialism.[13] Reid held no brief either for romantic Irish nationalist aspirations – although his fixation on boyhood was very 'Pearsian'[14] – and was happy enough to live in his detached way under the Stormont Unionist regime. Brian Taylor, his most recent biographer, hints that Reid had political friends in City Hall (also Unionist dominated) who got him the council house in Ormiston Crescent where he lived during the 1930s and 1940s.[15] The Catholic atmosphere in southern Ireland somewhat repelled him. In 1944, referring to an antagonistic review by a critic who urged him to stop writing about pagans and start studying Christian writers, Reid observed: 'It's this sort of thing, cropping up every now and then, that turns me against the South.'[16] Reid related to politics in general in a spirit of agnosticism: in a letter to Cunningham following the death of Craigavon, Prime Minister of Northern Ireland since partition, he poked fun at a member of his bridge circle and indirectly revealed his own disinterestedness: 'A terrible dilemma occurred. Lord Craigavon's funeral and the wedding of Norman Greaves happened on the same day, almost at the same hour. Picture poor Mrs. Joseph, torn between twin yearnings. In the end she elected for the funeral, though it was too late to get a ticket and she arrived home exhausted.'[17]

Reid's world was one into which the rancorous sectarian squabbles of Belfast did not intrude, and in relation to which Cunningham's defence of the *status quo* was more congenial than the idealism of Boyd and others.

Beyond this, however, Reid's letters indicate a more substantial objection to the fashionable political posturing of other writers and artists: Boyd's opinions he dismissed to Cunningham as 'ready made' and derived wholly from the Auden–MacNeice literary clique of the time.[18] This, it might be said, was not an unfair verdict on the self-consciously earnest and mechanically thinking Boyd. Reid's indifference to political radicalism was in any case more than offset by the unorthodoxy of his literary subject matter. This in turn dismayed Boyd, who recollected that he possessed no awareness of homosexuality and its importance to Reid's work.

Reid has been widely labelled a pederast, and his Hellenicism has been considered complementary to what Noel Annan has identified as the growth of 'a cult of homosexuality' during the inter-war years.[19] However, Taylor contends that such pigeon-holing does not help us understand Reid or his literary achievements and states that Reid considered the sex act 'degrading' and disapproved of homosexuals.[20] Certainly it is the case that Reid's novels champion the purity of the platonic male–male friendship; he disagreed profoundly with Forster's decision to have male lovers consummate their feelings physically in his novel *Maurice*, which was only published in 1971 after Forster's death.[21] In a letter to Cunningham in 1945 Reid was censorious about Yeats's published letters to his lesbian friend Dorothy Wellesley, finding distasteful 'the senile florescence of sex'.[22]

Yet there was a side to Reid revealed in his letters to Cunningham which was more knowing and playful than this suggests; moreover, Reid sometimes gave his descriptions of boys a gratuitous erotic charge which, it might be hazarded, he knew would be appreciated by the recipient. 'It looks as if he had Spanish blood in him', he wrote of thirteen-year-old 'Fred', 'with that colouring, a broad brow, the nose perhaps a little coarse, the mouth perfect, and dark eyes gleaming with friendliness and the joy of animal life. In summer he runs about half naked with an open shirt and a pair of crumpled shorts.'[23] 'The past few days have been very hot', he informed Cunningham in May 1944, 'and I've spent some hours round at Cabin Hill watching the boys playing cricket. Yesterday it was broiling, and they were running about practically naked.'[24] Reid swapped photographs of boys with Cunningham; a postcard sent by Reid bearing the image of HRH Prince Henry, then a strikingly attractive youth, is among the Cunningham papers. Moreover, there are several references to literature about male youth, of which genre Reid informed Cunningham he was making a collection. Of such a book, entitled *Schooling*, written by a young teacher, Reid vouchsafed to Cunningham that he was sure he would like it.[25] The intimacy between the two men was evident in asides relating to Reid's books, such as: 'You're the only person who will know'.[26] Their shared outlook is signalled by Reid's acknowledgement that his 'Young Tom' character in real life would have to face a 'cold world' lacking in 'Uncle Knoxes' or 'fond daddies'.[27] Reid seemed to be assuming a similar disposition towards boyhood fantasies on the part of Cunningham, and perhaps also a homoerotic approach to boys in real life.

Colin Cruise, in a discussion of Reid's fiction and its homosexual themes, has suggested that sports such as boxing stood in for sexual acts in certain of his works.[28] Intriguingly, Reid evinced interest in a boxing club run by Cunningham, a source of later speculation about Cunningham in connection with Kincora and other matters.[29] Indeed, through interests such as boys' boxing and his patronage of the YMCA, Cunningham can appear retrospectively as a closeted homosexual establishment figure, identified with what became clichéd codes of later twentieth-century gay culture.[30] Furthermore, the species of blimpish high Toryism which partly defined Cunningham's political life had long been a furtive male-centred phenomenon.

Perhaps Reid, in quoting a sentence written in the margin of a book borrowed from the Linenhall Library in Belfast in 1940, played to the clandestine tendency in Cunningham's make-up: 'If the reader', the sentence ran, 'will wait at the entrance to the Library on Thursday evening at 5pm wearing a red flower, I will introduce myself.'[31] Highlighting this Wildean invitation could hardly have been other than a knowing acknowledgement of the subterfuge adopted by homosexual men in order to meet in the repressive climate of the time, and it is significant that Reid should share it with the superficially strait-laced Cunningham. Equally, it does seem clear that Reid derived erotic fulfilment from the 'state of wonder' which Cruise suggests characterized his fictional treatment of boyhood – the eroticism of daring to dream – rather than physical acts; and Cunningham's interest in younger members of his own sex may have been similarly limited to his imagination, at least for a long time (or while he was still boxing). Robin Bryans has claimed that Cunningham indulged in gay sexual behaviour, but it is not clear what times in Cunningham's life Bryans is referring to, or how dependable is his testimony.[32] Conjecture has also surrounded Maurice Leitch's novel *The Liberty Lad*, first published in 1965, in which there is a fascinatingly drawn figure of an Ulster Unionist politician who combines the public appearance of a family man holding traditional views with a secret life seducing young men. Leitch, however, has denied that he had Cunningham specifically in mind while writing the novel.[33]

Reid's relationship with Cunningham, on the basis of these letters, also seemed to function as an emotional safety-valve for the older man. This is most marked in Reid's frankness about his feelings for Stephen Gilbert, whom he met when the latter was nineteen and whom he mentored until

Gilbert succeeded in becoming a novelist in his own right.[34] On the face of it Reid had cause to congratulate himself on adroitly playing the Socratic part in the development of a young man's talent, but his involvement clearly ran much deeper. Reid's feelings of desolation when Gilbert enlisted in the armed forces at the outbreak of war, and his sense of hurt and betrayal over Gilbert's engagement to two women, were displayed overtly to Cunningham, whose understanding was taken for granted. On Stephen's departure for France in November 1939 Reid wrote that their farewell meeting was 'affectionate, subdued, and on my part carefully restrained', but added: 'I have never known what he thought of me in any other capacity than as a tutor and a person to whom he could talk. The rest is guess work.'[35] What may be guessed at here is that Gilbert was the final – and most intense – love of Reid's life, and that frustration and thwarted emotional longings characterized the relationship, in the same manner as earlier involvements. The most significant of these was Reid's friendship with Andrew Rutherford during his late teenage and early adult years in Belfast. This formed the emotional substance and revelatory climax to his first volume of autobiography, *Apostate*, and the meditation on his feelings which opens the second, *Private Road*.[36]

Reid's personal reflections in correspondence with Cunningham indicate a man who preached the platonic ideal while privately yearning, perhaps in defiance of himself, for more.[37] Certainly the letters display emotional torment beyond what Reid would theoretically have viewed as the healthy confines of the tutor–pupil relationship. They show him to have been deeply possessive and jealous. In the light of this, Reid's rather tart comments to Cunningham that his friend Walter de la Mare's anthology of the literature of love, published in 1943, should have taken in 'all kinds', and that at the age of 70 de la Marc 'might have risked it', appear enigmatic.[38] Was he simply making a point about the neglect of love between males, or was he suggesting that the varieties of this category also deserved attention?

By 1945, when Gilbert was engaged for the second time, Reid admitted to Cunningham that he had acted selfishly the first time round, though he had not been mistaken about Stephen's choice of partner. 'At all events', he went on, 'we have both learnt from experience to avoid that unfortunate constraint which made everything so unhappy before. It will leave me extremely lonely, but it would be perfectly monstrous to let that interfere. The forty years of life he has before him are a good deal more important that the few I can count on.'[39] Letting go with dignity did not, however, preclude the deliciously feline observation on Stephen's intended made to Cunningham a week later: 'There was no lipstick etc: in appearance she is plump and solidly built, quite looking her age, which is 28 . . . what her tastes may be I don't know – beyond a taste for hiking.'[40] This kind of waspishness is somewhat at odds with the buttoned-up, Olympian and rather austere figure portayed in some accounts.[41]

III

Following Reid's death, Knox Cunningham strove to honour him and his literary achievements. He was executor of Reid's literary estate and worked closely in an advisory capacity with Reid's first biographer, Russell Burlingham, whose work was completed in 1952.[42] In the same year Cunningham joined with Forster to unveil a memorial plaque at Ormiston Crescent and to produce a celebratory collection of reminiscences. Forster delivered a tribute at a dinner in the Grand Central Hotel in Belfast, an event for which Cunningham acquired the official Ulster Unionist benediction of a message from Stormont Premier Lord Brookeborough.[43]

Reid's passing may have brought Cunningham and Forster closer; at the very best, it did not attenuate their relationship. Certainly, Cunningham's papers contain letters from Forster in the 1950s which carry explicit endearments: 'Please accept my love', he wrote in one, and 'much love' in others.[44] Forster's correspondence also touched on the subject of the status of homosexuality under the law. In one letter he mentions having done 'some protesting' but being of the view that it would not be helpful to 'the Society' or to himself to become part of 'a stage army'. 'I preferred to feel free', he wrote, before going on to reflect that he was wrong and that he ought to have joined 'the Society'. 'I hope you will!', he enjoined Cunningham. This letter is undated but can be confidently placed on the basis of Forster's following observation that nothing would be done in parliament as long as the government and the opposition were so 'indifferent' to the Wolfenden Report. The 'Society' referred to was in all probability the Homosexual Law Reform Society.[45]

The report of the committee chaired by John Wolfenden, whose public labours had already encompassed the YMCA and brought him to the attention of Cunningham, was concerned with the law as it related to homosexuality and prostitution. It was published in September 1957 and recommended that homosexual behaviour between consenting adults in private no longer be a criminal offence.[46] The report was debated in the House of Commons and there was notable intervention in favour of law reform by the Ulster Unionist MP for North Belfast and author of books on both Carson and Wilde, Harford Montgomery Hyde, a stance which contributed signally to his being de-selected by the local Unionist Party branch for the next election in 1959.[47] Knox Cunningham took no such political risks: he made no contribution to the debate and did not vote when the issue came to a division. In 1959 his discretion was perhaps rewarded when he became Parliamentary Private Secretary to Prime Minister Harold Macmillan, the closest an Ulster Unionist had been to the centre of power in British politics since the days of Edward Carson. Richard Aldous has speculated that Cunningham's advice to Macmillan on Irish matters was likely to have been of a hard-line Unionist variety, although he does not view Cunningham as 'a major political player'.[48] This assessment is reinforced in the light of improvement in British government relations with the Republic of Ireland and the tensions between London and Belfast during the period of Macmillan's government from (1959–1963). According to the indiscreet Bryans, Macmillan's family publishing house later refused to produce Cunningham's memoirs, and Macmillan claimed to have known little of what Bryans labels the 'complications' of the relationship between Cunningham and Anthony Blunt.[49] Cunningham, at any rate, was at the heart of the government when it was shaken by the Profumo scandal in 1963 and was the subject of much rumour about sexual misconduct.[50] Intriguingly, Bryans also alleges there was a falling-out between Cunningham and Forster during the former's spell as PPS to Macmillan.[51]

After leaving government with a baronetcy in Macmillan's farewell honours list, Cunningham became a focal point at Westminster for Ulster Unionist disaffection with Northern Ireland's new liberalizing Premier Terence O'Neill. In 1943, when thanking Cunningham for a photograph, Reid had complimented him on how well he looked in it and added with metaphorical if not literal prescience that 'it would make a grand centre-piece for an Orange banner and stranger things have happened'.[52] From the onset of the Ulster Troubles in 1969, Cunningham indeed cheered his Orange and traditional supporters with swingeing attacks on both Stormont and Westminster governments for 'appeasing' Nationalists. He flirted with William Craig's Vanguard movement when Stormont was prorogued in March 1972, but his essentially integrationist brand of unionism was at odds with Craig's tendencies towards greater Ulster independence. He was much closer to Ian Paisley, with whom he had farcically attempted to restore *The Clydevalley* in the mid-1960s, and he contributed to Paisley's *Protestant Telegraph* newspaper.[53]

In addition, Cunningham's involvement with William McGrath, the founder of a shadowy Loyalist paramilitary-style group called TARA, has led to claims that he knew about McGrath's sexual abuse of boys at the Kincora home in Belfast.[54] Bryans alleges that Cunningham also covered up the abuses of boys carried out by John McKeague, another extremist of the period, who later claimed that he knew too much about establishment figures to be prosecuted.[55] He was shot dead in January 1982, a killing claimed by the INLA, shortly before the inquiry into the Kincora affair. McGrath had been jailed for his part in Kincora in December 1981. In the course of the House of Lords debate on the Civil Partnership Bill (involving State recognition of gay relationships) in the summer of 2004, the Ulster Unionist peer, Lord Maginnis, invoked Kincora in advocating Northern Ireland's exclusion from the legislation, thus playing glibly to the pejorative perception of a widely applicable link between homosexuality and the abuse of minors.[56] Maginnis was spokesman for a phalanx of Ulster peers, including Cunningham's friend Lord Molyneaux and his 1960s adversary in the House of Commons, Lord Fitt.

IV

It would be too convenient to draw the conclusion from Knox Cunningham's relationship with Forrest Reid that the two men's preoccupation with boys in a literary context and the homosexual content of parts of their correspondence led Cunningham into scandalous pursuits. There is no firm evidence that he knew what was happening at Kincora, far less that he participated, although his association with McGrath begs obvious questions. However, the degree of familiarity displayed by Reid in his letters, and the predominance of boy-related and homoerotic themes, suggests strongly that Cunningham had decided homosexual leanings in spite of his marriage – it may or may not be significant that there were no children – and that he led something of a double life, or even several lives. There was nothing particularly unusual about this, nor about Cunningham's lack of public support for homosexual rights. In view of what has been claimed about him, Lord Boothby's declaration during the Wolfenden controversy that there was a 'homosexual underground threatening British youth' would appear to rank a lot higher on the hypocrisy scale.[57]

It might be speculated that Cunningham on the one hand desired to uphold the socially and culturally conservative nature of Ulster, for which he felt a nostalgic and sentimental allegiance, rather akin indeed to that of Reid,[58] while on the other he took advantage of the opportunities of escape into a kind of fantasy world in London, something again with a Reid-like quality, even if it is doubtful that Reid at any time took his passions to the point of sexual gratification. Perhaps Cunningham relished a secret layer of his life as Unionist politician,[59] confidant of the Prime Minister and married man, and saw it as providing emotional and erotic ballast. Like Reid, Cunningham probably did not welcome the prospect of homosexuality proclaiming itself in society. Yet, notwithstanding his establishment position and ancestral politics, Cunningham can be said to have represented a potentially subversive kind of outsiderness, much in the manner of the novelist whose deep affection he enjoyed.

Notes and References

1 Forrest Reid (1875–1947) wrote some fifteen works of fiction between 1904 and 1944, along with two volumes of autobiography, works of criticism and a volume of poetry. A good summary of his achievements and introduction to his work is provided by Robert Greacen in his *Rooted in Ulster* (Belfast: Lagan, 2000).
2 John Boyd, *The Middle of My Journey* (Belfast: Blackstaff, 1990), pp. 62–3.
3 *The Ulster-Scot*, December 2003.
4 See entry in *Who's Who*, Vol. VII, 1971–80 (London: A. & C. Black, 1981).
5 John Boyd, *The Middle of My Journey*, p. 63.
6 See Jeffrey Dudgeon, *Roger Casement: The Black Diaries* (Belfast: Belfast, 2002), p. 613.
7 Public Records Office of Northern Ireland (PRONI), MIC. 45.
8 See Chris Moore, *The Kincora Scandal* (Dublin: Marino, 1996).
9 Robin Bryans, *The Dust Has Never Settled* (London: Honeyford, 1992). Bryans was born in Belfast in 1928. He became a travel writer and published *Ulster: A Journey Through the Six Counties* in 1964. He also wrote, under the name Robert Harbison, four volumes of autobiography.
10 Moore, *The Kincora Scandal*, pp. 86–91; Martin Dillon, *God and the Gun* (London: Orion, 1997), pp. 216–19.
11 See Brian Taylor, *The Green Avenue: The Life and Writings of Forrest Reid, 1875–1947* (Cambridge: Cambridge University Press, 1980), pp. 148–9.
12 Reid to Cunningham, 10 November 1938. All letters from Reid to Cunningham in PRONI, MIC. 45/1.
13 Boyd, *The Middle of My Journey*, pp. 64–7.
14 See review by Ruth Dudley Edwards of Elaine Sisson's *Pearses's Patriots: St. Enda's and the Cult of Boyhood* in the *Irish Times*, 3 July 2004.
15 Taylor, *The Green Avenue*, Chapter 4.
16 Reid to Cunningham, 31 May 1940.
17 Reid to Cunningham, 30 November 1940.
18 Reid to Cunningham, 1 December 1944.
19 Noel Annan, *Our Age* (London: Fontana, 1991), Chapter 7.
20 Brian Taylor, *Green Avenue*, pp. 174–6.
21 See Colin Cruise, 'Error and Eros: The Fiction of Forrest Reid as a Defence of Homo-sexuality', in Eibhear Walshe (ed.), *Sex, Nation and Dissent in Irish Writing* (Cork: Cork University Press, 1997). The influence on Reid of the Cambridge 'Apostles' group is pertinent here: see W. McCann, '"Apostles" in Belfast: H. O. Meredith and E. M. Forster', *The Linenhall Review*, 1:4 (Winter 1984–5), 11–13.
22 Reid to Cunningham, 16 March 1945.
23 Reid to Cunningham, 15 October 1940. See also letter dated 3 May 1943.
24 Reid to Cunningham, 31 May 1944.
25 Reid to Cunningham, 7 November 1940.
26 Reid to Cunningham, postcard, 2 March 1943.
27 Reid to Cunningham, 16 September 1943.

28 Colin Cruise, 'Error and Eros'; see, for example, Reid's novel *Peter Waring* (London: Penguin, 1946), pp. 108–10.

29 Jeffrey Dudgeon, *Roger Casement*, p. 613, and Moore, *Kincora*.

30 See the treatment of such an establishment figure in the context of the gay subculture of 1980s London in Alan Hollinghurst, *The Swimming Pool Library* (London: Penguin, 1988).

31 Reid to Cunningham, 23 September 1940.

32 Bryans is the source for Moore's claims in *Kincora*. However, the latest biographer of Anthony Blunt is clearly sceptical of his reliability; see Miranda Carter, *Anthony Blunt: His Lives* (London: Macmillan, 2001), pp. 475–6.

33 Comments made by Leitch to the author and to Jeffrey Dudgeon.

34 See Taylor, *The Green Avenue*, pp. 138, 166. See comments on Gilbert's relationship with Reid in Greacen, *Rooted in Ulster*, p. 37.

35 Reid to Cunningham, 12 November 1939.

36 See Eamonn Hughes, 'Ulster of the Senses', in Damian Smyth (ed.), *Lost Fields*, a supplement to *Fortnight*, 306 (1993).

37 See letter from Reid to Cunningham, 15 June 1940.

38 Reid to Cunningham, 29 October 1943.

39 Reid to Cunningham, 14 August 1945.

40 Reid to Cunningham, 22 August 1945.

41 See, for example, V. S. Pritchett, 'Escaping from Belfast', *London Review of Books*, 5–18 February 1981.

42 Russell Burlingham, *Forrest Reid: A Portrait and a Study* (London: Faber, 1953). Burlingham shared Cunningham's conservative political views.

43 See letters concerning the memorial in PRONI, MIC. 45/2.

44 See letters and cards from Forster to Cunningham, *c.* 1954–5, in MIC. 45/2. Forster's tribute to Reid written in 1947 after Reid's death was subsequently published in his *Two Cheers for Democracy*.

45 The letter is probably from 1958, given that the Wolfenden Report was published in September 1957.

46 For the impact of Wolfenden, see Hugh David, *On Queer Street* (London: Harper Collins, 1997), Chapters 8 and 9; Jeffrey Weeks, *Sex, Politics and Society: The Regulation of Sexuality Since 1800* (London: Longman, 1989), pp. 239–44; and Roger Davidson and Gayle Davis, '"A Field for Private Members": The Wolfenden Committee and Scottish Homosexual Law Reform, 1950–67', *Twentieth-Century British History*, 15:2 (2004), 174–201.

47 See Dudgeon, *Roger Casement*, pp. 543–6; House of Commons Debates 1958–9, Vol. 596, *c.* 390–9.

48 See Richard Aldous, 'Perfect Peace? Macmillan and Ireland', in Richard Aldous and Sabine Lee (eds), *Harold Macmillan: Aspects of a Political Life* (Basingstoke: Macmillan, 1999).

49 Bryans, *Dust*, pp. 51–3.

50 See Anthony Summers and Stephen Dorrill, *Honeytrap* (London: Coronet, 1988). Bryans is also a source for claims made in this book. Macmillan's most authoritative biographer considers Cunningham to be one of those culpable for not informing the Prime Minister regarding the rumour and innuendo sweeping the House of Commons. See Alistair Horne, *Macmillan, 1957-86* (London: Macmillan, 1989), p. 493.

51 Bryans, *Dust*, p. 52.

52 Reid to Cunningham, 29 October 1943.

53 For example, *Protestant Telegraph*, 1 May 1971. For the *Clydevalley* episode, see Ed Moloney and Andy Pollak, *Paisley* (Dublin: Poolbeg, 1986), pp. 164–6.

54 See Moore, *Kincora*; Dillon, *God and the Gun*; and Aldous, 'Perfect Peace?'.

55 See Paul Foot, *Who Framed Colin Wallace?* (London: Pan, 1990), pp. 142–3.

56 Speech on Civil Partnership Bill, House of Lords, 1 July 2004.

57 See Davidson and Davis, '"A Field for Private Members"'.

58 See observations of E. M. Forster in his contribution to the Reid celebration in Belfast in 1952 in Cunningham's papers, MIC. 45/2.

59 See Aldous, 'Perfect Peace?', regarding the comments made about Cunningham resembling someone from the secret service.

Reviews

Subversive Law Subverted

Heather Laird, *Subversive Law in Ireland, 1879–1920*. Dublin: Four Courts Press, 2005. ISBN 1-815182-876-1. €45 hbk.

I should from the outset declare an interest: I am in the peculiar and perhaps unenviable position of reviewing a book that contains an extended critique of my own work. To be criticized is, for any postcolonial scholar, especially one working in or on Ireland, commonplace; to be critiqued interestingly and tellingly is, sadly, all too rare. But Heather Laird has written a book, *Subversive Law in Ireland*, which is of compelling interest throughout and as persuasive in its overall argument as it is in its detailed and original archival scholarship. The thesis of the book is clearly stated from the outset. Laird argues that 'resistance to an official legal system . . . created a space for the establishment of alternative legal concepts and structures that monitored and regulated the behaviour of rural communities'. Her work shows that, against what has often been implied in official reports and in historical works, the resistance to British law in Ireland led not to 'mere anarchy' but to the invocation and practice of a kind of 'counterlegality'. As Laird goes on to argue: 'Law in Ireland was not only a medium for the implementation of English rule; it was also a fundamental component of anti-colonial resistance, with the concept of an alternative system of control capable of supplanting a despised official law functioning as one of the most substantive threats to successive colonial administrations.' The elements of this 'alternative system' are both culturally complex and effective: they not only 'mimicked, paralleled, appropriated, parodied, [and] subverted' official law, they succeeded at critical moments in *displacing* it.

This is, I think, the crucial claim of Laird's work, which covers the period from the land war to the Dáil courts of the Anglo-Irish war. Although part of the appeal of popular resistance, and not only in Ireland, lies in its extravagant, ritualistic often theatrical use of symbolic forms of protest that express defiance and disaffection from colonial rule or class domination, Laird's point is that those symbolic elements are not merely symbolic but come to compose materially effective forms of resistance to colonial rule, forming 'one of the most *substantive* threats' that it faced. To argue this is to demand a serious accounting of forms of popular resistance that are often dismissed or underestimated as mere preludes to more organized, modern political movements guided by nationalism or Marxism, without which they remain inchoate, sporadic and aimless. And Laird does more than argue this point. Through extensive and original archival work, which reads the official archive of government papers, administrators' memoirs and the national and local press, she pieces together a detailed and interpretively imaginative picture of the resistance to British law and its social norms and of the alternative system of codes and sanctions that displaced the institutions that administrators struggled to normalize. As Laird points out, 'alternative law has functioned as a fundamental component of Irish agrarian agitation since at least the emergence of Whiteboyism in the 1760s' and it is notable that the issues around which it has been articulated most clearly have to do with land and tenancy rights.[1] A series of practices and sanctions emerged from the long-standing concern of agrarian movements to protect tenure and rights of commons, to defend against eviction or exorbitant rents, culminating in the land war in a set of institutionalized modes of social sanction. The most famous of these was the boycott, but all were able to gain more force than official law itself by virtue of the immediacy and effectiveness of their sanctions. What the administration thought of as *de jure* law was in fact to a very great extent displaced by the *de facto* legitimacy of popular institutions of an increasingly formal kind.

As Laird shows, the effectiveness of this alternative system derived from the accumulation of precedents and of customary practices and sanctions that could be mobilized and virtually codified for the purposes of land agitation in the 1870s and 1880s. But they could also form the basis for the legitimation and the conduct of more spontaneous if widespread forms of social protest. One fascinating, and often hilarious, segment of *Subversive Law* concerns the extensive resistance to the sacred Anglo-Irish rite of hunting that took place in many parts of Ireland in the season of 1881–2. The anti-hunting agitation was in part an expression of the community's 'desire to assert control over the land they occupied and determine the conditions under which others might gain access to it' and in that respect was a popular effort to challenge the property claims of the landlord class. But it also challenged a whole set of implicit and symbolic rights and rites of hunting that was itself an assertion – exclusive rights to game and to control of natural resources or access to land. Accordingly the protests included not only blocking the path of the hunt, but counter-symbolic activities such as the 'people's hunts' or organized and charitable poaching, the function of which was to protest against traditional landlord prerogatives and which were ritually based on such popular customs as the Stephen's Day wren hunt.

These protests were the product of clashing understandings of what constituted norms and rights in the context of colonial society and were the signs of deep cultural divisions that had prevented English law from ever attaining legitimacy or the appearance of impartiality. One chapter, which forms almost a self-contained essay, is a discussion of the impact of the resulting clash of 'conflicting systems of control' on Emily Lawless's *Hurrish*, a discussion which amply demonstrates how 'the novel compels us to rethink theoretical models and premises developed in the study of the metropolitan novel and question an uncritical application of such models to Irish literature'. Laird's analysis certainly makes one of the most effective cases to date for that proposition and suggests a culturally informed approach that could valuably be extended to other works. Another richly suggestive question raised throughout the book is that of the Irish attitude to property. Numerous English as well as Irish commentators, including John Stuart Mill and George Campbell, believed that the Irish maintained through the nineteenth century views of communal property based on older Gaelic laws and customs, notably those codified in the recently translated Brehon laws. Laird does not attempt to resolve the issue, which was widely debated and not, as she shows, in necessarily predictable ways, but her discussion does show in important ways how such earlier arguments enter into and help to explain the emergence in thinkers like James Connolly of concepts like Celtic Communism which have all too often been dismissed as romantic nostalgia. As Laird's work richly demonstrates, whatever the long history of their precedents, notions like the importance of the commons or of popular rights to land tenure are developed as much in the crucible of resistant practice as they are in discursive frameworks, an insight that is, I think, in keeping with Connolly's own analysis of Irish culture and history.

Mention of Connolly leads me to the final chapter of *Subversive Law*, 'Theories of Resistance', which is a sustained critique of Subaltern Studies and postcolonial theory and what Laird terms 'the damaging implications' of their 'constricted notions of resistance and subalternity'. The critique is forceful by virtue of Laird's intimate and scrupulous knowledge of the theory and practice of subaltern historiography and, unlike many criticisms of both subaltern and postcolonial theory, is distinguished by being sympathetic to the overall projects of both. The thrust of her argument is that, in jettisoning a progressive adherence to modern modes of both historiography and political mobilization, subaltern theory fails to offer any viable means either for the subaltern to exit the disabling conditions of subalternity (though in fact both Dipesh Chakrabarty and Gayatri Spivak have argued that, paradoxically, it is impossible 'not to not want' that exit to take place) or for the subaltern to offer a sustained and substantive resistance to the State. By the same token, 'the persistence of the non-modern [in subaltern formations] is not enough on its own to counter capitalism'. In effect, she argues, subaltern historiography (including my own work) consigns the marginal formations of society to a condition of perpetual marginality, to 'the vision of an unreformed/unreformable state going about its business more or less unaffected by fragmentary elements that often only have to be there to be resistant'. Accordingly, political independence itself, it is charged, might as well not have taken place or been struggled for. There will be great rejoicing in the courts of revisionism at this prospect.

There are, of course, numerous points of detail on which I would have to disagree with this account of either subaltern historiography's implications or my own, and, by implication, Irish postcolonialism generally, and it would be good to have space to do so fully. Failing that, let me commence where Laird ends, with her own claim that her work provides 'a credible alternative to approaches currently predominant in postcolonial studies . . . the Marxist perspective'. The problem is that Laird's own powerful and finely researched analysis scarcely adheres at all to what most readers would recognize as Marxist analysis. There is little discussion of economically determined social relations, except in the most general framework of landlord versus tenant conflict and, later, conflicts between 'strong farmers' and landless labourers. There is little at all on the vexed question of the 'colonial mode of production' and how it might be relevant to Irish conditions. There is little to suggest that what occurs in rural Ireland in the period she discusses is actually 'revolutionary' in the Marxist sense, although what occurs is indeed a considerable transfer of ownership in the land. To the contrary, the overarching tale is one of what Mary Kotsonouris (with whose work on the Dáil courts Laird's penultimate chapter is in tune) has dubbed 'retreat from revolution'. In a sense, then, Laird's actual work, against the grain of the theoretical reflections of her conclusion, confirms the general problematic that subaltern and postcolonial theory has been working, if not in every detail of its conclusions. The trajectory of anticolonial struggle, in Ireland as elsewhere, is shaped and dominated by a state-oriented nationalism that aims to contain and reduce the multiple forms of subaltern dissidence, generally in the name of well-regulated property relations or, in other terms, control of the means of production. Postcolonial theory, coming to the problem of ongoing emancipation from a perspective informed by the new nation state's arrest of decolonization, tries to prise the story of popular resistance and recalcitrance from its occlusion, not in order to celebrate a condition of eternal marginality or to declare the irrelevance of the independence struggle, but to trace the possibilities for alternative social imaginaries that have not been captured by the State. Over and again, those popular initiatives are, as Laird's work shows, suppressed or recuperated into élite-dominated forms of struggle or organization, but it is no less true that they provide continual evidence of the limits of domination. Such histories demand the rethinking of the terms and ends of Marxist as of standard nationalist and revisionist narratives, and in this respect are in tune with Frantz Fanon's overall analysis, which Laird invokes, of anticolonial resistance and its postcolonial fates. Above all, they are in tune with his insight in the concluding pages of *The Wretched of the Earth*, that decolonization demands something other than an imitation of the European state and its institutions. To the history and to the imagination of that endeavour, Heather Laird's *Subversive Law in Ireland* makes in the end a magnificent and indispensable contribution.

DAVID LLOYD

Note

1 It is worth noting, however, that Nassau Senior in 1843 associated the 'combinations' of urban workers with the agrarian movements in Ireland as equivalent instances of 'establishing a rival law with rules and sanctions of its own'. See Nassau Senior, 'Ireland', *Edinburgh Review*, January 1844, 200. He clearly grasped, as many British commentators on Ireland did, the existence and the extent of the 'alternative system' that Laird describes. It would be interesting to see an extension of Laird's work to the operation of urban organizations of labour in nineteenth-century Ireland.

Synthesizing Early Modern Women

Mary O'Dowd, *A History of Women in Ireland, 1500–1800*. Harlow: Pearson Education, 2005. ISBN 0-58240-429-0. £21.99 hbk.

Mary O'Dowd's new book is a culmination of more than a decade's work, during which she has both been a major contributor to Irish women's history and has encouraged many of those working in the field. The volume that she co-edited with Margaret MacCurtain in the early 1990s, *Women in Early Modern Ireland*, with its famous pink cover, has been the starting-point for those interested in the topic ever since its publication. The present work is a very readable synthesis of some of the work that O'Dowd and others have been doing since then. It also presents the results of a comprehensive trawl of other references to women in the secondary literature and an impressive array of primary sources.

The book is divided between four themes: politics, the economy, religion and education, and ideas, though naturally many issues cut across these categories. The political and economic aspects of marriage, widowhood and remarriage are dealt with particularly well. The role of marriage in the dynastic strategies of early modern families is a central theme. One of the most interesting sections of the book deals with the financial aspects of marriage, elucidating the dowry, jointure and dower arrangements made for women from different sections of society and ethnic backgrounds, as well as their inheritance rights. The influence of women within the home is also considered, alongside evidence for the promulgation in Ireland of literature and ideas prescribing their subordinate role within marriage. Information is provided about their everyday participation in the household economy and decision-making regarding domestic and family business matters, adding to the European picture of considerable hidden female influence in their husbands' affairs.

An account of the religious activities of women is to be found in the third part of the work. Certain late medieval laywomen are demonstrated to have been key patrons of the Church, though there were few female members of religious orders by the time of the dissolution of the monasteries. Opportunities for women to become nuns were few prior to the eighteenth century (when several convents were founded), though some pursued religious vocations in Europe or within their family homes. There is further proof here of the role of women within all religious denominations in preserving religious orthodoxy through the provision of spiritual guidance for their families and servants, as well as of their involvement in religious groups such as the Quakers, Baptists and Methodists. O'Dowd also considers some of the devotional practices that particularly attracted female participation. There is, however, little discussion of women's participation in religious conflict and controversy (though the ambiguous position of the wives of Protestant clergy is mentioned). Indeed, the book fairly consistently shies away from issues of conflict, violence and criminality.

There is a strong consciousness throughout of the changes that occurred in women's lives over the three centuries covered. For example, the centrality of marriage in the creation of political alliances declined as the old kin-based élites were undermined, though even in the eighteenth century 'family networks could also be political networks'. As a result, the political influence exercised by aristocratic women within marriage, especially those from Old English families, also declined. However, new opportunities for a public role for those women with wealth and leisure developed in the eighteenth century, through involvement in societies, patriotic movements such the 'Wear Irish' campaign, and involvement in charitable work in setting up hospitals and schools. Increased access to education, though it was often limited in its scope, allowed greater engagement with religion, business and politics. We see women reading for pleasure, and the erosion of the stigmatization of women's published writing is also traced. For women from the middling and poorer sorts, new employment opportunities might be offered by the expanding towns, and the concomitant expansion of commerce. O'Dowd identifies women in a variety of businesses, some of them short-lived, emphasizing their roles in the food and cloth trades and in shopkeeping. The number of positions available to domestic servants also grew, though the opportunities available to servants prior to the 1700s are probably underestimated.

An intriguing theme is the less advantageous position that Gaelic women enjoyed in comparison to their Old and New English counterparts. They were less likely to be literate. The continuation of divorce and serial marriage amongst the Gaelic élites meant that wives were easily put aside, thereby reducing their political influence. The fact that they were rarely entitled to hold property in their own right also had an impact on their place in society. Influence could be found, however, in hospitality and through patronage of poets and the Church. In the end, it was the expansion of English law in relation to dower and inheritance rights that most improved their practical position.

Throughout, the author weaves in vivid examples of women of very different characters glimpsed in diverse circumstances. Here find the well-known figures of Gráinne O'Malley, the pirate, and Nano Nagle, the founder of schools and a religious order. The less famous are here too: people like Fionnuala and Margaret O'Brien, founders of Franciscan friaries in Donegal and Leitrim; Christian Hamilton, temporarily disinherited for marrying without her father's permission, but reconciled with him when she presented him with a grandchild; and Elizabeth Kehoe and Mary Roche, inhabitants of the Magdalen Asylum set up by Lady Arabella Denny to assist in the education and rehabilitation of Dublin prostitutes.

This is in many ways a very traditional kind of women's history. Women are looked at in terms of their position in economic and public life, their participation in religion, their levels of education and literacy, and the ways in which they were represented in literary works that promoted the ideal of patriarchy, but whose precepts were generally mitigated in practice. The most significant omission, acknowledged by O'Dowd herself, relates to the emotional side of relationships with husbands and relatives, as well as the role of women as parents and grandparents, and in the community as neighbours, 'gossips' and friends. Though the sources that can tell us about these are patchy, they can be found. There is much more to be said also about women's participation in crime and incidents when they were victims of criminal acts and of violence, especially domestic violence. The lives of wealthy women come through better than those of the poor. But O'Dowd's work is not intended as a comprehensive survey of every aspect of women's lives. Such a survey would have added many more pages and would doubtless have swamped what is achieved here. This book will certainly help to 'set the research agenda for the history of women in Ireland, 1500–1800 for many years to come', both by providing a solid springboard for that research and identifying avenues for future investigation.

CLODAGH TAIT

Sophisticated Feminisms

Rosemary Cullen Owens, *A Social History of Women in Ireland, 1870–1970*. Dublin: Gill & Macmillan, 2005. ISBN 0-71713-681-7. €29.99 hbk.

Linda Connolly and Tina O'Toole, *Documenting Irish Feminisms: The Second Wave*. Dublin: Woodfield Press, 2005. ISBN 0-95342-935-0. €22 hbk.

These two publications are important milestones in the development of women's history and of feminist history in Ireland. Despite the wealth of scholarship published over the last three decades on aspects of women's lives in nineteenth- and twentieth-century Ireland, the efforts of teachers and researchers have been significantly hampered by the absence of a comprehensive survey history. As Rosemary Cullen Owens points out, the difficulties have been still greater for the general reader, for whom access to the published material is even more problematic. *A Social History of Ireland, 1870–1970* is intended to amend this situation and does so ably, attesting to the quantity and quality of contemporary research into Irish women's history but more particularly to Owens's breadth of scholarship, analytical strength and narrative skill. It is both an approachable and stylish introductory text and a gateway to further reading.

Owens's greatest contribution lies in the contextualization of her material. The campaigns for legislative and social reform, which provide the framework for the text, are related in turn to the economic and social circumstances that gave rise to them, the broader ideological and political agendas that informed them and the degree to which change resulted from the unanticipated interaction between social policy and social reality. Owens argues, for example, that, despite the preference of some Home Rule politicians and of Archbishop Paul Cullen for a domestic model of education for girls, academic standards rose due to the educational requirements of girls intending to emigrate and the intense competition for prizes between Protestant and Catholic schools in the wake of the Intermediate Education Act, 1878. At the heart of her analysis are class and land ownership as determinants of women's lives, as post-Famine patterns of inheritance – of the shop as well as the farm – gave rise to a society dependent on emigration and permanent celibacy and the position of women declined.

A Social History of Women in Ireland, 1870–1970 is divided into four chronological and thematic parts. The first traces the origins of the nineteenth-century women's movement, the suffrage campaign and the broadening agenda of the movement's social and legislative goals. The causes and consequences of increased access to education are given particular attention, as is the feminization of religious and philanthropic activism. Part Two examines the emergence of the radical suffrage campaign in 1908 and its relationships with the politics of unionism, nationalism, republicanism and labour. While the social structure of post-Famine Ireland informs both these parts, it is brought into sharper focus in Part Three, which examines rural and urban marriage and family life, work, paid employment and trade unionism. The treatment of women's experience post-1920 concentrates on independent Ireland, an approach that is mirrored in the final part, which considers the status of women in the new State and the surfacing of campaigns for equal citizenship and social improvement.

Owens argues that, broadly speaking, Irish women in the period between 1870 and 1970 fell into two categories: a minority of 'questioners' who moved, over time, from requesting social justice for all those in need to asserting the particular needs and rights of women. Although the 'questioners' determine the shape of *A Social History of Women in Ireland, 1870 1970*, its content provides the most thorough and nuanced treatment to date of what Owens describes as the 'accepting' majority.

Linda Connolly and Tina O'Toole's *Documenting Irish Feminisms: The Second Wave* is also a study of 'questioners', beginning where Owens ends, with the emergence of second-wave feminism in the early 1970s. The publication is one of the projects undertaken in connection with the fruitful PRTLI-funded 'Women in Irish Society Project', based at University College Cork. It demonstrates the increasing sophistication of Irish feminisms in interrogating their own past and critically analysing the 'dynamic of difference'.

Drawing on Connolly's earlier analysis of second-wave feminism from the perspective of social movements theory, *The Irish Women's Movement from Revolution to Devolution* (2001), *Documenting Irish Feminisms* is aimed at a less specialist audience. It also broadens the scope of analysis by moving beyond acceptance of the tactical advantages of difference in the context of liberal feminist mainstreaming, to examine the influence of a variety of feminisms on both the Women's Movement and Irish society.

The interaction between republican and non-republican feminisms and between the feminist movement and lesbian activism is examined. In a chapter on 'Feminism, Community and Class', Connolly and O'Toole draw attention to the recent debates on the exclusion of some women from feminist agendas and the historiographical neglect of socialist feminism. The most original and valuable result of the authors' concentration on difference and autonomous activism is in a chapter on feminist cultural projects incorporating graphics, the feminist press and publishing projects, such as those of Arlen House and Attic Press.

As the title suggests, the main aim of *Documenting Irish Feminisms* is to bring into the public domain the documentary legacy of second-wave feminism from a variety of archives. The authors argue that 'archives are political entities and collecting and preserving archival material is a political act' and suggest that feminist archives are distinguished by their willingness to collect ephemera and objects such as banners and t-shirts. Whether or not this approach challenges the traditional concept of an archive, its virtues are effectively demonstrated here by the representation of a wide range of 'documents', including badges, posters and Clodagh Boyd's wonderfully candid photographs. The decision to reproduce the more conventional documents as facsimiles is a particularly happy one and highlights the degree to which passion, imagination and humour made up for lack of material resources.

As with *A Social History of Women in Ireland*, teachers and researchers will have particular reason to be grateful for this publication. As part of the first government-funded 'university-led study and analysis of the legacy of feminism and the women's movement', it is itself part of the documentary legacy of one of the not wholly untroubled developments it chronicles, the establishment of feminist studies as an academic discipline.

SUSANNAH RIORDAN

Reflexive Images

Neil Corcoran, *Elizabeth Bowen: The Enforced Return*. Oxford: Oxford University Press, 2004. ISBN 0-19818-690-8. £45 hbk.

Elizabeth Bowen has been very well served critically in recent years, particularly by Roy Foster's two essays on her Irishness and also by Heather Bryant Jordan's, *How Will the Heart Endure: Elizabeth Bowen and the Landscape of War*, amongst others. Neil Corcoran's new book is a welcome development in the field of Bowen studies and draws fruitfully on these and other earlier studies. Sensibly, in his reading of Bowen, Corcoran eschews a chronological or linear approach to the trajectory of her writings, as Victoria Glendinning's biography and Hermione Lee's pioneering study, *Elizabeth Bowen* (revised and reissued in 1999), both use this approach to read her work within the context of her life and to good effect. Instead he opens his book with a useful discussion of Bowen's fictive representation of letters, of letter writing and even of imaginary letters and sees these moments in her writing as an indication of the centrality of literary production within Bowen's imagination. Writing, rewriting, the act of imagining and production are all interpreted by Corcoran as key metaphorical elements of Bowen's work and this supports his convincing and thoughtful argument that Bowen is 'a writer deeply impressed by the ambitions of High Modernism'. As a modernist, her fascination was with what had been written and this led her again and again to rewrite, to test what had gone before, and to enact processes of revision and return. Thus he structures his analysis of her writing around the idea of the enforced return, her return to earlier traditions of writing, attempts at modernist experimentation and generic revision. As he puts it himself: 'The "unexpected reflex" – what another essay calls "The Bend Back" – is the constant return in Elizabeth Bowen: the reflex as the thing you do without thinking, which you cannot prevent yourself from doing, but also as the reflection and self-reflection which is the writing self bent back, again and again, on images that will allow nothing to take their place, images that are therefore close to being obsessions. The most substantial of these in Bowen are, I believe, images of Ireland, childhood and war.'

As a result, Corcoran shapes his reading of most (but not all) of Bowen's writings to address these three central preoccupations in her imagination (Ireland, childhood and war), and this gives his non-linear approach a focus and a thematic coherence. In his introduction, he is one of the few writers on Bowen to pick up on a tiny but significant moment in her 1951 travel book, the bizarre but rewarding *A Time in Rome*, where Bowen visits Keats's grave in the Protestant cemetery but pays more attention to a nearby grave. This grave is of two young Anglo-Irish women, the Misses Moores of Moorehill in County Waterford, who died young in Rome in 1805. Bowen's whole project in *A Time in Rome*, a book rarely dealt with critically, is reflected in this moment and Corcoran picks up on her attempt to convert the centre of Catholicism, Rome, to an Anglo-Irish garrison town – her appropriation of the Misses Moores being part of this.

His first chapter, perhaps his most successful, deals with Bowen and Ireland, and, although Foster, Jordan and McCormack have all written on this aspect of Bowen's imagination to good effect, Corcoran manages to put his own stamp on this critical area and finds original ways in which to read Bowen's fractured and complicated relationship to her own Anglo-Irish identity. He opens with a reading of her 1942 family history, *Bowen's Court*, which then allows him to move back to her War of Independence novel, *The Last September* (1929), and then onwards to her least successful Irish fiction, *A World of Love* (1955). Corcoran's approach works best in this chapter, particularly in his account of *The Last September*, where his attention to tiny details is masterly. An example is his reading of the crack in Lois Farquar's wash hand basin becoming the fault line, the fissure where her incomplete, dissolving identity is made manifest. Likewise he finds in the naming of Lois's dead mother Laura the ghostly presence within the novel haunting the laurel bushes, reappearing as 'the Anglo-Irish ghost par excellence', the emblem of loss, dissolution and immanent disaster.

In his section on childhood, his appraisal of *The House in Paris*, her 1935 novel and possibly her strongest, is skilful and deft, seeing Bowen's portrayal of Max as 'there precisely to define the anti-Semitism of the Michealises and through them, of upper-class educated English liberal culture' rather than viewing him as a manifestation of Bowen's own anti-Semitism. Likewise his analysis of her most popular novel, *The Death of the Heart* (1938), is adroit, but I have some reservations about his account of her final novel, *Eva Trout* (1968). His argument here is that '[in] some of this critical work too, it can be almost seem as though the whole writerly career is being read backwards through the lens of *Eva Trout* and for me *Eva Trout* is, as I shall argue, a distorting mirror'. In my introduction to the 1999 re-issue of *Eva Trout* (cited in his excellent bibliography) I have argued that Bowen was moving gradually towards the nightmare vision of alienated self in *Eva Trout*, and I was hoping he might address some of the arguments I advanced in that introduction around the idea of displaced selfhood in this novel.

However, he is perceptive in seeing this as a novel where Bowen brings, as he puts it, 'into its foreground the lesbian element which is so often present but partly submerged in the earlier novels' but goes on to comment that Patricia Juliana Smith's idea that it works as a de-essentialization of heterosexuality and the establishment of lesbian panic 'makes *Eva Trout* seem more single minded that I find it'.

His section on war, encompassing her London Blitz writings, *The Demon Lover and Other Stories* and her masterpiece *The Heat of the Day*, is admirable and, overall, this tripartite thematic approach works. Thus, in this new study, Neil Corcoran both summarizes the formidable range of critical perspectives on Bowen and advances our engagement with this most rewarding Anglo-Irish novelist.

EIBHEAR WALSHE

North and South of the Lee

John Crowley, Robert Devoy, Denis Linehan and Patrick O'Flanagan (eds), *Atlas of Cork City*. Cork: Cork University Press, 2005. ISBN 1-89518-380-8. €59 hbk.

Cork University Press, which has launched ambitious and outstandingly successful books like the *Atlas of the Irish Rural Landscape* and Billy Colfer's *The Hook Peninsula*, is well served by this volume, which promises to be equally successful. Its form and its weight – almost two kilos – make it literally a coffee-table book, though its relatively modest price will ensure that it will reach the table of many homes, not only in Cork but beyond. Its appeal is enhanced by a profusion – one per page, on average – of maps, tables and remarkably fresh photographs.

While not forgetting a wider hinterland, its focus is the city and its immediate environs. The book starts with the natural environment, prehistory and early history, and ends with the changes and challenges in recent decades in the man-made environment. Sections number 1, 'The City in the Landscape: The Environmental Heritage', number 2, 'Transformation: A Minor Port Town becomes a Major Atlantic Port', and number 5, 'Contemporary Transformations', are very coherent. Coherence breaks down, however, in many of the intervening chapters in sections 3 and 4 (which account for some half of the book). While a geographical focus is maintained in an emphasis (with accompanying maps) on distribution patterns, the chapters, though interesting in themselves, still leave the reader with an impression of a loss of editorial control. Chapters are of variable length; the flow is interrupted by subjects such as Nano Nagle, Father Mathew, St Fin Barre's

Cathedral, architecture, great houses and their art collections, and the Famine. Repetition is commonplace: some of section 4 on Cork in the twentieth century (pp. 266–89) could have fitted more meaningfully into section 5. As a result, the volume as a whole is very much less than the sum of its well-written and rewarding chapters. Themes such as architecture and country houses could have been amalgamated into a jointly written section. More relevantly still, the emphasis maintained throughout the volume on distribution maps together with the often-repeated distinction between Cork north and south of the Lee could have been a vehicle for a very tight restructuring of much of the contents. Absorbing and novel accounts, one on the location and changes in hurling clubs since the 1880s, the other on the story of musical bands, while compelling on their own merits, underline the point. The literary chapter is an extreme instance of the lack of control and its consequences. As it stands, in emphasizing O'Faolain and O'Connor as the two literary glories of the city, as all too often happens it appraises these opinionated and difficult men on their own assessment of themselves and devalorizes the entire cultural life of the city. Their lives and the themes in their writing would, however, have fitted comfortably into reorganized chapters as an evocation of aspects of the city, north and south of the Lee. In passing, as others merit attention, one notes with surprise that Seán Ó Ríordáin, in many ways a quintessential Corkman, is not mentioned.

In its central sections the volume becomes an encyclopedia more than an atlas, a fact of which the editors are aware, thus writing defensively in the preface that 'The five sections of the Atlas are not encyclopedic, but present a broad canvas upon which the city is portrayed'. In one sense this is not a fault, and if the number of authors, some sixty, is perhaps too large to admit of a coherent structure, the volume gains greatly in authority by expert accounts, whether of Cork cooking, road bowling, houses, painting, institutional features, religious sects, individual Corkmen, or for that matter in the confines of a single page of the city's charters. The book thus covers a very wide range of topics, for many of which information is not readily available elsewhere (though, if one views it on its own terms, which reach beyond geography, the Gaelic League, passing reference on one page apart, is oddly ignored).

In the early chapters the story of how the first real township on two islands gradually occupied the remainder of thirteen islands in the sluggish waters at the end of the tidal reaches of the Lee is well told, and in turn the final chapters are an up-to-date and largely geographical analysis of modern change, highlighting positive achievements as well as the inevitable negative features in the process of modernization. The city that offers the closest comparison to Cork is Nantes. While Cork began to cover over its inlets earlier than Nantes, it halted the process, whereas Nantes continued to do so into the 1960s. As a result, the waterways of Nantes are concealed today below hectares of car parking or under the gracious curve of the Cours des Cinquante Otages (reminiscent on a larger scale of the sinuous character of Patrick Street). Cork remains a magic mix of land and water. While very modest structures (at any rate in scale), the location of St Fin

Barre's Cathedral, the North Chapel and Shandon on higher ground gives them a vital role in a visual drama rivalled by no other Irish city, played in many vistas across the city's built-up marshes and surviving waterways.

Residents of Cork and visitors alike will profit from a preliminary consultation before forays into the city. For this reviewer, who has often heard of 'The Lough' without knowing what it really was, the book makes him anxious to visit it the next time he finds himself in Cork. It is a very small and personal illustration of the success of the often affectionate as well as scholarly tone of the volume in communicating its enthusiasms to the reader.

L. M. CULLEN

South Munster's Golden Age

David Dickson, *Old World Colony: Cork and South Munster, 1630–1830*. Cork: Cork University Press, 2005. ISBN 1 85918 355 7. €49 hbk.

This book is an authoritative piece of scholarly investigation into what was one of the most culturally and economically vibrant regions of Ireland in the modern period. Few Irish historians have attempted regional studies on this scale, which makes Dickson's work all the more important. *Old World Colony* is written in the best traditions of the *Annales* school of historical thought. The region is studied over the *longue durée* of two hundred years, where geography and agrarian conditions set the pace of change and development. Dickson is primarily concerned with the social, economic, political and cultural impact that resulted from the settlement of New English colonists from the beginning of the seventeenth century.

While south Munster's geographic location placed it in easy reach of the transatlantic and trans-European commercial networks, it was the unfolding relationship between the colonists and the existing inhabitants that led to a set of conditions that encouraged economic growth and expansion. In this study, Dickson reveals the middling and lower strata of society that too rarely appear in other histories. The actions, thoughts and economic well-being of merchants, small farmers, labourers and others are placed alongside those of the élite classes. Thus, for example, he places the concerns of those wishing to 'improve' their estates and the countryside against the stark realities of agrarian practice and relations. The length and conditions of leases, subletting and the rise of a rural middling gentry whose interests often differed from those of their landlords sometimes hindered attempts to order the landscape.

Much of the book concerns the interdependency of agriculture and commerce, and their contrasting fortunes during war and peace. Dickson argues that wartime was often the more profitable for merchants and farmers, despite the disturbances caused to international trading networks. Peace could often spell disaster for stretched businesses, evident especially after the Napoleonic wars. For Dickson the period between 1630 and 1830 is a story of the rise and slump of an economic powerhouse. Using import and export statistics, he has, for the first time, measured the region's commercial weight. South Munster was successful in adapting to international trends and constraints for the most part, but by the 1820s the region could no longer muster the strength to aggressively compete in a changed economic, and increasingly industrial, environment. Dickson provides in minute detail the shifts from wool to beef and butter, and later the impact of corn and barley. These changing patterns of agriculture affected the demography of the countryside. He identifies eleven distinct areas across the region, each with individual farming cultures, defined by soil type and geographic location. These reveal a patchwork of internal variations within the region. Over the period Cork city assumed a greater hegemony over the produce of south Munster, though smaller towns like Dungarvan, Youghal and Kinsale often retained an important role in the national and sometimes international economy.

Besides trade, the impact of landed entrepreneurs and, latterly, the military and national bodies, such as the Fishery Board, altered the landscape, whether in the impetus given to urban development or the construction of roads and harbours. Dickson also deals with other less visible processes of change. The growing use of money and formal leasing arrangements from the seventeenth century, the development of a bilingual society helped by the spread of English among Catholics in the eighteenth and the role of education are all discussed.

Politics is interwoven as just another but vital ingredient contributing to a seamless story. As a result it receives less prominence than in other similar studies, though it remains an important factor in the formation of identity in the region. Dickson examines both Catholic and Protestant sentiments after calamitous events, usually, though not always, imported from outside the region, such as the 1641 rebellion, the Williamite wars, the Scottish rebellion in 1745, as well as the Union and Emancipation episodes. Thus, for example, he tests the viability of historians' arguments about how real Jacobitism was in south Munster, where much of the Irish-language poetry sympathetic to the Stuarts was written. Dickson argues that, besides these literati, most Catholics paid lip service to the 'King over the water', while their clergy gave only passive support. Protestants recycled older fears of the first New English settlers, which increasingly became jaded over time as the threat of invasion receded. But tensions remained and eventually older animosities surfaced again in the 1780s and 1790s. Dickson highlights the agrarian nature of much of these disturbances, though influenced by political motives and actors such as the United Irishmen.

Old World Colony is essentially a story of several identities bound together by economics but divided religiously, culturally and politically. Although much of what the author says is already known, much of it from earlier published work by him, the strength of the book is in the way that often diverse material seems to effortlessly unfold into a lucid and comprehensive story. The book's other great strength lies in the fact that the roles of individual actors and informal processes remain important components in the larger but slower processes of economic, social and cultural change. Besides this, Dickson does great service in rebalancing the relative positions of the provinces and Dublin. Studies like this are important in contextualizing Irish history overall. In highlighting the kaleidoscope of different ideas and interests within a relatively small area, Dickson has indirectly warned against the dangers of generalizing about politics, the economy and culture at the national level. For local historians of this region, the book will provide a context for their own work, and certainly none should ignore it. Overall, *Old World Colony* will set a daunting though justifiable precedent for others interested in regional studies to follow. For the reader the book is a *tour de force*, full of detail, imagery and insights into south Munster's golden age. Anybody who takes up this book will be amply rewarded.

DAVID FLEMING

Pre-modern Terrors

Stuart McLean, *The Event and Its Terrors: Ireland, Famine, Modernity*. Stanford, California: Stanford University Press, 2004. ISBN 0-8047-4439-4 cloth. ISBN 0-8047-4440-8 pbk. US$50.00 hbk. US$20.95 pbk.

'How does one give death its due?', asks Stuart McLean in the opening line of *The Event and Its Terrors*. In a sense, this has been the question that has driven Famine scholarship down its many avenues over the past few decades. What marks out Stuart McLean's work from many of his predecessors is his answer, for McLean seems to be suggesting that the attempt to 'give death its due' in relation to the Famine, rather than being an ethical or even purely scholarly response to trauma, has been yet one more stratagem by which modernity relegates to the realm of the unreal anything – including death – that threatens to seep through the iron coffin of rationality.

McLean bases his argument on an idea that goes back to Max Weber: the concept of modernity as 'disenchantment'. McLean mentions Weber only in passing, choosing instead to develop a theoretical framework that brings together elements of Walter Benjamin's critique of modernity (particularly the influential essay 'The Storyteller'), Derrida's meditations on 'the gift' as that which disrupts economies of exchange, with detours into subaltern studies, Artaud's Theatre of Cruelty, and Kristevan theorization of the body. In the wrong hands, this could turn into a fairly indigestible brew; however, McLean manages to put together a theoretical scaffolding that serves his argument without becoming bogged down in the minutiae of debate. By the same token, he uses the critical distance created by his theoretical framework to survey contentious issues more strictly within Irish Studies, such as historical revisionism and commemoration, without feeling the need to roll up his sleeves and engage in the hand-to-hand combat that such topics still, apparently, seem to demand from some writers.

For the most part, this polite disengagement from the debates of Famine historiography makes *The Event and Its Terrors* refreshing. However, there are points at which a slightly more hands-on approach might have enriched the argument, particularly in the chapter dealing with Malthus and Irish political economy in the nineteenth century (where the complexity of the current historiographical debate is not really done justice); the same is true in what is a fairly cursory exploration of the gendering of Famine near the end of the book. By the same token, McLean uses the Derridean figure of spectrality to good effect when exploring the ways in which images of the Famine dead (and dying) disrupted the regime of representation, but seems unaware of similar work published in *The Irish Review* in 1995.

Having said this, the basic argument has an appealing clarity. Weber writes of a disenchanted world as one that has been 'robbed of the gods' through a devaluation of mystery, and McLean never strays far from this central idea. He makes the point succinctly in his opening pages by turning to William Wilde's preface to *Irish Popular Superstitions* (1852), in which Wilde claims that the Famine constituted a 'revolution', in that it had almost obliterated an oral tradition that had once peopled the landscape with remembered presences, natural and supernatural. The depopulated post-Famine landscapes of the West of Ireland were, in this sense, quite literally 'robbed of their gods' when the bearers of this orature died or emigrated during the Famine. McLean suggests that this process of disenchantment invests folklore with an aura of loss at the moment of its recording, so that the very act which might seem to preserve a premodern past is actually containing and assimilating that past within the structures of modern rationality and the media of modernity, particularly print.

The Event and Its Terrors goes on to suggest that the process of containing a premodern past within the structures of modernity is not confined to a single moment, but is, in fact, a continuous process. The same gestures of containment that we find with Wilde in the 1850s, for instance, can be seen in the work of the Folklore Commission in the 1930s, and McLean devotes a particularly convincing chapter to the politics of the Commission's work. Following through on the logic of his argument, McLean might have extended the scope of argument in the opposite historical direction. For instance, in the introduction to the first volume of his *Traits and Stories of the Irish Peasantry*, published in 1843, two years before the potato crop failed, William Carleton is already writing of the Irish peasantry as being in 'a transition state'; and Carleton in turn is stating a commonplace in much of the folkloric writing that appeared in Irish periodicals in the 1820s and 1830s, in which – even before the Famine – recording premodern beliefs is understood as a way of exposing and containing their irrationality and sheer Otherness.

In the end, McLean argues in *The Event and Its Terrors* that the very possibility of a Famine historiography – or, indeed, any kind of historiography, including the construction of a national history – is in some way predicated upon disenchantment, the banishment of the small gods of the potato fields. The supernatural, so much a part of a premodern orature, must become 'inadmissible' for 'even the most democratically minded historian' in order for history as a modern form of discourse to function at all. Inevitably, of course, this leads McLean into the familiar paradox of anyone broaching a critique of rationality; he must do so within the bounds of a rational academic argument constructed within the same terms, and with the same standards of evidence, that are the object of his critique. At this point, perhaps, this paradox is so well-worn that it no longer even chaffs; indeed, in the case of *The Event and Its Terrors*, it would be the rare reader who would not appreciate the elegant clarity with which McLean weaves a complex argument. The result is a work that effectively caps one phase of Irish Famine scholarship, in the process making one of the most original and thought-provoking contributions to the field of the past decade.

CHRIS MORASH

Science Matters

David Attis and Charles Mollan (eds), *Science and Irish Culture: Why the History of Science Matters in Ireland*, Vol. 1. Dublin: Royal Dublin Society, 2004. ISBN 0-86927-047-5. €20 hbk.

In 1912 war was fomenting in Europe, the third Home Rule Bill was approved in parliament and one of the earliest journals devoted to the history of science was founded. Twelve years later, devotees of this relatively new subject formed the History of Science Society in order to support the continued publication of *Isis*. The force behind the journal and the society, George Sarton, believed the history of science would lead the way to a 'new humanism' in which man's inevitable scientific progress was tempered by the perspective of the humanities. For Sarton, telling the story of man's past and the story of nature were the great pursuits of human life. Dorinda Outram claimed in 1986 (in this journal) that Irish historians had ignored science. What had inspired this neglect? How could the void be filled?

The latter question has been answered by a growing literature on the history of Irish science. The editors of the new series, *Science and Irish Culture*, feel that a printed home for the subject will encourage the growth of a discipline in Ireland, just as *Isis* successfully fostered the history of science more generally. In response to the volume's subtitle, 'Why the history of science matters in Ireland', Jim Bennett, Charles Mollan and David Attis evince Sartonian idealism: now that science matters so much more in Ireland, the history of science matters as a tempering perspective. A similar answer has also been given to the question of why the history of science has been neglected here. As Bennett notes in his 'state of the literature' essay, some have argued that a new, self-consciously Catholic country wished to distance itself from a 'foreign', mainly Protestant and English, science. Thus, as scientific advancement returned with the Celtic Tiger, so did an interest in its place in Irish culture. However, the historical picture now developing indicates that science was never absent from Ireland and its practitioners were not only English and Protestant, but Irish, Catholic and often nationalist. This volume shows just how much science mattered to a variety of groups in Ireland's past, including university scholars, land speculators, priests, wealthy dilettantes, Fenians and middle-class industrialists.

In addition to Bennett's introduction and reprints of two of Outram's essays ('Negating the Natural' and 'Heavenly Bodies and Logical Minds'), the first volume of *Science and Irish Culture* carries six new essays covering a variety of time periods. Conscious of the need to place science within Irish history, the authors have not neglected cultural and political contexts. David Attis's excellent piece on William Petty in seventeenth-century Ireland offers a convincing picture of mathematics and the new science as a tool of British colonialism. In Gordon Herries Davies's essay, political violence ties the threads of his stories together. Through a brief tour of two centuries, Herries Davies details the impact that rebellions and political restlessness have had on men of science, concluding that Ireland's unsettled state hindered scientific development. By contrast, the story of John Phillip Holland, told by W. Garrett Scaife, demonstrates how important the nationalist movement was for the development of his submarine. A former Christian Brother, Holland moved to the United States in the late nineteenth century, where the Fenian Brotherhood of America gave nearly $60,000 towards the production of several early models.

War and domination are not the only areas of human life with which science is intertwined. The remainder of the essays examine science as an integral component of Irish culture. Greta Jones recovers the reactions of academics, the educated public and the churches in Ireland to Darwin's theories about the origin of life and man. Much historical research has been expended on the subject of reactions to Darwinism and evolutionism in Britain and thus this essay begins to draw the history of Irish science into the larger literature on the history of British science. Darwinism, and the materialistic extrapolations made from it, permeated cultural consciousness in a way that not all developments in science could. Aside from simply reacting to scientific theories, much of the Irish public participated in scientific activity. Ruth Bayles's essay shows how widespread the study of natural history was among the British and Irish middle classes. Bayles's study of the Belfast Natural History Field Club demonstrates how this society was a medium through which men and women formed opinions of their own on the latest biological theories, while also building local knowledge. As Sean Lysaght shows in his paper on 'Eagles in Mayo', such local knowledge, along with folklore and other cultural artefacts, can help modern scientists to reconstruct past habitats.

Clearly *Science and Irish Culture* contributes to increasing our knowledge of Ireland's scientific heritage. If future volumes do the same, it will be a valuable addition not just to the history of science, but to Irish history. The variety of approaches is to be welcomed, preserving what Bennett terms a 'more fluid intellectual milieu'. Of the contributors two are scientists, several others historians of science or scientific instruments and one a poet and lecturer in humanities. However, three less encouraging points are made clear from this mix of essays. First, perhaps only one of the contributors is engaged full time on work in the history of Irish science (Bayles, who is completing a PhD on the subject). Second, this same person is the only new voice on the subject to be aired in this volume. If history of science in Ireland is not to vanish as quickly as it appeared, more scholars must be attracted to the area. Perhaps the regular publication of *Science and Irish Culture* can accomplish this. This brings me to my third point, which is that, while the majority of work on the history of Irish science is conducted without the development of any unified vision or grand narrative, it may be impossible for the field to grow. Those working in this area have not often embraced the narratives offered by the history of British science (although the essays of Bayles, Jones and Attis in this volume are exceptions). Undoubtedly Ireland deserves her own story, told by her own historians. An overview of the changing role of science in Irish culture is needed, even if it be simplistic, to see how the individual pieces of work fit together and to provide a starting-point for undergraduate teaching in the subject. Without teaching, the future of ventures such as *Science and Irish Culture* will depend on the interest of a few relatively isolated individuals.

JULIANA ADELMAN

Trenchant Caution

Fintan O'Toole, *After the Ball*. Dublin: New Island Press, 2003. ISBN 190430138X. €10.99 pbk.

Julia Furay and Redmond O'Hanlon (eds), *Critical Moments: Fintan O'Toole on Modern Irish Theatre*. Dublin: Carysfort Press, 2003. ISBN 1904505031. €20 pbk.

Ireland: 'The most globalised country in the world' (E. T. Kearney/*Foreign Policy*, quoted in *After the Ball*); 'We spend half the proportion of our wealth looking after the old, disabled and the ill than Sweden, France or Germany does' (*Eurostat*, quoted in *After the Ball*); 'The sons and daughters of professionals are over 15 times more likely to enter college than students from lower socio-economic groups' (Higher Education Authority report, quoted in *After the Ball*). Contemporary Ireland can feel weirdly schizophrenic: feel-good Celtic Tiger euphoria dominates the airwaves despite evidence of a mounting social and political crisis associated with poverty and social exclusion. According to a recent UN report, Ireland's widening gap between rich and poor is second only to the United States. Alongside the idolization of the entrepreneur and championing of the private sector (for élite Ireland, to adjust Mary Harney's phrase, Boston is now infinitely preferred over Berlin), there exists a steady but savage deterioration in the conditions of our publicly funded hospitals, of our primary and secondary schools, and of social protection in general. And yet, for each of the major political parties, the panacea for such problems is presented not in terms of a radical change of political direction, but in terms of further privatization. Feel like not spending forty-eight hours on a hospital trolley? Then buy yourself expensive health insurance. Fancy enjoying proper fitness and leisure facilities? Join a private health club and forget the decrepit local swimming pool. Worried about your child's education? Put her name down for a private school.

Within this context – a context in which panegyrics to Celtic Tiger capitalism threaten to drown out the possibility of debate and criticism – Fintan O'Toole's *After the Ball* offers a welcome and incisive intervention. A rare and enjoyably accessible meditation on the origins and political implications of Ireland's recent affluence, *After the Ball* takes issue with the idea that the Celtic Tiger is the product of a right-wing agenda of tax cuts, wage 'moderation' and a relentless denigration of public-sector employment. To the contrary, argues O'Toole, the true story of Ireland's boom is that it is indebted to economic and social practices that derive from the liberal left: 'an interventionist government, public servants, the social democrats of the EU and the trade union movement'. Not doctrinaire adherence to the principles of free market ideology, then, but social partnership, state intervention and positive legislation regarding women's participation in the workforce (for example, the introduction of maternity leave in 1981) have led to the rise of Celtic Tiger prosperity. Forgetting the extent of this contribution by glamourizing individual entrepreneur capitalists (who in many cases owe their wealth not to business acumen and initiative, but to their opportunistic use of public institutions) threatens to kill off the sources of the boom and leads to a further egregious demonization of the public sector. Unless proper recognition is given to the role of social consensus and of public service, concludes O'Toole, then the gap between rich and poor in Ireland will deteriorate even further:

> If the Irish boom is misunderstood as the product of neo-conservative economics, the agenda for sustaining prosperity is obvious: more tax cuts, more privatisation, a weaker State, an expansion of the ethos in which Irish people are to be understood as consumers rather than as citizens. If the boom is understood for what it was – a complex product of left-of-centre values which has not ended the spectacle of social squalor even while removing the excuse for it – the agenda is equally clear. Without a strong, active, imaginative public sphere in which all citizens have the capacity to participate, we will look back on the boom years as a time of unfulfilled promises.

This is a timely and passionate exhortation. Carefully researched, methodically empirical and engagingly direct, *After the Ball* calls attention to the social injustices and inequalities that Celtic Tiger euphoria both propagates and attempts to conceal. This is, and will remain for some years, an important book for contemporary Ireland.

And yet, despite its welcome and stimulating trenchancy, *After the Ball* conveys a very restricted impression of what is possible in terms of political change. Political intervention is thought of in terms of a petitioning of the State, or of the political parties that comprise the State, rather than as a more radical form of agency. The role of the individual as a political actor, in other words, is to adopt a stance that is hortational, well-informed, supplicatory. Once an argument is methodically enunciated, O'Toole's assumption is that sense will prevail and that a more benevolent, liberal and well-managed capitalist economy will develop as a result. In the multi-locational world of contemporary global capitalism, this belief is quixotic. In any case, and more importantly, O'Toole's conception of politics is based on an acceptance of a particular way of thinking about representative democracy that needs to be questioned. Within this, albeit normative, frame, the citizen exercises political power by investing that power in an elected representative who then acts as her/his trusted delegate in a parliament governed by an agreed constitution. The individual exercises political power exclusively through elections and through petition. Thus, the agency of the individual operates according to an aesthetics of trust and delegation rather than according to any more radical conception of social and political intervention. Yet O'Toole's very argument concerning inequality in Irish society, and the repeated failures of Ireland's political establishment, points decisively to the dangers in asserting such trusting traditional politics. While there is no need, perhaps, for O'Toole to examine such issues theoretically, one is struck by the contradiction between the urgency of the calls for change in *After the Ball*, and the book's conclusion that change depends on the achievement of consensus and on traditional mechanisms of advocacy.

These difficulties are also conspicuous when O'Toole is writing about theatre. *Critical Moments* offers a comprehensive 400-page anthology of O'Toole's theatre writing from the early 1980s to the present. Published originally in the *Irish Times*, *Sunday Tribune*, *Magill*, *In Dublin* and the *New York Daily News*, as well as in *New York Review of Books* and *London Review of Books*, O'Toole's essays and reviews have had a major effect on Irish public debate and discussion, as well as on the popular perception abroad of Irish culture and society. Now available in Julia Furay and Redmond O'Hanlon's comprehensive and admirably edited compilation, *Critical Moments* shows that O'Toole's theatre writing is always stimulating, well informed and, like *After the Ball*, animated by the urgency of contemporary relevance. For Furay and Redmond, it is this focus on the immediate present that characterizes O'Toole at his best: seeking out 'the ultimate meaning, intent or significance in a piece of drama', O'Toole is 'unusually adept at dealing with the timeless and universal questions'. A successful theatre production for O'Toole is one that offers a clear and unambiguous critique of the exigencies of the contemporary moment. What O'Toole likes most about Brian Friel's *Dancing at Lughnasa*, for example, is that the play's August 1936 setting 'becomes every time and no time', whereas he finds the play to be at its weakest when it attempts to address specific political issues ('northern questions' like colonialism and cultural domination) or when mention of a character joining the International Brigade detracts from Friel's 'magical, universal quality'. Similarly Martin McDonagh's *The Leenane Trilogy* is praised for its 'utterly 1990s sensibility', whereas recent productions of *The Hostage* are criticized for not adequately addressing what O'Toole believes is the danger of IRA republicanism.

What emerges from the many short essays contained in *Critical Moments* is that O'Toole appraises plays and productions according to how they elucidate his conception of Irish history: a narrative of Ireland's inexorable progression towards modernity, frequently and lamentably interrupted by the siren call of an alternative, Irish republican, political ethics, 'the inward spiral of death we call the national question'. Thus Martin McDonagh's playwriting achievement, and the project of

Garry Hynes's Druid theatre, are praised because of their 'demythologisation of the West'. For O'Toole, cutting-edge theatre is that which confirms Ireland's contemporaneity, conceived of as a universal, all-encompassing timelessness in which history is flattened out into either a confirmation of the present or exists as the present's doomed and futile repudiation. There is no sense of history as involving multiple, co-existing or competing agencies. In much the same way as the brilliant trenchancy of *After the Ball* is weakened somewhat by its inability to imagine radical political alternatives, O'Toole's theatre writing – despite its undoubted intelligence and invigorating acumen – is moderated and curtailed by his cautious preference for the trusting aesthetics of the institutional theatre.

LIONEL PILKINGTON

Partial Visions

Rita Ann Higgins, *Throw in the Vowels: New and Selected Poems*. Highgreen: Bloodaxe, 2005. ISBN 1 85224 700 2. £9.95 pbk.

Where am I? Who am I? What am I? As both reader and writer I constantly ask myself these questions   always aware of the need to position myself and examine where it is I am speaking from. This is 'Embodied Locatedness' – a commitment to partial vision challenging what Donna Haraway terms 'the god trick of seeing everything from nowhere'. We need to make visible the dominant cultural paradigms operating to structure modes of seeing – how and what we see – examine how they privilege particular visionary locations, naturalizing them in the process, replacing their status of particularity with generality (the space of *everywhere* constructed from *nowhere*) – and unmask the conceptualization of universality itself. As Rita Ann Higgins herself puts it: 'It depends / on how you look at it' ('God Dodgers Anonymous') – seeing differently, that is the key, and it such a differencing of vision to which the work of Higgins is committed and which constitutes the defining feature of her latest poetic offering *Throw in the Vowels: New and Selected Poems*.

Higgins' work is noted for its critical social commentary and the astute attention it pays to the operation of class systems in contemporary Ireland. With Higgins locatedness is crucial, and the reader is always strongly aware of the position from which she is speaking. Throughout her career her poetry has sought to aestheticize and poeticize Irish working-class culture – a space left relatively unsymbolized and unexamined in the poetic sphere. Speaking from the margins, Higgins's work problematizes the universally legitimated visions of Irishness and Ireland (urban prosperity and rural idyllicism, respectively), constructing another perspective – a partial vision which makes evident the perspectivism inherent in the act of looking: 'Some people know what it's like, /. . . to be second-hand / to be second-class / to be no class / to be looked down on / to be walked on / to be pissed on / to be shat on / and other people don't' ('Some People'). *Throw in the Vowels*, containing both new and selected poems, is a powerful document of what Sandra Harding would term 'socially situated knowledges'. Well-known poems such as 'Poetry Doesn't Pay', 'The Blanket Man' and 'Lucky Mrs Higgins' operate alongside new pieces of work ('Loquacia L. Spake', 'Return to Sender') as a forcible social critique of the silencing of and refusal-to-see the unofficial underbelly of contemporary Irish society and, in turn, for the need to speak a language of alternative situated positions: 'This visionary is different / he knows exactly where he's not, / and when he's not up a ladder / he's not up a ladder' ('Fugued').

If a speaking-of-the-silenced is a definable characteristic of *Throw in the Vowels*, there is also an equivalent commitment to a respeaking-of-the-spoken, a reimagining of the ways in which things are positioned and configured in Irish cultural discourse. The female body as a commodified object is interrogated in the collection – with a particular emphasis on the 'mother-as-consumable-product' configuration and its impact upon the maternal body: 'Cop yourself on – / your shadow looks / better than ya, / pull yourself together / and for crying out loud / go and eat something / something decent' ('Mamorexia'). What this poem makes evident is the public norms imposed on the condition of motherhood – Mother as a consumable object starves, and this starvation is positioned in terms of an external consumption, sucking away at her body, her life energies, her productive powerful force: mother-as-product ravishingly consumed, so as to keep her powerful, amorphous body in check and under control. *Throw in the Vowels* contains a myriad of poems dedicated to freeing the female body, allowing it transformative power and energy – with such freedom being expressed through sexuality itself, and the possibility of 'woman' as a sexual subject rather than sexualized/de-sexualized object. 'The Did-You-Come-Yets of the Western World', 'I'll Have to Stop Thinking About Sex', 'It's Platonic' and 'The Temptation of Phillida' are but a few of the poems in this collection which address the issue of female sexuality and its limitless potentiality from a specifically feminine, embodied location. Higgins situatedly speaks – literally *through* the female body – and these often hilarious poems can be most productively read as a form of *écriture féminine*, a writing of the body through the body – a form of situated feminine sexual knowledge: 'If there was a night last week / he did not gratify then he owes you for that . . . you have to be compensated for off nights / or under the weather nights, think bat think bull' ('Throw in the Vowels').

Speaking through the body, or from a specific situated location, inevitably brings with it questions of accessibility, communicability and the way in which we use language to relate lived experience. *Throw in the Vowels* is a retrospective collection, organized in a linear format with selections from each of Higgins's published works, culminating in the final section of new poems subtitled 'Throw in the Vowels'. As such it is interesting to read the collection in terms of development and progression, charting Higgins's oeuvre and examining shifts, changes and nuances. Viewed in such a way, one of the most notable developments in her work is its relation to language – or rather, more specifically, the complex relation between language and lived embodied experience. As signalled in the title, many of the new poems of this collection are linguistically self-reflexive and pay attention to the borders and boundaries of language itself. While much of Higgins's earlier work bridged the gap between ontological existence and linguistic representation through a colloquial formal style, there is a marked shift in her new work whereby the difficulties of making such a bridge – of using language communicably – are explored: 'His eyes were empty, / except for that gulf of longing / that gaped around syllables, / making contact a cavity / language never reached' ('His i's Were Empty'). What Higgins is examining here – the gap, the 'cavity' – is the space which language can never reach, the excess which keeps it moving and in motion – the ongoing drive towards the 'unknowable' itself. If her earlier work can be said to be concerned with embodied speaking – speaking with another so as to make visible partial situated locations – then her more recent poems can be said to be an examination of the condition of embodied speaking itself – the drive to communicate always being marked by incommunicability, by that which is not yet (or cannot ever?) be known.

However, it is equally important – and as valid – to read *Throw in the Vowels* in non-linear terms, as an instance, a happening, a moment frozen in time in which then/now, before/after are unrecognizable and non-definable terms. Poetry collections do not necessarily require front-to-back reading strategies, but, rather, can be entered at any point, at many times, across many intersections. While it is important to consider this work in terms of Higgins's shifts and developments, it is just as productive to examine it as a standalone text – allowing for connections between poems to generate new interpretations, new engaged readings. The poems of this remarkable collection are wide-ranging and varied, but there is a common thread that runs throughout the work. As the reader journeys through the poetry she is faced again and again with instances of difference with which she is allowed to connect: connective difference – about as partially located as you can get!

CLAIRE BRACKEN

Not At All Bad

Leanne O'Sullivan, *Waiting for My Clothes*. Highgreen: Bloodaxe, 2004. ISBN 185224674. £7.95 pbk.

Rosita Boland, *Dissecting the Heart*. Loughcrew: Gallery, 2003. ISBN 9781852353438. €10 pbk.

Gerald Dawe, *Lake Geneva*. Loughcrew: Gallery, 2003. ISBN 9781852353414. €10 pbk.

John Montague, *Drunken Sailor*. Loughcrew: Gallery, 2004. ISBN 9781852353605. €11.95 pbk.

In his rather *de haut en bas* round-up for the *New York Review of Books* of the top ten bestsellers of 1973, Gore Vidal quotes the thriller writer Herman Wouk's characterization of F. D. Roosevelt and remarks, 'This is not at all bad, except as prose.' It's a devastating comment, rather than a merely snobbish one, because it acknowledges that few people read prose for the prose: they read it for information, for plot, character, suspense. If the prose is intelligible and does not distract it will do, except for the *NYRB* reader temporarily and vicariously slumming it in bestseller land. The poetry reviewer's equivalent of Vidal's quip does not come easily to hand, though the fish-in-a-barrel review is well enough established. Relatively recent examples include August Kleinzhaler on Garrison Keillor in *Poetry* and Andrew O'Hagan in the *LRB* on Daisy Goodwin; but for both reviewers the object of their vitriol is not so much the poems selected by these anthologists, but the cosy manner in which they are presented as material for self-improvement; 'mental flossing', as O'Hagan puts it. However much we may dislike the new variety of poetry bestseller, in which poems are packaged as tonics to get you through a tough day at the office, it is not possible to say 'not bad, except as poetry'. The poems are usually pretty good and, however hard Goodwin and her kind try to marginalize poetic form as something élitist or irrelevant, most readers do still, I think, read poems primarily for the poetry. Reading two, and perhaps a third, of these four collections, however, I became aware that there is a class of verse production that is *not at all bad*, *except as poetry*, that takes as its subjects events and feelings that may well be sympathetic and interesting in themselves, but quite fails to achieve the status of poetry. And where there is such a type of unpoetry, there is probably also an audience for it.

According to the author biography of her first collection, Leanne O'Sullivan's 'poems have been published or given awards when no-one knew her age'. No chance of that ever happening again: her age is mentioned, one way or another, no less than four times on the jacket of *Waiting for My Clothes*. O'Sullivan was twenty-one years old when the collection was published. The emphasis on her youth is unnecessary, since the contents of this collection (mostly written, I would guess from their tone and subject matter, some years ago) make the fact quite clear, but it is also unsettling, reminiscent of the infantilizing tags attached to the 'poetesses' of the past. Many reviews have suggested that O'Sullivan should attempt in future to resist the influence of Sylvia Plath; on the evidence of her PR, it's not Plath's ghost she should watch out for, but Letitia Elizabeth Langdon's. L. E. L., compelled to maintain into adulthood an artificial girlishness for a nineteenth-century public devoted to the notion of the infant prodigy, might have sympathized with this collection's powerful sense of the liminal. She would, though, have been able to teach O'Sullivan one or two things about versification. Most of the poems in *Waiting for My Clothes* are constructed on the principle that one grammatical clause = one line, and the little pleasures of language are so sparsely distributed that they must be regarded as happy accidents.

Nevertheless, O'Sullivan has a gift for evocation, not so much of the particular image, but of the mood of late adolescence. She creates a sharp portrait of a relentlessly self-dramatizing speaker, slinging her feet up on a car dashboard as she writes a poem on a napkin ('Crescendo'), pronouncing fustian phrases to her reflection ('Mirror'), posing with cigarettes and wearing black (*passim*). There is little or no sense of ironic comment on this posturing, so it is mostly just tiresome, but occasionally disturbing too:

> I am a dirty puddle of darkness after purging.
> In black clothes on a bed of polar tiles
> my back yawns bare between a belted waist
>
> and little top, silently awing the still tub.
>
> ('Bulimic')

Despite the wobbly grammar, O'Sullivan has captured something here: the bulimic's perverse need to be a sexualized object of someone's (some*thing*'s) gaze, even as she expels the nourishment that could make her into an adult capable of sexual desire in her own right. O'Sullivan's treatment of sexuality is strong: where a less sincere young writer might have affected knowingness, she reminds us that bewilderment at discovering one's own sexual nature persists far beyond childhood.

She is also candid about an adolescent's emotional dependence on family, and remarkably generous: the parental and grandparental figures in this collection are tolerant, devoted, almost without fault. This is as touching as it is unexpected from a poet whose chosen persona is a troubled adolescent. It also bodes well for O'Sullivan's future poetic career: preoccupation with family is common in first collections and usually results in desperately dull poetry. It's a great deal more forgivable in a twenty-one-year-old poet, though, than in those ten or fifteen years older. If we accept that a first collection will usually contain a large proportion of ill-digested material that will not contribute to the poet's long-term reputation, then O'Sullivan has acted astutely in choosing to publish so early, thereby getting the disposable stuff out of her system.

Rosita Boland doesn't have the excuse of youth or a first collection for the sometimes astonishingly poor poems presented in *Dissecting the Heart*. It is to her credit that she largely avoids sickly memorializing of her own family. 'My Mother's Winter Coat' could stand with the worst of them for witless sentimentality, but it is an exception. (Incidentally, O'Sullivan writes about wearing 'My Father's Fleece' – can't these poets afford their own clothes? Is there a hardship fund they can apply to?) Unfortunately, Boland's substitute for the homely material of so many young(ish) Irish poets seems to be derived from superficial browsing in books of popular history and science. The title poem is a case in point. Its epigraph is the comment of a transplant surgeon that 'People don't tend to donate hearts. They have romantic associations.' Is this then a poem about dissection or transplantation – very different procedures, with rather different metaphorical implications? We don't find out, though we do learn that Vesalius dissected executed criminals and worse:

> he awaited delivery of each cadaver
> with the eagerness of a lover
> impatient to solve all mysteries
> in the one he desires.

Did this grotesquery occur because of a simple unhappy insistence on the convergence of science and sexuality, or does Boland really think that empirical enquiry into human anatomy is tantamount to necrophilia? Instead of an answer, Boland gives us a conclusion of startling banality:

The heart has become the definable tissue
that stands for the indefinable:
for what makes us quicken and enliven
for what pulses through us and between us.

Boland's decision to base this collection on scientific matters must, originally, have seemed promising, but it is irretrievably damaged by her inability to do more than retell a piquant cutting. A rule of thumb: if you find yourself thinking of something seen in a museum or read in a newspaper, *now, that would make a good poem*, be warned. It probably won't, and certainly won't if the chosen snippet touches on a matter of current political or social importance. 'Lipstick', for example, juxtaposes the red peppers its speaker is chopping for supper with the facial mutilation inflicted on Iranian women for the 'crime' of wearing cosmetics. Mere confluence of imagery does not amount to a poem, still less political comment: on the contrary, this piece manages to imply, offensively, that metaphor can help us understand suffering, that the reader can know how it feels to have her lips sliced off just by looking at the 'delicate mouths' of chopped chillis. Boland has travelled in Iran: it is the peculiar achievement of 'Lipstick' to include none of that experience, suggesting a speaker whose knowledge of the world is mediated entirely by RTÉ.

By contrast, the strongest pieces in this collection are in the Irish parochial tradition that Boland is presumably trying to escape by frantically writing about revolutionary Russia, Charles Babbage's brain and Waterloo teeth. 'Looking at the Landscape' and 'The Last House on the Island' have a simplicity of diction that is absent from this collection's more sophisticated efforts, but these cannot compensate for *Dissecting The Heart*'s preponderance of weak verse.

Stevie Smith, who could be accused of neither sophistication nor simplicity, once complained: 'Why does my Muse only speak when she is unhappy? / She does not, I only listen when I am unhappy / When I am happy I live and despise writing.' Gerald Dawe is that rare poet who, apparently, does listen to his happy Muse, and takes it all down. *Lake Geneva* contains many poems of contentment and muted celebration, among which the brief sequence 'A Moving World' is outstanding for its artfully deployed colloquialism. Even in their darker moments Dawe's poems transmit contemplative calm, as in this impression of

ear-pierced, nose-pierced, head-shaven

detox kids in their thin sports gear
stare down the tracks at twenty years,
and the eyes dart, not seeing you or me
in the eggshell light that's everywhere.
('Pet Days')

At last, some awareness of the possibilities of language, in the assonance and consonance of 'gear', 'years' and 'everywhere'. There's a pun on 'dart' and a nice ambiguity about 'detox kids' – hippies or junkies? – at least until we glimpse 'their thin sports gear' and know they're the latter. Not entirely remarkable, perhaps, but bounty after the iron pemmican of O'Sullivan and Boland. Dawe's relaxed assurance is not quite immune to cliché: at a flip through this collection, there are 'manicured lawns', 'luminous faces', an 'empty beach / as far as the eye can see'. Sometimes the dead hand of fogeydom falls on poems otherwise remarkable for their informality: the italicized '*Indie* music' in 'Laughter and Forgetting' might just pass, distancing a middle-aged speaker from the students he observes, but the '"Glam" band', in 'The Buzz', corralled in its inverted commas, just won't do. More serious is a tendency towards sententious endings, or occasionally, whole sententious poems. In 'Delta', the poet is told about an 'old Vietnamese woman fishing' at a lakeshore. 'This, however, is Switzerland', pronounces the speaker, as if, in an age of mass global migration, we should be surprised. He gets into her head to discover that 'her / village sits at the back of her mind' and magnanimously grants her residency rights 'this / place which she's made her own / in the time it takes to catch a fish'. This kind of clumsy presumption is, however, thankfully uncommon in a collection characterized by understated, resonant speech and a nimble sense of form.

John Montague, by contrast, rarely deals in understatement. Now that he is seventy-five and, in the magnificent phrase of *Drunken Sailor*'s blurb, 'the doyen of Ulster poetry', we can indulge some of his windier moments, rather as we forgive Leanne O'Sullivan her gaucherie on grounds of youth. The publisher of *Drunken Sailor* is nearly as keen as that of *Waiting for My Clothes* to advertise its author's age, though the effort (naturally) has less of Svengali about it. The poet colludes: one of the collection's epigraphs is choice Montague, a comment on artistic theory, 'Written at the age of seventy-five years by me, formerly Hokusai, the old man, mad about drawing'. What might have been self-effacement in the Japanese master is transmuted into marvellous egotism by the poet who once mused 'I suppose [his home town of] Garvaghey will always be associated with my name'. The other epigraph is from *The Critique of Pure Reason*.

Nevertheless, within the casing of self-regard there is much to disarm the sceptical reader. A superb version of a poem by Cathal Ó Searcaigh, 'Clabber: the Poet at Three Years', uses unexpected, noisy alliteration on 'c', 'ch' and 'cl' to convey a creeping realization, 'through every fibre of my duds / the cold tremors of awakening knowledge'. 'Last Resort, Normandy' delivers on its splendidly off-beat and splenetic opening:

> 'There was an old woman
> who lived in a *blockhaus*';
> she was so slatternly
> she didn't know what to do

The mood of 'West Cork Annunciation', with its fine assonance ('People of the past, grown tortoise slow / their world will have gone before they do') and economic characterization ('Mary-Kate sighs, / thinking of something she can do for others') is marred a little by some unfortunate hackneyed rhymes (room / boom, child / mild), but the poem remains a moving, unsentimental evocation of old age and unadorned piety. In their firm confidence in the value of the parochial, these poems, set in West Cork or the poet's childhood home in County Tyrone, recall the later novels of John McGahern.

Montague quotes McGahern's last novel as an epigraph to 'The Plain of Blood', the long poem which constitutes the final part of *Drunken Sailor*. The poem is concerned with its speaker's search for the plain on which the legendary ruler Crom Cruach made human sacrifices. It is a poem in the *dinnseanchas* tradition, each place on the journey identified by some piece of local lore. The poet and his companion meet, at different points in their quest, two old men who each comment slyly on the companion's 'fair and Anglo-Saxon' appearance. Montague handles adroitly his conflation of ancient myth and modern sectarian tension. Rather than allowing his speaker to suggest an organic connection between violence past and present, he lets the old men articulate such sentiments, which normalize and apologize for bloodshed, or he distances them from his speaker by setting them as italicized liturgical fragments. The poet remains aloof from the mythicizing congruence of Crom Cruach and the Northern Troubles, able to deliver the poem's final twist: 'all this never happened, / or was told by a doting man'. If this makes the poem something of a confidence trick, it is to Montague's credit that he recognizes, and tries to avoid, a consolatory understanding of myth's relation to history. It is worth comparing 'The Plain of Blood' to Thomas Kinsella's treatment of the Crom Cruach myth in 'The Oldest Place', part of the sequence *One*. Kinsella sees no reason for the poet to stand back from his material, to act the tourist, complete with guidebook, as Montague does. Consequently, 'The Oldest Place' (in common with most of Kinsella's mythic poems) is always open to the charge of endorsing violence as inevitable, natural and chthonic; precisely the accusation Montague neatly sidesteps. But in its fierce commitment, its unselfconscious dalliance with melodrama, its supple open form, 'The Oldest Place' is simply a better poem than 'The Plain of Blood'. Even the efforts of *doyens*, it seems, might not be at all bad, except as poetry.

KIT FRYATT

Notes on Contributors

JULIANA ADELMAN is a PhD student in history at the National University of Ireland, Galway. She is studying the impact of the Queen's Colleges on science in nineteenth-century Ireland.

IVANA BACIK is Reid Professor of Criminal Law at Trinity College Dublin and barrister, and has written extensively on criminal law, criminology, feminist theory and human rights law. She is author of *Kicking and Screaming: Dragging Ireland into the 21st Century*.

WANDA BALZANO is Director of the Women's and Gender Studies Program at Wake Forest University, North Carolina.

CLAIRE BRACKEN is an IRCHSS PhD Scholar at the School of English and Drama, University College Dublin.

PATRICIA COUGHLAN is Professor of English at NUI Cork. She has edited *Spenser and Ireland* and co-edited *Modernism and Ireland: The Poetry of the 1930s*. With Tina O'Toole, she devised and led the research project that produced the bilingual *Dictionary of Munster Women Writers, 1800–2000*.

L. M. CULLEN is one of the leading economic historians of Ireland, with publications including *Economic History of Ireland Since 1660* and *The Irish Brandy Houses of Eighteenth-Century France*.

DAVID FLEMING works for Cork City Council.

KIT FRYATT is Faculty of Arts Fellow in the School of English and Drama at University College Dublin.

CATHY LEENEY lectures in Drama at University College Dublin and is co-editor of *The Theatre of Marina Carr*.

DAVID LLOYD is Professor in the Faculty of English at University of Southern California and author of *Ireland After History*.

EAMONN JORDAN lectures in Drama at University College Dublin and is author of *The Feast of Famine: The Plays of Frank McGuinness*

MARIA LUDDY is Professor of History at the University of Warwick and has published extensively on the history of women in nineteenth- and twentieth-century Ireland. She is one of the directors of the Women in Modern Ireland Project and was one of the editors of the *Field Day Anthology of Irish Writing: Women's Writings and Traditions*, Volumes 4 and 5.

SUSAN MCKAY is a journalist and author of *Sophia's Story*, *Northern Protestants: An Unsettled People* and *Without Fear: 25 Years of the Dublin Rape Crisis Centre*. The winner of several awards for journalism including Print Journalist of the Year (2000), Amnesty Print Journalist of the Year (2001) and Feature Writer of the Year (2002), she also founded Belfast RCC and was formerly a volunteer with DRCC.

GERARDINE MEANEY is Director of Irish Studies at University College Dublin. She is the author of: *(Un)like Subjects: Women, Theory, Fiction*; *Nora*; numerous articles on gender and Irish culture; and was also a co-editor of the *Field Day Anthology of Irish Writing: Women's Writing and Traditions*, Volumes 4 and 5.

CHRIS MORASH is Professor of English at NUI Maynooth and author of *A History of Irish Theatre, 1601–2000*.

PAT O'CONNOR is Professor of Sociology and Social Policy and Dean of the College of Humanities at the University of Limerick, Ireland. She has published extensively on gender and organizational culture, as well as gender and state policies and practices. Her books include *Friendships between Women* and *Emerging Voices*.

LIONEL PILKINGTON lectures in English at NUI Galway and is author of *Theatre and the State in Twentieth-Century Ireland*.

SUSANNAH RIORDAN lectures in the Department of History, Mary Immaculate College, Limerick.

AILBHE SMYTH is the founding Director of the Women's Education, Research and Resource Centre (WERRC) at University College Dublin. She has been actively involved in feminist, lesbian and gay, and radical politics for many years and has published primarily in the area of feminist politics and cultural analysis.

MOYNAGH SULLIVAN is a Lecturer in the Department of English, NUI Maynooth.

CLODAGH TAIT lectures in the Department of History at the University of Essex. She is author of *Death, Burial and Commemoration in Ireland, 1550–1650*.

GRAHAM WALKER is Professor of Politics at Queen's University Belfast. His most recent book is *A History of the Ulster Unionist Party*.

EIBHEAR WALSHE lectures in English at University College Cork and is author of *Kate O'Brien: A Writing Life*.